THE PURSUIT OF HISTORY

John Tosh is author of *Clan Leaders and Colonial Chiefs in Lango* (Clarendon Press, 1978), and a contributor to *African History in Maps*, edited by M. Kwamena-Poh (Longman, 1982).

THE PURSUIT OF HISTORY

Aims, methods and new directions in the study of modern history

John Tosh

LONGMAN
London and New York

D16
.4
.G7T67

LONGMAN GROUP LIMITED
Longman House, Burnt Mill, Harlow
Essex CM20 2JE, England
Associated companies throughout the world

*Published in the United States of America
by Longman Inc., New York*

© Longman Group Limited 1984

First published 1984
Second impression 1985
Third impression 1986

BRITISH LIBRARY CATALOGUING IN PUBLICATION DATA
Tosh, John
    The pursuit of history.
    1. History — Study and teaching
    I. Title
    907'.2   D16.2

    ISBN 0-582-49218-1

LIBRARY OF CONGRESS CATALOGING IN PUBLICATION DATA
Tosh, John
    The pursuit of history

    Bibliography: p.
    Includes index.
    1. History, Modern—Study and teaching (Higher)—Great Britain.
2. History, Modern—Study and teaching (Higher)
I. Title.
D16.4.G7T67 1984   907'.1141   84-885
ISBN 0-582-49218-1 (pbk.)

Set in 10/11pt Linoterm Times Roman
Produced by Longman Group (FE) Ltd
Printed in Hong Kong

CONTENTS

CONTENTS

PREFACE

The word *history* carries two meanings in common parlance. It refers both to what actually happened in the past and to the representation of that past in the work of historians. This book is an introduction to history in the second sense. It is intended for anyone who is sufficiently interested in the subject to wonder how historical enquiry is conducted and what purpose it fulfils. More specifically, the book is addressed to students taking a degree course in history, for whom these questions have particular relevance.

Traditionally history undergraduates were offered no formal instruction in the nature of their chosen discipline; its time-honoured place in our literary culture and its non-technical presentation suggested that commonsense combined with a sound general education would provide the student with what little orientation he or she required. This approach leaves a great deal to chance. It is surely desirable that students consider the functions served by a subject to which they are about to devote three years of study or more. Curriculum choice, which is a great deal more bewildering than it was twenty years ago, will be a hit-and-miss affair unless based on a clear grasp of the content and scope of present-day historical scholarship. Above all, students need to be aware of the limits placed on historical knowledge by the character of the sources and the working methods of historians, so that at an early stage they can develop a critical approach to the formidable array of secondary authorities which they are required to master. It is certainly possible to complete a degree course in history without giving systematic thought to any of these issues, and generations of students have done so. But an increasing number of universities and colleges now recognize that the value of historical study is thereby diminished, and they are providing introductory courses on the methods and scope of history to make good the deficiency. I hope that this book will meet the needs of students taking such a course. No work of comparable range has appeared in Britain since Arthur Marwick's *The Nature of History*, first published in 1970 and reissued with some modification in 1981.

Although my own research experience has been in the field of African history and has included oral as well as documentary evidence, it has not been my intention to write a manifesto for 'the new history'. I have tried instead to convey the diversity of current historical practice, and to situate recent innovations in the context of mainstream traditional scholarship which continues to account for a great deal of first-rate historical work and to dominate academic syllabuses. The book has been planned with this aim in mind. After an opening chapter on history's claims to social relevance, I concentrate on the traditional scope and methods of academic history (notably in Chapters 2, 3, 4 and 6), before turning to some of the approaches which have been developed over the past twenty or thirty years (Chapters 8 to 10).

The scope of historical studies is today so wide that it has not been easy to determine the precise range of this book; but without some more or less arbitrary boundaries an introductory work of this length would lose all coherence. I therefore say nothing about the history of science and very little about the history of art or environmental history. My treatment of historical sources is in practice limited to verbal materials (both written or oral) because it is in this sphere that the claims of historians to special expertise lie. My selection of quantitative history and Marxist history for extended treatment has been influenced by the dearth of clear introductions to these two fields. In general I have confined my choice to those themes which are of immediate practical use to students today.

Even within these limits, however, my territory is something of a minefield. Anyone who imagines that an introduction to the study of history will express a consensus of expert opinion needs to be promptly disabused. One of the distinguishing features of the profession is its heated arguments concerning the objectives and limitations of historical study. This book inevitably reflects my own views, and it is appropriate to declare them at the outset. The salient points are: that history is a subject of practical social relevance; that the proper performance of its function depends on a receptive and discriminating attitude to other disciplines, especially the social sciences; and that all historical enquiry, whatever the source of its inspiration, must be conducted in accordance with the rigorous critical method which is the hallmark of modern academic history. At the same time, I have tried to place these claims – none of which is of course original – in the context of recent debate among historians, and to give a fair hearing to views with which I disagree.

This book is intended to explore a number of general propositions about history and historians, rather than provide a point of entry into any one field of specialism. But since I anticipate that most of my readers will be more familiar with British history than any other, I have relied for my illustrative material mostly on that field, with some additional examples from Africa and Europe. The book is meant to be read as a whole, but I have included a certain amount of cross-referencing in the text to assist the reader who wishes to pursue only one theme.

In ranging so far beyond any one person's experience of research and writing, this book is more dependent than most on the help of other scholars. I am particularly grateful to my colleague Ben Fowkes who gave a careful appraisal of each chapter as it was written. David Henige performed a similar invaluable service at a distance (in Madison, Wisconsin). Others who have made helpful comments and suggestions include John Broad, Charles George, Doreen Jones, Michael Newman, Peter Seltman, Rosamond Tosh, Richard Waller and Andrew Wright. The Polytechnic of North London generously granted me two terms' study leave in 1981–82. I am also grateful to Isobel Clark for the speed and efficiency with which she typed the final draft. More years ago than I care to recall, my wife Norma Clarke gave me the idea of writing a book of this kind and suggested the title. Neither she nor anyone else is responsible for what I have made of her suggestion.

JOHN TOSH
London, November 1983

For Nick and William

Chapter 1

THE USES OF HISTORY

Contemporary society is sometimes portrayed as dominated by the experience of change. The break-neck speed of technological innovation, the erosion of traditional values and loyalties, the fickleness of electorates, and the instability of international relations are all from time to time cited as evidence that we live in a world radically different from the past, in which a sense of history and the lessons which can be drawn from it are dispensable. This is a superficial assessment to say the least. In all spheres of life, from personal relationships to political judgements, we constantly interpret our experience in time perspective, whether we are conscious of it or not. The mere fact of living alongside people older than ourselves makes us conscious of the past. Our sense of personal identity demands roots in the past which are sought in the first instance in genealogy and family history. We know that we cannot understand a situation in life without some perception or where it fits into a continuing process or whether it has happened before. We take it for granted that other people reveal themselves less in a specific action than in their behaviour and our interaction with them over an extended period. Our sense of what is practicable in the future is formed by an awareness of what has happened – or not happened – in the past. We learn, in short, by experience.

To assert the indispensability of history is only another way of saying that what holds good for us as individuals applies with equal force to our lives as members of society. History is collective memory, the storehouse of experience through which people develop a sense of their social identity and their future prospects. People who profess to ignore history are nevertheless compelled to make historical assumptions at every turn. Our political judgements are permeated by a sense of the past, whether we are deciding between the competing claims of political parties or assessing the feasibility of particular policies. We are all naturally curious about how our society came to be the way it is, and we all entertain some explanation on the subject, however half-baked and ill-founded it may be. The pace of contemporary change

1

does not render the past irrelevant; it merely shifts the perspective from which we weigh its influence and interpret its lessons. Racial conflict in modern British society is due not only to unequal access to employment and housing here and now, but to the legacy of plantation slavery and colonial rule which moulds racial attitudes, both black and white. Assessments of what can be done to rescue the ailing British economy depend on interpretations of how and why it has reached its present condition. Western strategies for dealing with the Soviet Union are based on a reading of Soviet objectives and policies since 1945, and often considerably earlier. These examples could be extended indefinitely.

But whereas the individual's sense of his or her past arises spontaneously, historical knowledge has to be *produced*. Society has a past which extends back far beyond the lives of the individuals who happen to comprise it at any one time. The raw materials out of which a historical consciousness can be fashioned are accordingly almost unlimited. Those elements which find a place in it represent a selection of truths which are deemed worthy of note. Who produces that knowledge, and who validates it for general consumption, are therefore important questions. How well the job is done has a bearing on the cohesion of society and its capacity for renewal and adaptation in the future. That is why what historians do should matter to everyone else. Their work can be manipulated to promote desired forms of social consciousness; it can remain confined to academic circles, powerless to influence society for good or ill; or it can become the basis for informed and critical discussion of current issues. In this chapter each of these possibilities is considered with a view to defining the proper social role of historical knowledge.

I

In January 1980 the inquest on the death of Lord Mountbatten and three others in the previous August was concluded at Sligo in the Irish Republic. In his closing remarks the coroner was reported as saying:

> I believe it is necessary to stress again the great responsibility that parents and teachers of any nation have in the way they interpret history and pass it on to the youth of their country. I believe that if history could be taught in such a fashion that it would help to create harmony among people rather than division and hatred, it would serve this nation and all other nations better.[1]

Outside commentators customarily deplore the powerful sense of the past which animates political passions in Ireland, the implication being that if the Irish could live fully in the present the cleavage between Catholics and Protestants would no longer divide them so deeply. Such a view not only underestimates the intensity and persistence of the sufferings of the Irish people over many centuries; it also fails to recognize how far the aspirations and antipathies of all societies are influenced at every turn by historical perspective. The Sligo coroner, on the other hand, did not suggest that his countrymen could be emancipated from the hand of history. His contention was rather that Irish history is still being used to sustain sectarian solidarities to the exclusion of other, more positive values.

The Irish case is only a pronounced and baleful illustration of a universal phenomenon. One of the strongest bonds uniting a large social grouping is its members' awareness of a common history. Without that awareness men and women could not easily acknowledge the claims on their loyalty of large abstractions. This is manifestly true in the case of the most powerful group identification in modern times – the nation. The present day nationalities of Europe have been formed through the accumulation of distinctive national experiences, sancti-fied as so many national pasts. Indeed history is probably a stronger force than language in the moulding of national consciousness. This was certainly so during the nineteenth century when the growth of nationalism reached its climax on the European continent at the same time as history was assuming a pivotal position in education and research. Each process fed on the other. The writing of national histories offered to peoples such as the Italians, Germans and Slavs one of the most effective means of sustaining a popular sense of national identity at a time when its full political expressions still eluded them. During a lifetime of historical work, František Palacký re-covered the Czech past virtually single-handed, and when he died in 1876 he was mourned as the father of the Czech nation.[2] Once the resources of the state were harnessed to the task, the consolidation of a national past was rapidly pushed forward. By the late nineteenth century most European countries were moving towards parliamentary institutions based on a wide franchise which required a strengthening of national consciousness at the expense of class or regional loyalties. This was one of the considerations which led to the development of mass education under close state control, with national history featur-ing prominently in the curriculum. Both in new nation-states like Germany and Italy, and in well-established ones like France, the state promoted historical research, encouraged the publication of source materials, and appointed the university professors who were re-sponsible for the training of history teachers in schools. A powerful alliance was forged between historical scholarship and officially approved nationalism.[3]

Outside Europe the materials from which a national consciousness could be fashioned have usually been less promising, yet the political need for a national past has been if anything greater. Here the United States was the prototype. Before the Revolution colonial Americans regarded British history as their own. After the Revolution it gradually became clear that the consolidation of a national identity among the thirteen colonies required a distinctively American past. The new school textbooks which were published in Massachussetts and elsewhere during the 1820s represented the first attempt in this direction. By the 1850s the task had been accomplished: in the writings of historians like George Bancroft, Americans were invited to identify with a flattering self-image – in taming the wilderness far away from the corruptions of the old society in Europe, their ancestors had developed the values of self-reliance, honesty and liberty which were now the heritage of all Americans.[4] What a later generation has dismissed as 'mindless patriotism'[5] seemed at the time a valid and necessary expression of the nation's identity.

In today's black African states too, the most pressing charge laid upon historians by their wider audience has been the writing of national histories. Most African states acquired their present boundaries less than a hundred years ago, when they were laid down by European diplomats and administrators with scant regard for geographical or cultural considerations. The history which Africans were taught in schools during the colonial period was essentially a white man's history in which African achievements were disparaged or ignored. Conversely since independence history has been an important instrument for undermining the colonial psychology of dependence and inferiority. One of the resolutions carried by the International Congress of African Historians meeting in Dar es Salaam in 1965 was:

> that an African philosophy of history which would serve as a liberation from
> the colonial experience must be a vital concern of all historians studying in
> Africa.[6]

In the past twenty years a great deal of history has been published in Africa which rightly emphasizes the historical evidence of African creativity. School and university syllabuses feature the great experiments in state-building in pre-colonial Africa like the Medieval empires of Ghana and Zimbabwe, and the record of resistance to white incursions like the rebellion against the Rhodesian settlers of 1896 or the Maji-Maji revolt in German East Africa in 1905 (both significantly based on inter-tribal cooperation). Topics such as these, which previously had very limited currency, are now part of the historical consciousness of school-educated Africans all over the continent. Within each country the struggle for independence provides material out of which a national identification, as well as a pride in African culture, can be nurtured. As the optimism engendered by the arrival of independence dissolves into an increasing awareness of exploitation among the mass of the people, a shared historical perspective must seem more than ever desirable to the governing elites of the new African states.

In Britain national consciousness in history has taken more varied forms, but their cumulative effect has been significant. During the nineteenth century national identity could be taken much more for granted and the legitimacy of the state was less open to challenge than in many continental countries. But against the background of an expanding and increasingly literate electorate, history came to be seen as an important unifying element in the country's political culture. At the turn of the century Britain's imperial past was much emphasized: the migration of the British people overseas, the colonial conquests, and the provision of 'civilized' government over inferior races were presented as achievements in which everyone could take pride. Along-side the imperial interpretation the older tradition of English history as 'the story of our liberty' continued as strong as ever. According to this view, all Englishmen were beneficiaries of the centuries-long evolu-tion of constitutional liberties, achieved for the most part by gradualist methods which respected the heritage of the past. Though usually known as the 'Whig interpretation of history', it was in fact bipartisan and effectively reinforced the legitimacy of the country's political institutions. In its foremost champions it inspired an almost mystical reverence for the English way in politics.[7] More crudely, British national history to this day celebrates those moments in the past when the country was united behind a leader who embodied the national consensus, usually in war-time: Elizabeth I, Pitt the Younger, and above all Winston Churchill. It was that tradition that Margaret Thatcher sought to invoke in the spring of 1982 in support of her military adventure in the Falkland Islands. During this century all these themes have come to be associated with the monarchy – as the most visible bond between Britain and her former colonies, the focus of national consensus, and paradoxically the symbol of the political liberties which were once wrested from a reluctant monarchy but now seem guaranteed by the sovereign's respect for constitutional convention.

However, the state's interest in history does not arise only from the desirability of promoting a national consensus among its subjects. It also springs from an awareness of the subversive possibilities of untrammelled historical enquiry. To know about the past is to know that things have not always been as they are now, and by implication that they need not remain the same in future. History can be the basis for scepticism about received ideas, which is why in totalitarian societies history-writing is not regarded as a harmless escape from the present. In some instances the state has set out to rid history of this subversive potential. In his powerful novel, *Nineteen Eight-Four* (1949), George Orwell depicted an imaginary state which expunged

5

from the record anything which might suggest that its rulers had ever failed or been mistaken. The book was no mere flight of fancy, but a political satire partly inspired by the Soviet Union: under Stalin Russian history was radically revised in order to enlarge the reputation both of the Communist Party, and of Stalin at the expense of Trotsky. Nor is suppression of the past the invention of twentieth-century totalitarian regimes. It is documented in the case of one of the great civilizations of the Ancient World. The political unity of China dates back to the reign of the Ch'in emperor, Shih-huang-ti (246–210 BC) who sct up one centralized monarchy in place of a multitude of warring feudal states. The measures he took to secure his regime included not only the elimination of the old political elites and the construction of the Great Wall of China, but also the notorious 'Burning of the Books'; an imperial decree of 213 BC ordered the destruction of all histories of the feudal states circulating outside the official archives, in order to confound those scholars who, as the emperor's Grand Councillor is reported to have said, 'study the past in order to criticize the present age'.[8] The limited knowledge we have of the pre-Ch'in period and the long survival of the idea – if not always the reality – of a united China testify alike to the success of this ruthless policy.

Ch'in China and Stalinist Russia are certainly exceptional cases. Most regimes do not resort to such drastic methods. But from the political establishment's point of view, an important by-product of a national historical consensus is that it displaces other, more dangerous readings of the past. In Britain the Whig interpretation remains significant because it encourages people in the belief that British liberties are a fact of history, a closed chapter, not an agenda for change. The popular identification with the national tradition – 'our heritage' – is a powerful check on political radicalism and has been officially promoted partly for this reason. Contrary to common belief, most of the pageantry which keeps the monarchy in the public eye is not traditional at all, but has been improvised and enlarged by deliberate policy since the death of Queen Victoria in 1901.[9]

Yet if history has always ministered to authority, it has also been many times enlisted in the cause of dissent and rebellion. In any political culture which retains some vitality the state's appropriation of the past does not go unchallenged. If other groups whose aspirations conflict with the approved consensus are to mobilize effectively, they too need the sanction of the past. The purpose of much labour history written by politically committed historians is to sharpen the social awareness of the workers, to confirm their commitment to political action, and to reassure them that history is 'on their side' if only they will keep faith with the heroism of their forebears. In Britain this approach is reflected in the History Workshop movement of socialist historians (both academic and extra-mural) which began in the late 1960s; for them, the historical reconstruction of working people's experience serves as 'a source of inspiration and understanding'.[10] Their aim is to rescue working-class memories of work, locality, family and politics – with all the pride and anger so often expressed through them – before they are pushed out of popular consciousness by an approved national version (see Ch. 10).

The women's movement has been if anything more conscious of the need for a usable past. For feminists this requirement is not met by studies of exceptional women like Elizabeth I who operated success-fully in a man's world; the emphasis falls instead on the economic and sexual exploitation which has been the lot of most women, and on the efforts of activists to secure redress. These are the themes which, to quote from the title of a popular feminist text, have been 'hidden from history'.[11] For socially deprived groups – whether in a majority like workers and women, or in a minority like blacks in America and Britain – effective political mobilization depends on a consciousness of common experience in the past. As an American feminist historian has put it:

> It is not surprising that most women feel that their sex does not have an interesting or significant past. However, like minority groups, women cannot afford to lack a consciousness of a collective identity, one which necessarily involves a shared awareness of the past. Without this, a social group suffers from a kind of collective amnesia, which makes it vulnerable to the impositions of dubious stereotypes, as well as limiting prejudices about what is right and proper for it to do or not to do.[12]

'Oppositional' history has the immediate effect of raising the con-sciousness of the group in question. In the longer term it may also lead to an adjustment in other people's historical perceptions – a recogni-tion that women or blacks have a collective identity which merits a certain respect.

The morale of all 'outsider' groups in society is also enhanced by recalling earlier traditions of popular protest and revolutionary politics which can now be treated as their common property. The English Revolution of the seventeenth century, which threw up ideas about democracy, communal living, women's emancipation and sexual freedom, is one phase in Britain's past which nourishes radical dissent today; the popular resistance to proletarianization during the early nineteenth century is another.[13] One practical outcome of these and other episodes of struggle was the achievement of a body of popular rights *vis-à-vis* authority. In Britain, where much of the constitution and the law rests on precedent, it can be argued that historians have a special responsibility in this area. This was certainly the view taken by the lawyers who challenged the early Stuart monarchy by citing Medieval precedent – misleadingly as it seems to historians today – to protect the rights of the subject. In our own day the historian and campaigner E. P. Thompson has sought to preserve the powers of juries and the public accountability of the police from authoritarian encroachment by showing how these liberties have the force of precedent on their side, and how vigilant their champions have needed to be in their defence.[14] Awareness of the antiquity of these rights and of the popular struggles which helped to entrench them is potentially a powerful support for political radicalism today.

So history is a political battleground. The sanction of the past is sought by those committed to upholding authority and by those intent on subverting it, and both are assured of finding plenty of ammunition. Near-universal literacy raises the stakes. In the days when only a minority could read and write, popular memory took shape more spontaneously and relatively free from interference; but today the mainstream establishment interpretations of our history penetrate everywhere through school textbooks, the press and television. At the same time, the several variants of oppositional history can, if they gain access to the media, achieve a much wider distribution than previously and can aim for a common historical consciousness with wider terms of reference than was possible in the pre-literate age. Fifteen years ago, the Cambridge historian J. H. Plumb argued that the power of the past to validate authority and group consciousness was on the wane and would shortly disappear.[15] That judgement seems premature in 1983. There are signs that the history syllabus in British schools is about to become a bone of contention once more, as conservatives and radicals shape up for a struggle for control.[16] History is evidently still too powerful a force in our consciousness to be shrugged off as an idle intellectual pastime.

II

Clearly, then, history has a social role. Society requires a usable past, and different conceptions of the social order produce rival histories. Many historians have been proud to enlist on one side or another, believing that they have a social responsibility to promote this or that group identity, or to reinforce the authority of the state. But is this the only practical application of history? Is history simply something to be manipulated in support of an ideology (however estimable), or does it also have a value as an independent body of knowledge? Does it confer wisdom, or merely reinforce pre-conceived world-views? Can we, in short, *learn* from history? Generations of historians and their readers have believed that we can. They have turned – and still turn – to history for two kinds of guidance: for lessons on how to act in situations which have occurred before, and for a broader intimation of where they stand in the flow of time and thus of what may lie in the future.

The first of these follows logically from the proposition that history is to society what remembered experience is to the individual. Human beings strive to learn from their mistakes and successes in their collective life just as they do in everyday individual experience. Historical biography is said to feature prominently in the leisure reading of British politicians. Indeed a few of them have written distinguished works of this kind – Winston Churchill and Roy Jenkins, for example.[17] That politicians have a lively interest in the historical context in which posterity will judge their own standing is only part of the explanation. The real reason for their study of history is that politicians expect to find a guide to their conduct – in the form not of moral example (though this was taken seriously in all centuries prior to our own) but of practical lessons in public affairs. This approach to history has a long pedigree. It was particularly pronounced during the Renaissance when the record of classical antiquity was treated as a storehouse of moral and practical examples. Machiavelli's prescriptions for his native Florence and his famous political maxims in *The Prince* (1513) were alike based on Roman precedent. He was justly rebuked by his younger contemporary, the historian Francesco Guicciardini:

> How wrong it is to cite the Romans at every turn. For any comparison to be valid, it would be necessary to have a city with conditions like theirs, and then to govern it according to their example. In the case of a city with different qualities, the comparison is as much out of order as it would be to expect a jackass to race like a horse.[18]

Guiccardini put his finger on the principal objection to the citing of precedent, that it usually shows scant regard for historical context. For the precedent to be valid, the same conditions would have to prevail, but the result of the passage of time is that what looks like an old problem or a familiar opportunity requires a different analysis because the attendant circumstances have changed. Acting on the strength of historical analogies is a most uncertain guide, as likely to lead to frustration as success.

The second approach is rather more sophisticated and less at odds with the notion of historical change: this is that the broad pattern of the future can be inferred from the direction of history up to the present. The idea that mankind is always in a state of transition towards a new condition in the future is a relatively recent one in Western civilization. Medieval thinkers believed that the world was moving inexorably according to God's purpose towards the Last Judgement, but this eschatological interpretation did not carry with it any notion of historical change in secular affairs. The Renaissance saw a revival of the cyclical view of history which was popular in classical times: civilization was thought of as subject to a life-cycle of growth, maturity and decay, which ruled out the prospect of long-term cumulative change. Not until the eighteenth century was there a widespread confidence that mankind had a future in the sense that it could move beyond what had been achieved before in classical antiquity. The historians and philosophers of the Enlightenment interpreted the past according to the idea of progress, which for them meant the moral and material improvement of mankind by the application of reason. The extent to which eighteenth-century society had turned its back on the barbarism and superstitions of the past offered grounds for optimism about mankind's prospects for complete self-fulfilment in the future. A more circumscribed version of the same idea was current during the nineteenth century, when a number of nation-states – notably Germany and the USA – appropriated the optimistic predictions of the Enlightenment and proclaimed their 'manifest destiny' as the nations of the future. Marx offered an alternative, subversive version of the future as the triumph of socialism achieved by proletarian revolution (see Ch. 8). As these examples demonstrate, there is an element of wishful thinking, if not outright manipulation, about most grand predictions. Even the writers of the Enlightenment, who were freer than most from sectarian loyalties, had only a very crude notion of what circumstances had facilitated progressive change in the past or might do so in the future.

As will shortly be made apparent, history's claims to offer precedents or to yield predictions about the future are not entirely without foundation; but it is certainly true that the writing of history with these aims primarily in view was not conducive to historical understanding. The quest for precedents tended to stress superficial similarities at the expense of fundamental differences between one age and another, while the exponents of 'history as progress' interpreted the past from the standpoint of modern 'enlightened' standards, and so were ill-equipped to understand periods like the Middle Ages whose guiding principles were so very different. In fact the modern academic discipline of history originated as a sharp reaction against these practically inspired modes of historical enquiry.

This reaction took shape during the early nineteenth century, initially in Germany, though it soon spread all over the Western world. It is usually known as *historicism* (from the German *Historismus*). The fundamental premise of historicism was that each age is a unique manifestation of the human spirit, with its own culture and values. For one age to understand another, there must be a recognition that the passage of time has profoundly altered both the conditions of life and the mentality of men and women – even perhaps human nature itself – and that an effort of the imagination must be made to relinquish present-day values and to see an earlier age from the inside. But historicism was more than an antiquarian rallying cry. Its proponents maintained that the culture and institutions of their own day could only be understood historically. Unless their growth and development through successive ages were grasped, their true nature would remain elusive. History, not reason, was the key to understanding the world.

The causes of this shift in approach are complex. In part it was a reaction against the rationalism of the Enlightenment, and it also reflected a growing interest in the primitive roots of Western civilization. These were features of Romanticism, the dominant movement in European thought around 1800. But the growth of historicism owed most to the impact of the French Revolution. To conservatives, the political excesses in France were a terrifying instance of what happens when radicals turn their backs on the past. For them society was an organic whole, rooted in tradition; to apply first principles without respect for inherited institutions was a threat to the very fabric of the social order. But as the Revolution went off course, many of the radicals acquired a new respect for history too. They were disillusioned by the corruption of revolutionary principles under Napoleon, and still more by the restoration of monarchy and church in 1815. They were compelled to recognize that mankind was not so free from the hand of the past as they had supposed, that progressive change must be built on the cumulative achievements of earlier generations. In the early nineteenth century, therefore, there was a particularly acute sense among politically conscious people that history imposes constraints which society ignores at its peril.

The conservative reaction against the French Revolution was a strong formative influence on the man who did more than any other to establish historicism as the dominant mode of historical scholarship – Leopold von Ranke. Ranke rejected both the Revolution, which had resulted in the French occupation of Germany, and the Enlightenment's cult of progress. His views were typical of German conservatives of his day, and after settling in Berlin he identified strongly with the Prussian monarchy. He was a professor at Berlin University from 1824 until 1872 and was author of over sixty volumes. He approached the past with humility and detachment. Ranke did not maintain that historical research served no purpose outside itself; indeed, he was probably the last major historian to believe that the outcome of studies like his own would be to reveal the hand of God in human history. But he did not look for practical lessons from the past. As Ranke explained in the much-quoted Preface to his first book:

> History has had assigned to it the task of judging the past, of instructing the present for the benefit of the ages to come. To such lofty functions this work does not aspire. Its aim is merely to show how things actually were (*wie es eigentlich gewesen*).[19]

By this Ranke meant more than an intention to reconstruct the passage of events, though this was certainly part of his programme.[20] The notion that the past is recoverable dates back to the Renaissance, and since then antiquarian scholarship had achieved considerable precision in matters of historical fact. What was new about the historicists' approach was their realization that the atmosphere and mentality of past ages had to be reconstructed too, if the formal record of events was to have any meaning. The main task of the historian became to find out why people acted as they did by stepping into their shoes, by seeing the world through their eyes and as far as possible judging it by their standards. And this obligation extended to *all* periods in the past, however alien they might seem to modern observers. Ranke himself strove to meet this ideal in his treatment of the wars of religion in the sixteenth and seventeenth centuries. Others tackled the Middle Ages in the same spirit.

Whether Ranke is the greatest historian who has ever lived is open to question. But he certainly founded the modern discipline of academic history – largely because he developed the techniques of research necessary for the fulfilment of the historicists' programme, especially the use and interpretation of primary documentary sources (see Ch. 3). Modern historical consciousness comprises two elements: an awareness of the disparity in circumstances and mentality which creates a gulf between all previous ages and our own, and a recognition that our world owes its distinctive character to the way in which it has grown out of those past circumstances and mentalities. It was in the mid-nineteenth century that the full implications of these ideas were explored for the first time and realized in the practice of historians. They have remained the hallmark of historical scholarship ever since.

III

Although historicism readily lends itself to antiquarianism – and has attracted countless antiquarians to its banner – it is by no means without important practical implications. To study the past 'for its own sake' or 'from the inside' may be the essence of the historian's enterprise, but it is not necessarily the whole of it. What practical advantages accrue to society from supporting thorough and faithful historical reconstruction? The answer is threefold.

In the first place, the effort to recapture the essence of every epoch in the past alerts us to the sheer variety of human mentality and achievement – and thus to something of the range of possibilities at our disposal now. Partly this is a matter of imaginative range. History, after all, offers insights into a very wide range of human mentalities. Few people could have foreseen the rise to power of an Adolf Hitler or an Idi Amin; but to someone with a historical education their personalities were at least credible, as being within the range of recorded human deviance, and an effort of imaginative comprehension was possible – not, it should be added, to excuse their crimes but to provide a basis for dealing realistically and effectively with them. From this point of view, the broader the scope of historical study the better; dynastic China and pre-colonial Africa have no less a claim than do the Middle Ages or the wars of religion in European history.

History is also, of course, the record of human achievement, an inventory of assets whose value may be realized by later generations. This is a familiar idea in the creative arts. The work of painters and sculptors is periodically enriched by contact with the styles of the past; since the Renaissance if not earlier, Western art has been marked by a pronounced tendency to feed on its own history. More broadly, historical knowledge serves as a reminder that there is usually more than one way of interpreting a predicament or responding to a situation, and that the choices open to us are often more varied than we might have supposed. As the process of historical change unfolds, old arguments or programmes may once more become relevant. This has been a persistent theme in the work of the foremost historian of the English Revolution, Christopher Hill:

> Since capitalism, the protestant ethic, Newtonian physics, so long taken for granted by our civilization, are now at last coming under general and widespread criticism, it is worth going back to consider seriously and afresh the arguments of those who opposed them before they had won universal acceptance.[21]

Secondly, what of the more immediate appeal of history as a source of precedent and prediction? From all that was said earlier about the gulf that separates us from all previous ages, it will be clear that the citing of precedents from the distant past is a pretty fruitless enterprise. Only the recent past can be usefully treated in this way, which is one reason why contemporary history is worth careful study. But even here the task is a daunting one. Consider the case of the arms race. The decade before the Second World War is commonly regarded as an object lesson in the dangers of military weakness and of appeasing an aggressive power. But one could equally cite the precedent of the First World War, one of whose causes was the relentless escalation in armaments from the 1890s onwards. Which precedent is valid? The answer must be: neither as it stands. Even within the timespan of a hundred years, history does not repeat itself. No one historical situation has been, or ever can be, repeated in every particular. If an event or tendency recurs, as the arms race has done, it will be as a result of a unique combination of circumstances, and the strategies we adopt must have regard primarily to those circumstances.[22] At the same time, the drawing of historical analogies, often half consciously, is a habitual and unavoidable part of human reasoning, to which people in public life are especially prone. Conducted in a critical spirit, it can be illuminating: if a number of alternative parallels are compared with each other, with due regard for their varying and distinctive circumstances, we can be alerted to hitherto unsuspected aspects of the present situation which may be highly relevant to the formulation of policy. Comparisons across time do illuminate the present by highlighting both what is recurrent and what is new – provided we do not look to the past for a short cut to the solution of today's problems.[23]

The truth that history never repeats itself also limits the confidence with which historians can predict. However probable it may seem that a recurrence of this or that factor will result in a familiar outcome, the constant process of historical change means that the future will always be partly shaped by additional factors which we cannot predict and whose bearing on the problem in hand no-one could have suspected. Moreover, when people do perceive their situation as 'history repeating itself', their actions will be affected by their knowledge of what happened the first time. But there is another kind of prediction which promises better prospects of success: the identification of past trends and their projection into the future. This might be described as the *sequential* – as opposed to the *repetitive* or *recurrent* – model of historical prediction. In a very crude way this is what the 'history as progress' school of interpretation was all about. But the kind of sequential prediction in demand today is less concerned with the destiny of mankind than with trends in specific areas of social activity and within specific societies. Anyone interested in the future of South Africa, for example, would be well advised to take note of a prediction to which most historians would subscribe on the strength of what has happened there since the beginning of the gold-mining industry a hundred years ago: that, given a white culture of extreme racial prejudice and an economy based on artificially cheap non-white labour, South Africa will experience an increasingly violent confrontation between the races for the foreseeable future. This is not a watertight forecast, since a change of heart among the ruling minority cannot be completely discounted, but it does indicate the strength of the trend with which any countervailing policy will have to contend. Historical knowledge provides the basis not for categorical predictions, but for projection into the future of social, political or economic trends which provide a vital insight into the conditions in which future action will unfold.

Given the historian's characteristic interest in growth and development, this is the kind of prediction which the profession is best qualified to offer. But few historians would stake their discipline's claim to social relevance on either prediction or the citing of precedents. More important is the awareness it conveys of what is enduring and what is ephemeral in our present circumstances: this is what is meant essentially by 'historical perspective'. Justifications along these lines sometimes read like a half-hearted attempt to salvage 'relevance' for history by those who shrink from offering significant analogies or gazing into the crystal ball. But the point is an important one, with practical implications for the management of social and political change. There is a tendency for most people to take for granted many of the institutions and conventions in which their own lives are interwoven, in the sense of assuming that they have prevailed over time out of mind. Family morality is a case in point. A loving marriage 'till death us do part' is generally assumed to represent the traditional norm in Western society, against which the present divorce-rate seems a shocking decline in standards. Certainly in pre-industrial society (and for some time beyond the onset of industrialization) the social sanctions against departure from the norm were much more severe than they are today; but there was also less cause to contemplate separation. People married later and died much younger than they do now, so that the span of married life was much shorter, while the expectations which spouses entertained of each other had more to do with domestic production and reproduction than with happiness or love. The rate of marital breakdown today reflects these changes. Marriage *looks* the same, but its nature and function have changed radically in the past two hundred years.[24] It is also all too easy to make the opposite error of supposing that a very old and entrenched feature is of relatively recent origin. The great French Medievalist, Marc Bloch, liked to point out that the wasteful strip pattern of land tenure in northern France was not the consequence of the Napoleonic Code's laws of inheritance, as impatient reformers assumed, but was rooted in farming practice dating back to prehistoric times.[25]

One of the most valuable 'lessons' which history teaches, then, is the sense of what is durable and what is transient or contingent in our present condition. That sense will be helpful in estimating how easily particular changes can be accomplished – something that all radical reformers surely need to know. This was the approach of R. H. Tawney, the foremost social historian of England between the two World Wars, and an influential social reformer. In his best-known historical work, *Religion and the Rise of Capitalism* (1926), his purpose was to show how the disengagement of Christian social ethics from the conduct of business, which in his day was so total and (from Tawney's viewpoint) so disastrous, had first come about; the book traces the reciprocal relationship between Puritanism and the capitalist spirit during the seventeenth century, culminating in the triumph of economic individualism after the Restoration of 1660. As Tawney put it in a characteristically elegant metaphor:

> If he [the historian] visits the cellars, it is not for love of the dust, but to estimate the stability of the edifice, and because, to grasp the meaning of the cracks, he must know the quality of its foundations.[26]

This kind of historical perspective is very different from the old idea that we can look to the past for the solution of current problems. It is also a far cry from the determinist perspective from which the various schools of 'history as progress' interpret the past. History is not being quarried for 'meaning' to validate particular values, but is here treated as an instrument for maximizing our control over our present situation. To be free is not to enjoy total freedom of action – that is a Utopian dream – but to know how far one's action and thought are conditioned by the heritage of the past. This may sound like a prescription for conservatism. But what it offers is a realistic foundation for radical initiatives. Strategies for change which fail to take the measure of institutions integral to our culture over many centuries are likely to founder; through underestimating the obstacles to change they will end as futile political gestures.

The third practical implication of a historicist approach to the past relates to the links between history and political power with which this chapter began. The examples which I cited – nationalist history, women's history, etc. – may suggest propaganda rather than history. In fact the quest for a group identity in the past does not necessarily lead to myth-making; as I hope to show later in the book (Ch. 7), *all* history, whether or not it bears directly on current social needs, is selective, and one principle of selection is intrinsically no more true than any other. But obviously an urgent and overriding political commitment *may* produce a mythical version of history, and myths can be dangerous. They induce misguided attitudes and responses, and they stand in the way of the lessons which *can* be learnt from the past. As we saw earlier, the ruling groups in society have an interest in promoting mythical pasts which serve to legitimize their power or win support for particular policies. In Britain today a Victorian myth is being sedulously cultivated. Conservative politicians seek to justify the piecemeal dismantlement of the welfare state and the retreat from state economic planning by an appeal to the Victorian values of self-reliance and competitive individualism which, it is claimed, made Britain a powerful and respected nation in the nineteenth century. But do we really want a return to the scale of human destitution and the entirely uncontrolled destruction of the environment which characterized the hey-day of Victorian *laissez-faire*? The myths which one society entertains about another can also be particularly enduring and harmful. When Britain's African empire was at its zenith during the early twentieth century, her imperial morale was sustained by the notion that Aficans were economically feckless and passive. In fact in the late nineteenth century the continent had been traversed by far-flung indigenous trade-routes linking the interior with the coast, and most of the food requirements of the towns which later sprang up in the wake of the colonial occupation were met by African peasant farmers responding quickly to market opportunities.[27] Yet the mythical stereotype of economic ineptitude persists, and it contributes to the often specious authority with which outside experts pronounce on Africa's development needs today, with such disastrous results.

As for oppositional histories, the problem here is that a view of the past which serves to raise consciousness may be less helpful as a guide to action. A great deal of such history is frankly 'inspirational' or 'triumphalist'; that is, it romanticizes the past by emphasizing heroism in adversity, and in doing so may lead to faulty prescriptions for the future. Most recent labour history in Britain has tended to emphasize traditions of political radicalism and of struggle against capital; yet if it is to provide a realistic historical perspective in which political strategies can be planned, labour history cannot afford to ignore the equally long tradition of working-class Toryism, still very much alive today. Peter Burke put it this way at a conference of socialist historians in 1979:

> (although I consider myself a socialist and a historian) I'm not a socialist historian; that is, I don't believe in socialist history. I believe that to use history as a weapon in political struggle is counter-productive. One comes to believe one's own propaganda, to overdramatise the past, and hence to forget the real complexity of the issues at any time. One comes to idealise one's own side, and to divide human beings into Us and Them.[28]

Myth-making about the past, however desirable the end it may serve, is incompatible with *learning* from the past.

So the historian has a significant negative function in undermining myths which simplify or distort popular interpretations of the past. In this role he has been likened to 'the eye-surgeon, specializing in removing cataracts'.[29] In addition to correcting myths about our own society, the historian can make a positive contribution by exploring the myths which mould the consciousness of *other* societies. The ability to step outside one's own assumptions and into the shoes of other countries which inherit different national traditions is indispensable to the effective conduct of international relations. Some of the errors which British statesmen made in their policies towards central Europe during the 1930s can be attributed to their ignorance of the powerful myths then current in Nazi Germany. Ireland is a classic example of the serious consequences of believing one's own myths too much and knowing too little about other people's. The Irish suffer not, as is often maintained, from too much history, but too little – that is to say, too little awareness of the real context in which their country and its sectarian myths have developed. The British also paid dearly for their historically ill-informed policies towards Ireland during the formative period from the 1880s to the 1920s; indeed they still do.[30]

The Irish case demonstrates only too clearly what a major assignment this is for historians. The fact that a more faithful and fair-minded view of the past has been constructed – and historians in Ireland have done a great deal towards this in recent years – does not necessarily mean that it will prevail over popular distortions. The mental reflexes of a lifetime are hard to give up, especially when they are grounded in strong self-interest (at least in the short term). There is too little appreciation of the distinction between the two meanings of the word 'history' – between history as what actually happened and history as a collective *representation* of what happened. Above all, myths flourish when historical knowledge is superficial and no alternative perspective is freely available. A sound historical education consists of a certain depth of historical knowledge together with a grasp of the principles of historical criticism. The prevalence of myth demonstrates that this programme is a social necessity, not a luxury for the cultivated minority.

IV

Granted, then, that history has a varied and significant practical relevance, the question remains whether this should influence the way in which historians set about their work. Prior to the Rankean revolution this question could hardly have arisen. Historians believed what their audience assumed, that a historical education offered a training for citizens and statesmen alike. As we saw earlier, many historians were interested in the lessons which could be drawn from the past and in the meaning of history. They took it for granted that history furnished the basis for a rational analysis of politics; indeed, many of the best historians, from Guicciardini in the sixteenth century to Macaulay in the nineteenth, were active in public life. All this was changed by the professionalization of history. By the late nineteenth century the subject featured prominently in the university curriculum all over Europe, controlled by a new breed of historians whose careers were largely confined to academic life. Their subject's traditional claim to offer practical guidance seemed irrelevant – almost an embarrassment. They adhered strictly to the central tenet of historicism, that the study of history 'from the inside' was an end in itself. This attitude still represents the conventional professional approach among British historians. G. R. Elton, the leading authority on Tudor government, is an outspoken champion of the prevailing orthodoxy:

> Teachers of history must set their faces against the necessarily ignorant demands of 'society' . . . for immediate applicability. They need to recall that the 'usefulness' of historical studies lies hardly at all in the knowledge they purvey and in the understanding of specific present problems from their prehistory; it lies much more in the fact that they produce standards of judgement and powers of reasoning which they alone develop, which arise from their very essence, and which are unusually clear-headed, balanced and compassionate.[31]

Apart from providing an intellectual training, the study of history is a personal pursuit which at most enables the individual to achieve some self-awareness by stepping outside his or her immediate experience.[32] Neither of these justifications is peculiar to history: training the mind is part of all academic disciplines worth the name, while the claim to enlarge the individual's experience can be argued with equal, if not greater, conviction by teachers of literature.

One positive result of 'history for its own sake' is a whole-hearted commitment to the re-creation or resurrection of the past in every material and mental dimension. There are historians for whom a fascination with the past as it was really lived and experienced over-rides all other considerations. A notable case is Richard Cobb, a leading historian of the French Revolution:

> The historian should, above all, be endlessly inquisitive and prying, con-stantly attempting to force the privacy of others, and to cross the frontiers of class, nationality, generation, period, and sex. *His principal aim is to make the dead live.* And, like the American 'mortician', he may allow himself a few artifices of the trade: a touch of rouge here, a pencil-stroke there, a little cotton wool in the cheeks, to make the operation more convincing.[33]
> [emphasis added]

Cobb's marvellously evocative studies of the seamy side of life in revolutionary France, notably in *Death in Paris* (1978), certainly vindi-cate his approach. Probably all historians can trace their vocation back to a curiosity about the past for its own sake, often aroused in child-hood by the visible relics of the past around them. And there will always, one hopes, be historians like Cobb with special gifts in the re-creation of the past. But it is quite wrong to suppose that historians in general should be content with this. For most of them it is the essential preliminary to *explaining* the past. Their purpose is to iden-tify trends, to analyse causes and consequences – in short to interpret history as a process and not just as a series of brightly coloured lantern-slides. Thus historians of the English Revolution approach their work with a view to discovering not only what happened in the Civil War or what it felt like to be a soldier in the New Model Army, but why the war occurred and what changes it brought about in the nature of English politics and society. This represents the other side of historicism. Without it history's practical explanatory functions could not be fulfilled at all. (The distinction between re-creation and ex-planation is further explored in Chapter 6.)

However, it is perfectly possible for historical explanation to be pursued without reference to the claims of social relevance, and this, rather than the strictly 'resurrectionist' position, represents the main-stream academic view. For explanation too can be sought 'for its own sake'. Topics such as the origins of the First World War or the social welfare provision of the Victorians can be tackled in an entirely self-contained way without any recognition that they might have a bearing on the choices available to us today. Academic syllabuses are sometimes drawn up on the assumption that history consists of a number of core themes and periods of permanent significance which, because they have generated extensive research and debate, offer the best material for training the intellect. New areas of study like the history of Africa or the history of the family are dismissed as passing fancies peripheral to 'real history'.

It is hard not to detect a fundamental conservatism in these attitudes: if history is defined to exclude anything that smacks of 'relevance', it is less likely to call in question the dominant mythologies of today or suggest radical alternatives to current institutions. This explains why, to conservatives, 'relevant' historical enquiry seems like irreverent muck-raking. Tawney's work on the history of English class relations and business ethics has come in for strong words here, with Elton in the van of the attack:

> The whole collapse of self-confidence which we have encountered in this present generation . . . owes an immense amount to the influence of this one man and his school.[34]

There can be little doubt that conservatives are disproportionately represented in the ranks of the historical profession. As noted earlier, the triumph of historicism during the nineteenth century owed much to the strength of the conservative reaction to the French Revolution. It remains the case that the study of the past often attracts those who are hostile to the direction of social and political change in their own day, and who find comfort in an earlier and more congenial order. This outlook has been marked in English local history: the writings of W. G. Hoskins, a formative influence on this field, are suffused with a nostalgic regret for the passing of the old English rural society.[35]

Disclaimers of social relevance are not, however, usually couched in explicitly conservative terms. They are more commonly defended on the grounds that 'relevant' history is incompatible with the historian's primary obligation to be true to the past, and with the requirements of scholarly objectivity. This argument has a wide currency among academic historians, being supported by many who are not conservative in other respects but who see their professional integrity at stake. But whether grounded in a conservative attitude or not, the denial of practical relevance is timid and in the last resort irresponsible. It is entirely understandable that the original champions of the new historical consciousness should have distanced themselves from issues of current concern, because they were only too aware how severely their subject had suffered at the hands of prophets and propagandists in the past. But the battle for scholarly standards of historical enquiry has long since been won. Practical purposes can be entertained without sacrificing standards of scholarship – which anyway continue to be zealously upheld by institutions of learning.

Historians should, of course, strive to be true to the past; the question is, which past? Faced with the almost limitless evidence of human activity in the past and the need to select certain problems or periods as more deserving of attention than others, the historian is entirely justified in allowing current social concerns to affect his or her choice. The notable broadening of the scope of historical enquiry during the past thirty years is largely the result of a small minority of historians responding to the demands of topicality. The crisis in America's cities during the 1960s brought into being the 'new urban history', with its stress on the history of social mobility, minority group politics and inner-city deprivation. African history was developed at about the same time in Africa and the West by historians who believed that it was indispensable both to the prospects of the newly independent states and to the outside world's understanding of the 'dark continent'. More recently, the history of the family has attracted much attention in the context of contemporary debate in Britain and the USA about the merits of the nuclear family-unit and of marriage-for-life.

Obviously new areas of history which proclaim their relevance are more likely to be manipulated by ideologues than the traditional staple fare of scholarship. But the responsibility of historians in these cases is clear: it is to provide a historical perspective which can inform debate rather than to service any particular ideology. Responding to the call of 'relevance' is not a matter of falsifying or distorting the past, but rather of rescuing from oblivion aspects of that past which now speak to us more directly. Historians of Africa, for example, should be concerned to explain the historical evolution of African societies, not to create a nationalist mythology, and one of the consequences of thirty years' research and writing is that it is now much easier to distinguish between the two than it used to be. Our priorities in the present should determine the questions we ask of the past, but not the answers. As will be shown later in the book, the discipline of historical study makes this a meaningful distinction. At the same time, it is a fallacy to suppose that the aspiration to reconstruct the past in its own terms carries the promise of objectivity: no essay in historical re-creation is proof against the values of the enquirer (see Ch. 7).

But historians who renounce relevance in the cause of objective knowledge are not only pursuing a chimera; they are also evading a wider responsibility. Intellectual curiosity about the past for its own sake is certainly one reason why people read history, but it is not the only one. Society also expects an interpretation of the past which is relevant to the present and a basis for formulating decisions about the future. Historians may argue that, since their expertise concerns the past not the present, it is not their job to draw out the practical import of their work. But they are in fact the only people qualified to equip society with a truly historical perspective and to save it from the damaging effects of exposure to historical myth. If professionally trained historians do not carry out these functions, then others who are less well-informed and more prejudiced will produce ill-founded interpretations. What Geoffrey Barraclough, a veteran champion of contemporary values in history, said thirty years ago applies with equal force today:

> Man is an historical animal, with a deep sense of his own past; and if he cannot integrate the past by a history explicit and true, he will integrate it by a history implicit and false. The challenge is one which no historian with any conviction of the value of his work can ignore; and the way to meet it is not to evade the issue of 'relevance', but to accept the fact and work out its implications.ey

One clear implication is that contemporary history, which can be roughly defined as the period since 1945, has a strong claim on historians. It can be argued that scholars today are too close to the events of this period to achieve sufficient detachment, and that they are further handicapped by their limited access to confidential records (see Ch. 2). But although the job cannot be done as well as historians would like, it is important that they do it to the best of their ability. For it is the recent past on which people draw most for historical analogies and predictions, and their knowledge of it needs to be soundly based if they are to avoid serious error. The recent past has also often proved a fertile breeding ground for crude myths – all the more powerful when their credibility is not contested by scholarly work. Academic neglect of contemporary history therefore has dangerous consequences. But the fulfilment of history's practical functions does not mean the abandonment of more distant periods: far from it. So many facets of the contemporary scene are rooted in the remote past that the tradition of studying the classical, medieval and early modern epochs can never be given up: without it our historical perspective on current problems would be seriously defective. And as evidence of the range of human achievement and mentality in the past, those periods are indispensable.

Responding to society's expectations does not, therefore, impose a limitation as regards periods – or as regards countries. But it does suggest that the selection of themes for research should be influenced by a sensitivity to those areas of current concern which stand most in need of a historical perspective; the examples cited in this chapter could easily be multiplied. Finally, the proper performance of history's social role demands that historians take seriously the task of diffusing as widely as possible their findings and the practical implications to be drawn from them. Scholarly historical writing should not just be directed at the academic community, important though the critical scrutiny of other scholars is; it concerns all who want informed perspectives on the present. One of the criticisms which can most fairly be made of the historical profession today is that too little history is written with this wider audience in view (see Ch. 6).

V

The argument of this chapter can be briefly summed up by situating history in the context of its neighbours among the academic disciplines. Traditionally history has been counted, along with literary and artistic studies, as one of the humanities. The fundamental premise of these disciplines is that what mankind has thought and done has an intrinsic interest and a lasting value irrespective of any practical implications. The re-creation of episodes and ambiences in the past has the same kind of claim on our attention as the re-creation of the thought expressed in a work of art or literature. The historian, like the literary critic and art historian, is a guardian of our cultural heritage, and familiarity with that heritage offers insight into the human condition – a means to heightened self-awareness and empathy with others. In this sense history is, in Cobb's phrase, 'a cultural subject, enriching in itself'[37] and any venture in historical reconstruction is worth doing.

By contrast the social sciences owe their position to their promise of practical guidance. Economists and sociologists seek to understand the workings of economy and society with a view to prescribing solutions to current problems, just as scientists offer the means of mastering the natural world. Historians who believe in their subject's practical functions habitually distance it from the humanities and place it alongside the social sciences. E. H. Carr did so in *What is History?* (1961), probably the finest reflection by a historian on the nature of his subject in our time:

> Scientists, social scientists, and historians are all engaged in different branches of the same study: the study of man and his environment, of the effects of man on his environment and of his environment on man. The object of the study is the same: to increase man's understanding of, and mastery over, his environment.[38]

On this reading, historical re-creation has value primarily as a preliminary to historical explanation, and the kinds of explanation which matter are those which relate to questions of social, economic and political concern.

In this discussion I have given pride of place to the practical uses of history because these continue to arouse such strong resistance among many professional historians. But the truth is that history cannot be defined as either a humanity or a social science without denying a large part of its nature. The mistake that is so often made is to insist that history be categorized as one to the exclusion of the other. History is a hybrid discipline which owes its endless fascination and its complexity to the fact that it straddles the two. If the study of history is to retain its full vitality, this central ambivalence must continue to be recognized, whatever the cost in logical coherence. The study of history 'for its own sake' is not mere antiquarianism. Our human awareness is enhanced by the contemplation of vanished eras, and historical re-creation will always exercise a hold over the imagination, offering as it does vicarious experience to writer and reader alike. At the same time, historians also have a more practical role to perform, and the history which they teach, whether to students in schools and colleges or through the media to the wider public, needs to be informed by an awareness of this role. In this way a historical education achieves a number of goals at once: it trains the mind, enlarges the sympathies *and* provides a much-needed historical perspective on some of the most pressing problems of our time.

NOTES

1. *The Times*, 10 January 1980.
2. Richard G. Plaschka, 'The political significance of František Palacký, *J. of Contemporary History*, VIII, 1973, pp. 35–55.
3. Felix Gilbert, 'The Professionalization of history' in the nineteenth century', in John Higham (ed.) *History*, Prentice-Hall, 1965.
4. See David D. van Tassel, *Recording America's Past*, Chicago University Press, 1960.
5. Richard Hofstadter, *The Progressive Historians*, Cape, 1969, p. 17.
6. T. O. Ranger (ed.) *Emerging Themes of African History*, Heinemann, 1968, p. 218.
7. For a late and eloquent example, see Herbert Butterfield, *The Englishman and His History*, Cambridge University Press, 1944.
8. Quoted in Derk Bodde, *China's First Unifier*, E. J. Brill, 1938, p. 82.
9. David Cannardine, 'The context, performance and meaning of ritual: the British monarchy and the "invention of tradition", *c*. 1820–1977', in Eric Hobsbawn and Terence Ranger (eds.) *The Invention of Tradition*, Cambridge University Press, 1983.
10. *History Workshop Journal*, I, 1976, p. 2 (editorial).
11. Sheila Rowbotham, *Hidden from History*, Pluto Press, 1973.
12. Sheila R. Johansson, ' "Herstory" as history: a new field or another fad?', in Berenice A. Carroll (ed.) *Liberating Women's History*, Illinois University Press, 1976, p. 427.
13. Christopher Hill, *The World Turned Upside Down*, Penguin, 1975; E. P. Thompson, *The Making of the English Working Class*, Penguin, 1968.
14. See E. P. Thompson, *Writing by Candlelight*, Merlin, 1980, especially 'The State of the Nation', for popular and polemical writing in this vein.
15. J. H. Plumb, *The Death of the Past*, Macmillan, 1969, pp. 14–15, 142–5.

16. See reports by Martin Walker in *The Guardian*, 19 and 20 June 1983, and feature article by Christopher Hill, 30 July.

17. W. S. Churchill, *Marlborough: His Life and Times*, (4 vols), Harrap, 1933–38; Roy Jenkins, *Asquith*, Collins, 1964.

18. Francesco Guicciardini, *Maxims and Reflections of a Renaissance Statesman (Ricordi)*, Harper & Row, 1965, p. 69.

19. L. von Ranke, *Histories of the Latin and German Nations from 1494 to 1514*, extract translated in G. P. Gooch, *History and Historians in the Nineteenth Century*, 2nd edn, Longman, 1952, p. 74.

20. Unfortunately this is the impression conveyed by the most frequently cited translation, 'What actually happened': see Fritz Stern (ed.) *The Varieties of History*, 2nd edn, Macmillan, 1970, p. 57.

21. Christopher Hill, *Change and Continuity in Seventeenth-Century England*, Weidenfeld & Nicolson, 1974, p. 284.

22. David H. Fischer, *Historians' Fallacies*, Routledge & Kegan Paul, 1971, Ch. 9.

23. Geoffrey Barraclough, *From Agadir to Armageddon*, Weidenfeld & Nicolson, 1982, is an explicit and controversial attempt to apply a historical analogy.

24. Michael Anderson, 'The relevance of family history', in Chris Harris (ed.) *The Sociology of the Family*, University of Keele, 1980.

25. Marc Bloch, *The Historian's Craft*, Manchester University Press, 1954, pp. 39–40.

26. R. H. Tawney, *History and Society*, Routledge & Kegan Paul, 1978, p. 55.

27 Richard Gray and David Birmingham (eds.) *Pre-Colonial African Trade*, Oxford University Press, 1970; Robin Palmer and Neil Parsons (eds.) *The Roots of Rural Poverty in Southern and Central Africa*, Heinemann, 1977.

28. Peter Burke, 'People's history or total history' in Raphael Samuel (ed.) *People's History and Socialist Theory*, Routledge & Kegan Paul, 1981, p. 8.

29. Theodore Zeldin, 'After Braudel', *The Listener*, 5 November 1981, p. 542.

30. D. W. Harkness, *History and the Irish*, Queen's University of Belfast, 1976.

31. G. R. Elton, 'Second thoughts on history at the universities', *History*, LIV, 1969, p. 66. See also his *The Practice of History*, Fontana, 1969, pp. 66–8.

32. V. H. Galbraith, *An Introduction to the Study of History*, C. A. Watts, 1964, pp. 59–61; David Thompson, *The Aims of History*, Thames & Hudson, 1969, pp. 11–12.

33. Richard Cobb, *A Second Identity: Essays on France and French History*, Oxford University Press, 1969, p. 47.

34. G. R. Elton, *The Future of the Past*, Cambridge University Press, 1968, p. 16.

35. See W. G. Hoskins, *The Making of the English Landscape*, Penguin, 1970.

36. Geoffrey Barraclough, *History in a Changing World*, Blackwell, 1955, pp. 24–5.

37.   Richard Cobb, *A Sense of Place*, Duckworth, 1975, p. 4.
38.   E. H. Carr, *What is History?*, Penguin, 1964, p. 86.

Chapter 2

THE RAW MATERIALS

Such is the range of motives and the variety of interests which draw people to the past that history can be said to embrace the human experience of every place and period in the past. No part of that past can be dismissed as falling outside the proper domain of historical knowledge. But how far it can be made the subject of well-founded research depends on the availability of historical evidence. Whether the historian's main concern is with re-creation or explanation, with the past for its own sake or for the light it can shed on the present, what he or she can actually achieve is determined in the first instance by the extent and character of the surviving sources. Accordingly it is with the sources that any account of the historian's work must begin. This chapter describes the main categories of documentary material, showing how they came into being, how they have survived down to the present, and in what form they are available to the scholar.

I

Historical sources encompass every kind of evidence which human beings have left of their past activities – the written word and the spoken word, the shape of the landscape and the material artefact, the fine arts as well as photography and film. Among the humanities and social sciences history is unique in the variety of its source materials, each calling for specialist expertise. The military historian of the English Civil War can examine the arms and armour surviving from the seventeenth century, the terrain over which the battles were fought, as well as the military dispatches of each side. A rounded picture of the General Strike of 1926 calls for a study of government and trade union records, the press and broadcasting, together with the collection of testimonies from survivors. The reconstruction of a pre-colonial kingdom in black Africa is likely to depend not only on the excavation of its capital but on the contemporary observations of European or Arab visitors and the oral traditions handed down over many generations. No single historian can possibly master all these tools. The more technical of them have become the province of distinct specialisms. The excavation of ancient sites and the interpretation of the material remains found there is the business of the archaeologist, assisted these days by the aerial photographer and the chemical analyst. The art historian has established a comparable hold over the study of the visual arts. The historian frequently draws on the findings of archaeologists and art historians, and he or she may feel qualified to draw inferences from a wide range of material evidence – from the design and structure of a Norman castle, for example, or the imagery employed in contemporary portraits of Elizabeth I and on the coinage of her reign; but these are regarded by most historians as 'extras', peripheral to their discipline. During the past thirty years the range of sources in which historians claim expertise has certainly increased. It now includes place-names, landscape patterns and – for recent history – film. The fact remains, however, that the study of history has nearly always been based squarely on what the historian can read in documents or hear from informants. And ever since historical research was placed on a professional footing during Ranke's lifetime, the emphasis has fallen almost exclusively on the written rather than the spoken word – though oral sources, as we shall see, have recently begun to attract attention once more (see Ch. 10). For the vast majority of historians, research is confined to libraries and archives.

The reason is not just academic conservatism. From the High Middle Ages (*c.* 1000–1300) onwards, the written word survives in greater abundance than any other source for Western history. The fifteenth and sixteenth centuries witnessed not only a marked growth in record-keeping by the state and other corporate bodies, but also the rapid spread of printing which encouraged literate production of all kinds and transformed its prospects of survival. Written sources are usually precise as regards time, place and authorship, and they reveal the thoughts and actions of individual men and women as no other source can do. One has only to read an account of a society for which virtually no written records exist – for example Iron Age Britain or Medieval Zimbabwe – to see how lacking in human vitality history can be when denied its principal source material. Moreover, the written word has always served many different purposes – information, propaganda, personal communication, private reflection and creative release – all of which may have relevance for the historian. The interpretation of texts serving a variety of functions from an age whose habits of mind differed sharply from our own calls for critical abilities of a very high order. Written sources are at the same time the most rewarding and (in most cases) the most plentiful. Small wonder, then, that historians seldom look elsewhere.

The use of written materials as the principal historical source is complicated by the fact that historians communicate their findings through the same medium. Both in their choice of research topic and in their finished work, historians are influenced to a greater or lesser extent by what their predecessors have written, accepting much of the evidence which they uncovered and, rather more selectively, the interpretations which they put upon it. But when we read the work of a historian we stand at one remove from the original sources of the period in question – and further away still if that historian has been content to rely on the writings of other historians. The first test by which any historical work must be judged is how far its interpretation of the past is consistent with all the available evidence; when new sources are discovered or old ones are read in a new light, even the most prestigious book may end on the scrap-heap. In a very real sense the modern discipline of history rests not on what has been handed down by earlier historians, but on a constant reassessment of the original sources. It is for this reason that historians regard the original sources as *primary*. Everything which they and their predecessors have written about the past counts as a *secondary* source. Most of this book is concerned with secondary sources – with how historians formulate problems and reach conclusions, and how we as readers should evaluate their work. But first it is necessary to examine the raw materials a little more closely.

The distinction between primary and secondary sources, fundamental though it is to historical research, is rather less clear-cut than it might appear at first sight, and the precise demarcation varies between different authorities. By 'original sources' is meant evidence contemporary with the event or thought to which it refers. But how far should our definition of 'contemporary' be stretched? No-one would quibble about a conversation reported a week or even a month after it took place, but what about the version of the same episode in an autobiography composed twenty years later? And how should we categorize an account of a riot written shortly afterwards, but by someone who was not present and relied entirely on hearsay? Although some purists regard the testimony of anyone who was not an eye-witness as a secondary source,[1] it makes better sense to apply a broad definition, but to recognize at the same time that some sources are more 'primary' than others. The historian will usually prefer those sources which are closest in time and place to the events in question. But sources more remote from the action have their own significance. The historian is often as much interested in what contemporaries *thought* was happening as in what actually happened: British reactions to the French Revolution, for example, had a profound influence on the climate of politics in this country, and from this point of view the often garbled reports of events in Paris which circulated in Britain at the time are an indispensable source. As this example suggests, to speak of a source as 'primary' implies no judgement of its reliability or freedom from bias. Many primary sources are inaccurate, muddled, based on hearsay or intended to mislead, and (as the next chapter will show) it is a vital part of the historian's work to scrutinize the source for distortions of this kind. The distinction between primary and secondary is further complicated by the fact that sometimes primary and secondary material appear in the same work. Medieval chroniclers usually began with an account of world history since the Creation to the life of Christ, based on well-known authorities; but what modern historians value them most for is the entries which they recorded year by year concerning current events. Equally a work can be primary in one context and secondary in another: Macaulay's *History of England* (1848–55) is a secondary source whose reputation has been much undermined by modern research; but for anyone studying the political and historical assumptions of the early Victorian elite, Macaulay's book, in its day a best-seller, is a significant primary source. These examples might suggest what is often assumed, that 'historical documents' are the formal, dignified records of the past. It is true that records of this kind are more likely to endure, but the term should carry the widest possible reference. Every day all of us create what are potentially historical documents – financial accounts, private correspondence, even shopping lists. Whether they actually become historical documents depends on whether they survive and whether they are used as primary evidence by scholars of the future.

In order to make sense of the vast mass of surviving primary sources, the first requirement is some system of classification. Two types are in common use. The first draws a distinction between the published – which in the modern period has usually meant printed – and the unpublished or manuscript source. The second emphasizes instead the authorship of the sources, drawing a distinction between those produced by governments and those produced by corporations, associations or private individuals. Each of these methods lends itself to the precision required by the cataloguer, and bibliographies published by historians at the end of their works are normally arranged along these lines. But the criteria which historians actually apply in the course of their research, although related to these two types of classification, are rather less cut and dried. In the historian's hierarchy of sources those which carry most weight are the ones which arise directly from everyday business or social intercourse, leaving open the task of interpretation. In every age men and women have sought to make sense of their times, and to interpret the pattern of events through books, broadsheets and newspapers. Such statements offer valuable insights into the mentality of the age, but for the historian they are no substitute for the direct, day-to-day evidence of thought and action provided by the letter, the diary and the memorandum: these are the 'records' of history *par excellence.* The historian wishes to be as nearly as possible an observer of the events in question; he does not want to deliver himself into the hands of a narrator or commentator. The most revealing source is that which was written with no thought for posterity. Marc Bloch called this 'the evidence of witnesses in spite of themselves';[2] it has all the fascination of eaves-dropping.

II

We begin, however, with primary sources written for the benefit of posterity. These tend to be the most accessible because their survival was seldom left to chance. Often they have a literary quality which makes them a pleasure to read. They provide a ready-made chronology, a coherent selection of events, and a strong sense of period atmosphere. Their drawback is that they recount only what people found worthy of note about their own age – which may not be what interests us today. Prior to the Rankean revolution in the nineteenth century it was on primary sources of this kind that historians tended to rely. For Roman history they turned to Caesar, Tacitus and Suetonius, while Medievalists drew on the Anglo-Saxon Chronicle and the works of men like Matthew Paris in the thirteenth century and Jean Froissart in the fourteenth. Nor do modern historians disparage these narrative sources. They owe their continuing importance to the fact that they survive from periods which have left only a limited amount of record sources. In the Middle Ages most of the early chronicles were written by monks without personal experience of public affairs, but increasingly from the twelfth century they were joined by secular clergy who had served the king in responsible positions and could to some extent record political history from the inside. Gerald of Wales was a royal chaplain who became acquainted with Henry II towards the end of his reign in the 1180s. The following passage well conveys the restless energy of one of England's most remarkable kings:

> Henry II, king of England, was a man of reddish, freckled complexion with a large round head, grey eyes which glowed fiercely and grew bloodshot in anger, a fiery countenance and a harsh, cracked voice. His neck was somewhat thrust forward from his shoulders, his chest was broad and square, his arms strong and powerful. His frame was stocky with a pronounced tendency to corpulence, due rather to nature than to indulgence, which he tempered by exercise . . .
> In times of war, which frequently threatened, he gave himself scarcely a modicum of quiet to deal with those matters of business which were left over, and in times of peace he allowed himself neither tranquility nor repose. He was addicted to the chase beyond measure; at crack of dawn he was off on horseback, traversing waste lands, penetrating forests and climbing the mountain-tops, and so he passed restless days. At evening on his

return he was rarely seen to sit down either before or after supper. After such great and wearisome exertions he would wear out the whole court by continual standing.[3]

The autobiography is essentially a modern variant of the chronicle, with the personality of the author brought to the front of the stage. Invented by the self-conscious Italians of the Renaissance,[4] this form is favoured by artists, writers, and perhaps most of all by politicians. Their fascination derives from the fact that they are the recollections of an insider. Indeed they often provide the only available first-hand account because in all countries recent government records are closed to public inspection (see below p. 43–4); in Britain former Cabinet ministers, when writing their memoirs, are permitted to consult official papers relating to their term of office, though they may not cite or quote from them. But the author's purpose is less to offer an objective account than to justify his or her actions in retrospect and to provide evidence for the defence before the bar of history. Autobiographies may be very revealing of mentality and values, but as a record of events they are often inaccurate and selective to the point of distortion. The historian of the Suez crisis of 1956 who could use no other source than the third volume of Sir Anthony Eden's memoirs (*Full Circle*, 1960) would be in an unenviable position.

The eighteenth century understood the term 'memoirs' in a rather different sense: it denoted a personal chronicle written by someone in public life and intended for publication only after – sometimes long after – his or her death; its purpose was to record facts and opinions which it would have been indiscreet or dangerous to make known at the time, and it therefore makes much more exciting reading than the usually bland and evasive political autobiography. The master of this genre was the Duc de Saint-Simon whose ambition was to leave what has been aptly called 'a minority or dissenting report'[5] on the Versailles of Louis XIV and Louis XV; his *Memoirs*, written in a superb prose style, cover the years from 1691 to 1723. His nearest English rival was Lord Hervey, a favourite of George II's Queen Caroline, who composed a malicious picture of palace intrigue between 1727 and 1737.[6]

The chronicles and memoirs which people write for future generations are, of course, only a small minority of what is published in any period. Most publications are issued with little thought for posterity; they are rather intended to inform, influence, mislead or entertain contemporaries. The invention of printing in the fifteenth century greatly facilitated the dissemination of such writings, while the growth of literacy among the laity increased the demand for them. Governments were quick to profit from the revolution in communications, and by the nineteenth century statements of policy, propaganda, and digests of information on trade, revenue and expenditure were flowing from the official presses. In Britain perhaps the most impressive of these publications were the census reports published every ten years from 1801, and the reports of royal commissions set up from the 1830s onwards to take evidence and make recommendations on major social problems such as public health and conditions of work. Another official publication of great interest is the reports of parliamentary proceedings. Thomas Hansard began publication of the debates in the Lords and Commons as a private venture in 1812 (though not quite the first of its kind). The series assumed its modern format in 1909 when the government, through His Majesty's Stationery Office, took it over; first-person, verbatim reporting became the rule. Few other sources convey so well the public face of political discourse.

But the most important published primary source for the historian is the press, which in Britain has a continuous history dating back to the early eighteenth century, the first daily newspaper having been founded in 1702. Newspapers have a threefold value. In the first place, they record the political and social views which made most impact at the time; indeed the earliest newspapers, which had developed out of the vigorous tradition of pamphleteering during the Civil War and Commonwealth (1642–60), contained little else and are remembered now for the brilliant polemics of Addison, Steele and Swift. To this day the leaders and correspondence columns of the great London dailies offer the best entry into the current state of establishment opinion – provided due allowance is made for the editorial bias of the paper in question. Secondly, newspapers provide a day-to-day record of events. During the nineteenth century this function began to be filled much more fully, particularly when the development of the electric telegraph in the 1850s enabled journalists in distant postings to file their copy home as soon as it was written. W. H. Russell of *The Times* was one of the first to take advantage of this revolution in communications. His celebrated despatches from the Crimea during the war of 1854–56, which provided shocking evidence of the disarray of the British forces, had a major impact on public opinion at home and still make compelling reading.[7] As sources of straight reporting, newspapers are likely to become even more valuable to historians in the future. For despite the vast archives which governments and corporations continue to amass, important decisions are increasingly communicated by telephone rather than by letter, and information obtained informally by journalists at the time may provide the only contemporary written record of what has taken place. Lastly, newspapers from time to time present the results of more thorough enquiries into issues which lie beyond the scope of routine news-reporting. The founder of this tradition was Henry Mayhew, an impecunious writer briefly employed by the *Morning Chronicle* in 1849–50. As 'Special Correspondent for the Metropolis' he wrote a series of articles exposing social conditions among the London poor in the aftermath of the great cholera epidemic of 1849, which later formed the basis of his book, *London Labour and the London Poor*

(1851). Few investigative journalists since then have equalled Mayhew in the thoroughness of his research or in his impact on contemporary opinion.[8]

There is one other kind of source intended for the eyes of contemporaries (and often for posterity too) which historians have to consider, though it is rather a special case: this is creative literature. Novels and plays cannot, of course, be treated as factual reports, however great the element of autobiography or social observation may be. Nor, needless to say, do historical novels – or Shakespeare's history plays for that matter – carry any authority as historical statements about the periods to which they refer. But all creative literature offers insights into the social and intellectual milieu in which the writer lived, and often vivid descriptions of the physical setting as well. The success of an author is often attributable to the way in which he or she articulates the values and preoccupations of literary contemporaries. So it makes good sense to cite Chaucer as a spokesman for the attitudes of the fourteenth-century laity to abuses in the Church, or Dickens as evidence of the frame of mind in which middle-class Victorians considered the 'condition of England' question.

III

Because newspapers, official publications and parliamentary speeches are composed mostly with a view to their impact on contemporary opinion, historians attach greater weight to them than to the chronicles and memoirs written with the requirements of posterity in mind. But the very fact of publication sets a limit on the value of all these sources. They contain only what was considered to be fit for public consumption – what governments were prepared to reveal, what journalists could elicit from tight-lipped informants, what editors thought would gratify their readers, or MPs their constituents. In each case there is a controlling purpose which may limit, distort or falsify what is said. The historian who wishes, in Ranke's phrase, 'to show how things really were' (see above p. 11) must go behind the published word, and that is why the greatest advances in modern historical knowledge have been based on research into 'records' – that is, confidential documents such as letters, minutes and diaries. It is in these forms that men and women record their decisions, discussions and sometimes their innermost thoughts, unmindful of the eyes of future historians. Time and again, historians have found that a careful study of the record sources reveals a picture very different from the confident generalizations of contemporary observers. Whether the question at issue is the motives of the participants in the English Civil War, or the impact of the

Industrial Revolution on standards of living, or the volume of the Atlantic slave trade, there is no substitute for the painstaking accumulation of evidence from the record sources of the period.

In most countries the largest single body of unpublished records is that belonging to the state, and since Ranke's day more research has been devoted to government archives than to any other kind of source. In the West the oldest surviving state archives took shape during the twelfth century, which saw a marked advance in the sophistication of government organization all over Europe. In England a continuous series of revenue records – the Pipe Rolls of the Exchequer – extends back to 1155, and the records of the royal courts (King's Bench and Common Pleas) to 1194. The beginning of systematic record-keeping can be dated precisely to 1199. In that year King John's chancellor, Hubert Walter, began the practice of making copies on parchment rolls of all the more important letters dispatched from Chancery in the king's name. Even after the emergence of other departments in the thirteenth and fourteenth centuries, the Chancery remained the nerve-centre of royal administration, and its enrolments are the most important archival source for the Middle Ages in England.

During the period 1450–1550 the Medieval system was superseded by a more bureaucratic administrative structure controlled by the Privy Council. The most powerful single official within this structure was the king's secretary (later called the secretary of state), and from the reign of Henry VIII his records, known as the State Papers, become the most rewarding source for the policies and actions of the government. In contrast to Chancery records the State Papers, to quote Galbraith,

> are not the routine products of an office, but the intimate and miscellaneous correspondence of an official whose duties knew no fixed limits . . . The veil that separates us from character and personality in the Middle Ages is torn aside.[9]

Among the State Papers for 1536 there survives this letter summoning an unfortunate priest from Leicestershire to an interrogation, probably in connection with treason; the menacing tone is unmistakable:

> I commend me unto you. Letting you wit the King's pleasure and commandment is that, all excuses and delays set apart, ye shall incontinently upon the sight hereof repair unto me wheresoever I shall chance to be, the specialties whereof ye shall know at your coming. Without failing thus to do, as ye will answer at your peril. From the Rolls, the 8th day of July. Thomas Crumwell (sic)[10].

It is this category of document which proliferated in the following centuries as additional secretaries of state were appointed to run new departments which could keep abreast of the expanding scope of government. By the nineteenth century each department of state was keeping a systematic record of letters and papers received, copies of letters sent out, and memoranda circulating within the department. At the apex of this complex bureaucratic structure stands the Cabinet. For the first two hundred years of its existence, its deliberations were entirely 'off the record', but since 1916 the Cabinet Secretariat has kept minutes of the Cabinet's weekly meetings and prepared papers for its use.

Another aspect of the enlargement of government under the Tudors was the beginning of routine diplomacy conducted by resident accredited ambassadors. The Italian states set the pattern in the 1480s and 1490s; other countries soon followed, and England's diplomatic network had taken shape by the 1520s. The Venetian ambassador who, in the course of twelve months in 1503–4, sent back from Rome 472 despatches was more industrious than most,[11] but regular reporting home was from the start an essential part of the ambassador's duties. These reports not only document the conduct of foreign policy more fully than ever before; they also record the diplomat's appraisal of the court and country to which he was accredited. Ranke relied on them heavily for both political and diplomatic history, and there have been many historians since whose expertise is almost entirely limited to diplomatic documents. By the late nineteenth century – often thought of as the 'golden age' of diplomatic history – the documentary record is so full that the historian can reconstruct every stage in a diplomatic initiative from the first tentative proposal of a ministry official to the completed report on the negotiations.

Two other types of record share the official character of central government records. In the first place, during the Middle Ages the Church wielded as much, if not more authority than the state, and in most European countries retained many of its powers in the secular sphere until the early nineteenth century. Its history is fully documented by the immense quantity of church records which are available to historians today, many of them still virtually untouched. Royal charters granting land and privileges to the Church have been preserved from the early Middle Ages, and copious records document the efficiency of episcopal and monastic administration. The records of the church courts are more interesting than might seem likely at first glance, because so many moral misdemeanours of ordinary people came within their jurisdiction. In sixteenth- and early seventeenth-century England, for example, when the established Church's position *vis-à-vis* the Puritan sects was under threat, strenuous efforts were made through the church courts to discipline the laity, and the records of these courts are therefore an important source for the social historian. The church courts also retained jurisdiction over wills in England until 1858, and from Elizabeth I's reign onwards they insisted on detailed inventories of all moveable property, which can now tell the historian a great deal about wealth, status and standards of living.

Secondly, there are the records of local government. During the thirteenth century in England lords of the manor began to follow the king's example and keep records – and particularly judicial records since they had legal jurisdiction over their tenants and servants. One result is that changes in landholding are relatively well documented for rich and poor alike. The first justices of the peace were commissioned by the Crown in the fourteenth century, and under the Tudors they were saddled with a mounting load of responsibility – for matters as various as policing, poor relief, wage regulation and military recruitment. Much of this burden was discharged during quarter sessions held at three-monthly intervals in each county, and recorded by a clerk of the peace. This remained the basis of local government in England until the modern system of county and borough councils was established during the nineteenth century. Until that time a high proportion of local records are legal: the same individuals – whether lords of the manor or JPs – were charged with judicial as well as administrative duties. Of all public records, the court records of everyday and often trivial disputes and misdemeanours shed most light on the wider society beyond the small world of government.

Church and state are the oldest record-keeping institutions in Western society. But from the fifteenth century onwards the historian can supplement them with an ever-increasing volume of records generated by private corporations and associations – guilds, universities, trade unions, political parties and pressure groups. Prior to the nineteenth century those that survive in the greatest number are the estate records of landed families, many of which endured over several centuries: their deeds, account books, maps and business correspondence are indispensable material for agrarian historians. Another source within this general category which has atracted much attention – from historians of the Industrial Revolution especially – is the records of businesses and firms. For example, the papers of the Stockport textile manufacturer, Samuel Oldknow, were discovered quite by chance in a disused mill in 1921; covering the period 1782–1812, they provide vivid documentation for the transition from the domestic to the factory system of production.[12] Many companies today have cashbooks, inventories and ledgers dating back to the same period or earlier; the historian of England's brewing industry recalls,

> The family continuity in the industry has been such that in most cases I found myself working on the letters and the accounts of the ancestors of the present owners and managers of the concerns, reading their records on the same site where they had brewed in the eighteenth century.[13]

The records he examined included those of such well-known names as Whitbread, Charrington and Truman.

IV

As a general rule, those activities which leave most evidence behind are *organized* activities, and especially those controlled by bodies which have a lifespan beyond the careers of the individuals who happen to staff them at any one time – whether they be governments, religious bodies or businesses. For the greater part of recorded history, literate people have probably done most of their writing in the course of their professional or official duties. Nevertheless there survives a vast mass of written material which has been set down by men and women as private individuals, outside the office or the counting house. Much the largest proportion is accounted for by private correspondence. Among the earliest and most intimate is that between a successful fourteenth-century merchant of Prato (a Tuscan cloth town) and his wife. For eighteen years (1382–1400) pressure of business kept Francesco Datini away from home in Florence and Pisa, and twice a week he wrote to Margherita, and she almost as often to him. On Datini's instructions, most of these letters, along with his extensive business correspondence, were preserved after his death in his house at Prato. The result is a unique chronicle of a Medieval marriage. Something of the strain which frequent separations imposed on the marriage is conveyed in this extract from a letter written by Margherita in 1389:

> As to your staying away from here until Thursday, you can do as you please, being our master – which is a fine office, but should be used with discretion . . . *I* am fully disposed to live together, as God wills . . . and I am in the right, and you will not change it by shouting.
>
> Methinks it is not needful to send me a message every Wednesday, to say you will be here on Sunday, for I trow on every Friday, you repent. It would suffice to tell me on Saturday that I could buy something more at the market: for then at least we would fare well on Sundays.[14]

There are no other sources which bring to life so clearly the family and social relationships of people in the past. Without private correspondence the biographer must be content with the public or business life of his subject – which indeed is all that Medieval biographies can usually attain. But private letters are an essential source for historians of politics as well. This is because government records are more concerned with decisions and their implementation than with the motives of the people who made them. The private correspondence of public figures reveals much that is scarcely hinted at in the official record. It is the 522 volumes of the Duke of Newcastle's papers (supported by many other private collections), rather than the State Papers or the proceedings of the House of Commons, which underpin Namier's classic analyses of electoral and parliamentary management in the mid-eighteenth century.[15] The nineteenth and early twentieth centuries were the eve of the telephone era and the great age of personal correspondence, when close colleagues in public life wrote to each other daily. Much of this correspondence by-passed official channels and was intended to be seen by none but the recipient. Some politicians confided to a remarkable degree in friends who were without any formal position in politics at all. For three of the years (1912–15) during which he was prime minister, H. H. Asquith wrote once or twice a day to a young lady called Venetia Stanley. In these letters he could frankly express all his political anxieties and frustrations (as well as many more trivial reflections) confident that his remarks would go no further. Here, in a letter of March 1915, is his assessment of Winston Churchill, then First Lord of the Admiralty:

> As you know, like you, I am really fond of him; but I regard his future with many misgivings . . . He will never get to the top in English politics, with all his wonderful gifts; to speak with the tongue of men & angels, and to spend laborious days & nights in administration, is no good, if a man does not inspire trust.[16]

Private letters are associated with another source which is in some ways even more revealing of personality and opinion – the diary. Diary-keeping began in the sixteenth century and soon became a common literary accomplishment among the educated, especially in England, which in John Evelyn and Samuel Pepys produced two of the greatest masters of the art. Unlike the chronicler or annalist, the diarist is as much preoccupied with his own subjective response as with the external events which he has witnessed. The considerations which induce someone to devote several hours each week to keeping up a diary are anything but frivolous. For creative writers the diary satisfies the compulsion to observe and reflect, free of the constraints imposed by the formal requirements of the novel, poem or play. Of politicians it is sometimes assumed that a diary serves as little more than an *aide-mémoire* to be drawn on when the time comes to compose an autobiography. But for most political diarists this is a secondary consideration compared with the release from the intense pressures of life in the public eye which a diary affords. The diary which Gladstone kept from 1825 to 1896 has almost the character of a confessional: the record of daily engagements and political commentaries is broken up by long passages of painful self-analysis, an unremitting quest for purity of soul.[17] No historian who has not read the diary can hope to understand the personality of this giant among Victorian statesmen. In the case of the Labour politician, Hugh Dalton, diary-writing seems to have filled a psychological need directly related to his political performance. As Ben Pimlott explains, the diary, which spans the years 1916 to 1960, acted both as a 'sounding-board for ideas' and as a safety-valve for Dalton's 'very strong instinct towards political self-destructiveness', being fullest for those times when he was consumed by feelings of resentment or irritation against his closest political associates.[18]

For the historian of twentieth-century politics letters and diaries are of particular significance, despite the almost limitless volume of official records. In the course of the last two generations ministers and civil servants have tended to become more discreet in their official correspondence. During the nineteenth century such correspondence was occasionally published by authority, for example in the Blue Books laid by British ministers before Parliament; but this was usually done almost immediately, for pressing propaganda reasons, and the published despatches had in some cases been composed with that express purpose. In the 1920s, however, the select publication of official records grew out of all proportion, as governments strove to excuse themselves, and blame others, for responsibility for the First World War, often with scant regard for the reputation of individual officials twenty or thirty years earlier. Ministers and civil servants, especially those concerned with foreign policy, became much more inhibited in their official correspondence; what they wrote to each other privately, or recorded in their diaries, therefore gains in interest. Moreover, much that politicians *do* say in the course of their ministerial duties does not find its way into the official record. The civil servants who compile Cabinet minutes, for example, are primarily concerned with the decisions reached; the heated political arguments, which are what interests the historian most about Cabinet meetings, go largely unrecorded. Richard Crossman, who served as a Cabinet minister under Harold Wilson from 1964–70, kept a weekly diary which was intended, as he put it, to do something towards 'lighting up the secret places of British politics', among which the Cabinet featured prominently.[19] Crossman's diary is unusual in that, almost from the outset, he envisaged its publication within a few years; his work bears comparison with 'memoirs' in the sense understood by Saint-Simon or Hervey. By contrast, the vast majority of the diaries and letters available to the historian were written without thought of a wider readership. Of all sources they are the most spontaneous and unvarnished, revealing both the calculated strategems and the unconscious assumptions of public figures.

V

From this discussion about the different categories of source material it will be apparent that a variety of factors has contributed to the survival of so much documentation from the past. Private letters and diaries have owed their survival to the writer's desire for posthumous fame, or the family piety of the heirs, or perhaps their inertia in leaving trunks and drawers undisturbed. In the case of public records the reasons are more straightforward and more compelling: they arise from the central role of written precedent in law and administration since the High Middle Ages. To put it bluntly, governments needed an accurate record of what was due to them in taxes, dues and services, while the king's subjects cherished evidence of privileges and exemptions which had been granted to them in the past. As the royal bureaucracy grew bigger and more unwieldy, it became increasingly necessary for officials to have a record of what their predecessors had done. As the practice of diplomacy became more formalized from the fifteenth century onwards, ministers could review the earlier relations of their governments with foreign powers and be briefed on their obligations and entitlements under foreign treaties. What was true of governments applied *mutatis mutandis* to other corporate bodies such as the Church, or the great trading companies and financial houses. The only way in which institutions with this sort of permanence could have a 'memory' was if a careful record of their transactions was preserved.

But practical motives are not everything. Written documents are also fragile, and the fact that they have weathered the hazards of fire, flood and sheer neglect in such profusion also requires explanation. Continuity of government and of basic law and order are vital. Throughout most of Europe the fabric of literate civilization has endured without a break since the early Middle Ages. Within Europe the distribution of the surviving documentation is largely explained by the incidence of warfare and revolutionary upheaval. It is because England has had little of either that English Medieval public records are so plentiful. Last but not least, the growth of historical consciousness itself has had important consequences in minimizing the destruction of documents once they have ceased to be of practical use. Here the Renaissance was the turning point. Curiosity about classical antiquity bred an antiquarian mentality which valued the relics of the past for their own sake – hence the beginning of both archaeology and the systematic conservation of manuscripts and books. It is the combination of these factors which accounts for the uniquely rich documentation for the history of Western society, and distinguishes it from the other great literate cultures of China, India and the Muslim world where the survival of written sources has been much more patchy.

Only relatively recently, however, has it become a reasonably simple matter to locate the sources and secure access to them. Without the coming of age of historical studies in the mid-nineteenth century and the growing political awareness of the need to preserve the raw materials of a national past, historians today would face a much more daunting prospect. Their task is easiest in the case of published sources. In England there is a good chance that the researcher, assisted by bibliographies and catalogues, will find what he or she wants in one of the great 'copyright' libraries which by Act of Parliament are entitled to a free copy of every book and pamphlet published in the United Kingdom; the most complete is the British Museum (reorganized as the British Library in 1973) whose entitlement dates back to 1757, and has been rigorously enforced since the 1840s. But what of the unpublished sources? The conservation of public and private documents, many of them written with no thought for the requirements of storage and reference, presents much greater problems.

In some cases the problems have been partially solved by publication. An immense effort was devoted to this task during the nineteenth century when the historical value of records gained common acceptance for the first time. The pattern was set by the *Monumenta Germaniae Historica* series, which began publication with government support in 1826 under the direction of the best historians of the day; by the 1860s most of the raw materials for Medieval German history were in print.[20] Other countries quickly followed suit, including Britain, where the equivalent Rolls Series began to appear in 1858. The original promoters of these projects intended to publish *all* the extant primary sources. Even for the Medieval period this was an ambitious goal; for later, more lavishly documented periods it was an obvious impossibility. In the late nineteenth century, therefore, attention was increasingly switched to the publication of 'calendars', or full summaries of the records. Calendars are an immense help to the researcher, but only because they indicate which documents are relevant to his or her purpose; they are no substitute for perusal of the originals. There is therefore no evading the need to spend long and often tedious hours reading primary sources in manuscript.

The historian's task is in most countries greatly eased by an elaborate archive service. But this is a relatively recent development, and the survival of documents from the remote past has often owed more to luck than good management. Many archival collections have perished by accident: the Whitehall fire of 1619 destroyed many of the Privy Council papers, and the fire which swept the Palace of Westminster in 1834 took with it most of the records belonging to the House of Commons. Other holdings have been deliberately destroyed for political reasons: a prominent feature of the agrarian revolts which broke out in the French countryside in July 1789 was the burning of manorial archives which authorized the exaction of heavy dues from the peasantry.[21] In Africa during the 1960s departing colonial officials sometimes destroyed their files for fear that sensitive material would fall into the hands of their African successors.

In England, as elsewhere in Europe, the conservation of archives by the state dates back to the twelfth century. But until the nineteenth century each department of government retained its own archives. They were housed all over London in a variety of buildings, many of them highly unsuitable. Throughout the seventeenth and eighteenth centuries the Chancery records in the Tower were kept above the

Ordnance Board's gunpowder stores,[22] while other repositories were exposed to the ravages of damp and rodents. These conditions not only frustrated private litigants (and the occasional historian) wishing to track down precedents, but were an embarrassment to the government itself: it was not unknown for the original of an important treaty to elude the most diligent search.[23] The mid-nineteenth century was a period of reform in this as in so many other spheres of administration. The Public Record Office was set up by Act of Parliament in 1838, and within twenty years it had gained custody of all the main classes of government record. Without that reorganization the immense progress made in the study of English Medieval history – the greatest achievement of British historians in the late nineteenth and early twentieth centuries – would scarcely have been possible. Today the Public Record Office is the largest archive in the world (with over 80 miles of shelving) and, in its new premises at Kew, offers probably the most up to date facilities to be found anywhere. In the course of the nineteenth century the archives of most other European countries were reorganized and made available to researchers. A comparable process has taken place in the new states of Asia and Africa which won independence between the 1940s and 1970s. The consolidation of the records of colonial administration into a national archive has been one of the first tasks undertaken in pursuit of a properly documented national past.

As the interests of historians have been enlarged to cover social and economic themes (see Ch. 5), the conservation and organization of local records has been increasingly taken in hand. This has been a formidable undertaking which has won scant public recognition. Under legislation passed in 1963 every county in England and Wales is required to maintain a county record office whose job is to gather together the different categories of local record – quarter sessions, parish, borough and manorial records, etc. Many of the record offices originated in local initiatives taken before the Second World War, and they have extended their search well beyond the semi-official categories to include the records of businesses, estates and associations. Today the holdings of all the county record offices almost certainly exceed those of the PRO. Local and regional studies have become a practicable proposition for professional historians for the first time.

Nowhere, however, have historians been granted complete freedom of access to public records. If historians were allowed to inspect files as soon as they had ceased to be in current use, they would be reading material which was only a few years old. All governments, whatever their political complexion, depend on a measure of confidentiality, and they tend to interpret this requirement very rigorously. Civil servants expect to be reasonably secure in the knowledge that what they set down officially shall not be publicly discussed in the foreseeable future. In Britain the 'closed period' laid down for public records varied considerably according to the department of origin until it was standardized at fifty years in 1958. Nine years later, after a vigorous campaign by historians, this period was reduced to thirty years. France followed suit in 1970, but in some countries, for example, Italy, fifty years is still the rule. Everywhere governments do not hesitate to withhold indefinitely documents which relate to particularly sensitive episodes – for example the Irish crisis of 1916–22 and the abdication of 1936 in Britain, and in France several issues which arose during the decline of the Third Republic in the late 1930s. In the USA the Freedom of Information Act of 1975 allows both historians and the general public much wider access, but elsewhere the reduction of the closed period to thirty years is probably as far as the liberalization of access to public records is likely to go. Clearly this has major implications for the study of contemporary history, where historians are forced to rely much more than they would like on what was made public at the time, or what has been disclosed retrospectively in memoirs and diaries.

Yet, however galling these restrictions may seem, government archives are at least centralized and accessible. The same broadly applies to local public records. The case is entirely different with records in private hands. These are widely dispersed and subject to varying – and sometimes perverse – conditions of access; and while governments have usually acknowledged the need for some kind of archive conservation, however rudimentary, family and business records, which may serve no practical function, have often been completely neglected. Nor can the historian whose interest is confined to official documents afford to ignore these private collections. Until the Cabinet Secretariat laid down firm guidelines after 1916, it was common for retiring ministers and officials to keep official papers in their possession; from the sixteenth century onwards, a steady flow of State Papers passed out of public custody in this way,[24] and to this day most of the State Papers dating from Robert Cecil's tenure of office (1596–1612) are at Hatfield House.

In most European countries one of the functions of the national libraries which were set up during the nineteenth century has been to secure possession of the most valuable private manuscript collections. Britain's national library dates back to the foundation of the British Museum in 1753. Of the Museum's foundation manuscript collections, the most important from the historian's point of view is that of Sir Robert Cotton, the early seventeenth-century collector and antiquarian; this numbered among its treasures a great many State Papers, one version of the Anglo-Saxon Chronicle, and two of the four surviving 'exemplifications' of Magna Carta (i.e. copies made at the time of the agreement between King John and the barons in 1215). Purchases and bequests since then have made the British Museum far and away the largest repository of historical manuscripts in this country outside the PRO. Even so, the number of important documents held elsewhere is incalculable. Many private collections have been given or loaned indefinitely to public libraries, or to the county record offices. But many more remain in the hands of private individuals, companies and associations. For over a hundred years the Historical Manuscripts Commission has promoted the care of manuscripts privately held in Britain and located their whereabouts, but there is still scope for the historian with a nose for detective work. Several of the collections of private papers on which Namier relied for his studies on eighteenth-century English politics were discovered during what he called his 'cross-country paper-chases'.[25]

The position is worst in the case of the personal and ephemeral materials in the hands of ordinary people – the account books of small businesses, the minute books of local clubs, everyday personal correspondence and the like. Neither the local record offices nor the Historical Manuscripts Commission cast their net as widely as this, yet the recovery of everyday documentation is important if historians are ever to make good their oft-stated aspiration to treat the masses and not just their masters. This is a task for historians with a local focus everywhere, but it is seldom energetically pursued. Since people are usually unaware that they hold material which might be historically significant, historians cannot wait for documents to be brought forward; they need to engage in propaganda and go out in search of them. The Manchester Studies Unit of Manchester Polytechnic began an adventurous programme of archive retrieval in 1975. Appeals for material appeared in the local press and on radio, and a field officer was appointed who approached likely holders of papers and organized house-to-house canvassing in selected neighbourhoods: the results were rewarding.[26]

It might be supposed that a clear division of labour exists between archivists and historians, with the former locating the materials and the latter putting them to use. These examples show that historians cannot in practice leave the task of tracking down documentation to others. The first step in any programme of historical research, then, is to establish the full extent of the sources. Considerable perseverence and ingenuity may be required even at this early stage.

NOTES

1. Louis Gottschalk, *Understanding History: A Primer of Historical Method*, Knopf, 1950, pp. 53–5.
2. Marc Bloch, *The Historian's Craft*, Manchester University Press, 1954, p. 61.

3.   Extract from Gerald of Wales, *Expugnatio Hibernica*, translated from the Latin in D. C. Douglas & G. W. Greenaway (eds.) *English Historical Documents, 1042–1189*, Eyre & Spottiswoode, 1953, p. 386.

4.   The best example is the autobiography of Pope Pius II, composed in the late 1460s. See Leona C. Gabel (ed.) *Memoirs of a Renaissance Pope: the Commentaries of Pius II*, Allen & Unwin, 1960.

5.   D. W. Brogan, introduction to Lucy Norton (ed.) *Historical Memoirs of the Duc de Saint-Simon*, Vol. I, Hamish Hamilton, 1967, p. xix.

6.   Romney Sedgwick (ed.) *Lord Hervey's Memoirs*, William Kimber, 1952.

7.   See Kellow Chesney, *Crimean War Reader*, Severn House, 1975.

8.   E. P. Thompson and Eileen Yeo (eds.) *The Unknown Mayhew: Selections from the Morning Chronicle, 1849–50*, Penguin, 1973.

9.   V. H. Galbraith, *An Introduction to the Use of the Public Records*, Oxford University Press, 1934, pp. 54–5.

10.   Thomas Cromwell to John Harding, 8 July 1536, quoted in G. R. Elton, *Policy and Police*, Cambridge University Press, 1972, pp. 342–3.

11.   Garrett Mattingly, *Renaissance Diplomacy*, Cape, 1962, pp. 110, 306.

12.   George Unwin, *Samuel Oldknow and the Arkwrights*, Manchester University Press, 1924.

13.   Peter Matthias, *The Brewing Industry in England, 1700–1830*, Cambridge University Press, 1959, p. xii.

14.   Monna Margherita to Francesco di Marco Datini, 29 August, 1389, translated and quoted in Iris Origo, *The Merchant of Prato*, Cape, 1957, p. 166.

15.   L.B. Namier, *The Structure of Politics at the Accession of George III*, Macmillan, 1929, and *England in the Age of the American Revolution*, Macmillan, 1930.

16.   H. H. Asquith, *Letters to Venetia Stanley*, ed. M. and E. Brock, Oxford University Press, 1982, p. 508.

17.   M. R. D. Foot and H. C. G. Matthew (eds.) *The Gladstone Diaries*, Oxford University Press, in progress.

18.   Ben Pimlott, 'Hugh Dalton's Diaries', *The Listener*, 17 July 1980. An edited version of the diaries is shortly to be published by LSE in association with Jonathan Cape.

19.   Richard Crossman, *The Diaries of a Cabinet Minister*, Vol. I, Hamish Hamilton and Cape, 1975, p. 12.

20.   David Knowles, *Great Historical Enterprises*, Nelson, 1963, pp. 65–97.

21.   Georges Lefebvre, *The Great Fear of 1789*, New Left Books, 1973, pp. 100–21.

22.   Elizabeth M. Hallam and Michael Roper, 'The capital and the records of the nation: seven centuries of housing the public records in London', *The London Journal*, IV, 1978, pp. 74–5.

23.   R. B. Wernham, 'The public records in the sixteenth and seventeenth centuries', in Levi Fox (ed.) *English Historical Scholarship in the Sixteenth and Seventeenth Centuries*, Oxford University Press, 1956, pp. 21–2.

24.   Ibid., pp. 20–3.

25.   Julia Namier, *Lewis Namier: a Biography*, Oxford University Press, 1971, p. 282.

26. Audrey Linkman and Bill Williams, 'Recovering the people's past: the archive rescue programme of Manchester Studies', *History Workshop Journal*, VIII, 1979, pp. 111–26.

Chapter 3

USING THE SOURCES

If the historian's business is to construct interpretations of the past from its surviving remains, then the implications of the vast and varied array of documentary sources described in the previous chapter are daunting. Who can hope to become an authority on even one country during a narrowly defined timespan when so much spadework has to be done before the task of synthesis can be attempted? If by 'authority' we mean total mastery of the sources, the short answer is: only the historian of remote and thinly documented epochs. It is, for example, not beyond the capacity of a dedicated scholar to master all the written materials which survive from the early Norman period in England. The vicissitudes of time have drastically reduced their number, and those which survive – especially record sources – tend towards the terse and economical. For any later period, however, the ideal is unattainable. From the High Middle Ages onwards more and more was committed to paper or parchment, with ever increasing prospects of survival to our own day. Since the beginning of the twentieth century the rate of increase has surged ahead at breakneck speed. Between 1913 and 1938 the number of despatches and papers received annually by the British Foreign Office increased from some 68,000 to 224,000.[1] Additions to the Public Record Office at present fill approximately one mile of shelving a year.[2] Amid this documentary surfeit, where does the historian begin?

I

Ultimately the principles governing the direction of original research can be reduced to two. According to the first, the historian takes one source or group of sources which fall within his or her general area of interest – say the records of a particular court or a body of diplomatic correspondence – and extracts whatever is of value, allowing the content of the source to determine the nature of the enquiry. Recalling his first experience of the French Revolutionary archives, Richard Cobb describes the delights offered by a source-orientated approach:

> More and more I enjoyed the excitement of research and the acquisition of material, often on quite peripheral subjects, as ends in themselves. I allowed myself to be deflected down unexpected channels, by the chance discovery of a bulky *dossier* – it might be the love letters of a *guillotiné*, or intercepted correspondence from London, or the account-books and samples of a commercial traveller in cotton, or the fate of the English colony in Paris, or eyewitness accounts of the September Massacres or of one of the *journées*.[3]

The second, or problem-oriented approach is the exact opposite. A specific historical question is formulated, usually prompted by a reading of the secondary authorities, and the relevant primary sources are then studied; the bearing which these sources may have on other issues is ignored, the researcher proceeding as directly as possible to the point where he or she can present some conclusions. Each method encounters snags. The source-oriented approach, although appropriate for a newly discovered source, may yield only an incoherent jumble of data. The problem-oriented approach sounds like commonsense and probably corresponds to most people's idea of research. But it is often difficult to tell in advance what sources *are* relevant. As will be shown later, the most improbable sources are sometimes found to be illuminating, while the obvious ones may lead the historian into too close an identification with the concerns of the organization that produced them. Moreover, for any topic in Western nineteenth- or twentieth-century history, however circumscribed by time or place, the sources are so unwieldy that further selection can hardly be avoided, and with it the risk of leaving vital evidence untouched.

In practice neither of these approaches is usually pursued to the complete exclusion of the other, but the balance struck between them varies a good deal. Some historians begin their careers with a narrowly defined project based on a limited range of sources; others are let loose on a major archive with only the vaguest of briefs. The former is on the whole the more common, because of the pressure to produce quick results which is imposed by the Ph.D. degree – the formal apprenticeship served by most academic historians. A great deal of research – probably the majority – consists not in ferreting out new sources but in turning to well-known materials with new questions in mind. Yet too single-minded a preoccupation with a narrow set of issues may lead to evidence being taken out of context and misinterpreted – 'source-mining' as one critic has called it.[4] It is vital, therefore, that the relationship between the historian and his or her sources is one of give and take. Many historians have had the experience of setting out with one set of questions, only to find that the sources which they had supposed would furnish the answers instead directed their research on to quite a different path. Emmanuel Le Roy Ladurie first turned to the land-tax registers of rural Languedoc with a view to documenting the birth of capitalism in that region; he found himself instead investigating its social structure in the broadest sense, and in particular the impact of demographic change:

> Mine was the classic misadventure; I had wanted to master a source in order to confirm my youthful convictions, but it was finally the source that mastered me by imposing its own rhythms, its own chronology, and its own particular truth.[5]

At the very least there must be a readiness to modify the original objective in the light of the questions which arise directly from the sources. Without this flexibility historians risk imposing on their evidence and failing to tap its full potential. The true master of the craft is someone whose sense of what questions can profitably be asked has been sharpened by a lifetime's exposure to the sources in all their variety. Mastery of all the sources must remain the ideal, however improbable its complete accomplishment may be.

The reason why the ideal remains for the most part unattainable is not only that the sources are so numerous, but that each of them requires so much careful appraisal. For the primary sources are not an open book, offering instant answers. They may not be what they seem to be; they may signify very much more than is immediately apparent; they may be couched in obscure and antiquated forms which are meaningless to the untutored eye. Before the historian can properly assess the significance of a document, he or she needs to find out how, when and why it came into being. This requires the application of both supporting knowledge and sceptical intelligence. 'Records', it has been said, 'like the little children of long ago, only speak when they are spoken to, and they will not talk to strangers.'[6] Nor, it might be added, will they be very forthcoming to anyone in a tearing hurry. Even for the experienced historian with green fingers, research in the primary source is time-consuming; for the novice it can be painfully slow.

Historians have long been aware of the value of primary sources – and not merely the more accessible sources of a narrative kind. A surprising number of Medieval chroniclers showed a keen interest in the great state documents of the day and reproduced them in their writings. William Camden, the leading English historian in Shakespeare's generation, was granted access to the State Papers in order to write a history of Elizabeth I's reign. But scholarly source criticism is a much more recent development. It was largely beyond the historians of the Renaissance, for all their sophistication. Camden, for example, regarded his record sources as 'infallible testimonies'.[7] Many of the technical advances which underpin modern source criticism were made during the seventeenth century – notably by the great Benedic-

tine scholar Jean Mabillon. But their application was at first confined
to monastic history and the lives of the saints, and historians continued
to live in a different world from that of the source critic *(érudit)*.
Edward Gibbon, the greatest historian of the eighteenth century, drew
heavily on the findings of the *érudits* in his *Decline and Fall of the
Roman Empire* (1776–88), but he did not emulate their methods.

The introduction of a critical approach to the sources into mainstream history-writing was Ranke's most important achievement. He
owed his early fame and promotion to a merciless exposé of
Guicciardini's faults as a scholar. His appetite for archival research was
truly prodigious. And through his seminar at the University of Berlin
he brought into being a new breed of academic historians trained in the
critical evaluation of primary sources – and especially the many
archival sources which were being opened to research for the first time
during the nineteenth century. It was with pardonable exaggeration
that Lord Acton saluted Ranke as 'the real originator of the heroic
study of records'.[8] Ranke won acceptance for the idea that the evaluation of sources and the writing of history must be kept in the same
hands. The spread of Rankean method to Britain came comparatively
late; it was primarily due to William Stubbs, Regius Professor of
History at Oxford from 1866 to 1884, whose reputation rested not only
on his studies of English constitutional history, but on his scrupulous
editing of Medieval historical texts. To this day, what Marc Bloch
called 'the struggle with documents' is what distinguishes the professional historian from the amateur.[9]

II

The first step in evaluating a document is to test its authenticity; this is
sometimes known as *external* criticism. Are the author, the place and
the date of writing what they purport to be? These questions are
particularly relevant in the case of legal documents such as charters,
wills and contracts, on which a great deal could depend in terms of
wealth, status and privilege. During the Middle Ages many royal and
ecclesiastical charters were forged, either to replace genuine ones
which had been lost, or to lay claim to rights and privileges never in fact
granted. The Donation of Constantine, an eighth-century document
which purported to confer temporal power over Italy on Pope
Sylvester I and his successors, was one of the most famous of these
forgeries. Documents of this kind might be termed 'historical forgeries', and detecting them may tell us a great deal about the society
that produced them. But there is also the modern forgery to be
considered. Any recently discovered document of great moment is

open to the suspicion that it was forged by somebody who intended to make a great deal of money or to run rings round the most eminent scholars of the day. The Vinland Map did just that. In 1959 an anonymous benefactor of Yale University paid a large sum for the map in the belief that it dated from the mid-fifteenth century; since the map clearly showed the north-eastern coast of North America ('Vinland'), the implication was that the earlier Viking discoveries were not unknown in Europe at the time when Columbus was planning his first voyage across the Atlantic. Several experts had committed themselves to the hilt in favour of the map before it was exposed beyond reasonable doubt as a forgery in 1974.

Once suspicions are aroused, the historian will pose a number of key questions. First, there is the issue of provenance; can the document be traced back to the office or person who is supposed to have produced it, or could it have been planted? In the case of great finds which suddenly materialize from nowhere, this is a particularly significant question. Secondly, the content of the document needs to be examined for consistency with known facts. Given our knowledge of the period, do the claims made in the document or the sentiments uttered seem at all likely? If the document contradicts what can be substantiated by other primary evidence of unimpeachable authenticity, then forgery is strongly indicated. Thirdly, the form of the document may yield vital clues. The historian who deals mostly in handwritten documents needs to be something of a palaeographer in order to decide whether the script is right for the period and place specified, and something of a philologist to evaluate the style and language of a suspect text. (It was philological tests which clinched Lorenzo Valla's case against the Donation of Constantine as early as 1439.) More specifically, official documents usually conform to a particular ordering of subject matter and a set of stereotyped verbal formulae, the hallmarks of the institution which issued them. *Diplomatic* is the name given to the study of these technicalities of form. Lastly, historians can call on the help of technical specialists to examine the materials used in the production of the document. Chemical testing can determine the age of parchment, paper and ink; the hand of the Vinland Map forger was betrayed by microphobe analysis of the ink which revealed a substantial percentage of a man-made pigment unknown before about 1920.[10]

It would be misleading, however, to suggest that historians are constantly uncovering forgeries, or that they methodically test the authenticity of every document that comes their way. This procedure is certainly appropriate to certain branches of Medieval history, where much may depend on a single charter of uncertain provenance. But for most historians – and especially the modern historian – there is little prospect of a brilliant detective coup. Their time is more likely to be spent perusing an extended sequence of letters or memoranda, recording humdrum day-to-day transactions, which would scarcely be in anyone's interest to forge. And in the case of public records under proper archival care the possibility of forgery is pretty remote.

For the Medievalist some of these skills of detection have another application – to help in preparing an authentic edition out of the several corrupt variants which survive today. Before the invention of printing in the fifteenth century, the only means whereby books could be circulated was by frequent copying by hand; for most of the Middle Ages the *scriptoria* of the monasteries and cathedrals were the main centres of book production. Inevitably errors crept into the copying, and they increased as each copy was used as the basis of another. Where the original (or 'autograph') does not survive, which is frequently the case with important Medieval texts, the historian is often confronted by alarming discrepancies between the available versions. This is the unsatisfactory form in which some of the major chroniclers of the Medieval period have come down to us. However, close comparison between the texts – especially their scripts and the discrepancies of wording – enables the historian to establish the relationship between the surviving versions and to reconstruct a much closer approximation to the wording of the original. The preparation of a correct text is an important part of a Medievalist's work, requiring a command of paleography and philology. It is made easier now that the texts, which may be held by widely scattered libraries, can be photographed and examined alongside each other.

III

The authentication of a document and – where applicable – cleansing the text of corruptions are only preliminaries. The second and usually much more demanding stage is *internal* criticism, that is the interpretation of the document's content. Granted that author, date and place of writing are as they seem, what do we make of the words in front of us? At one level this is a question of meaning. This involves more than simply translating from a foreign or archaic language, difficult though that may be for the novice trying to make sense of Medieval Latin in abbreviated form. The historian requires not merely linguistic fluency but a command of the historical context which will show what the words actually refer to. Domesday Book is a classic example of the difficulties that can arise here. It is a record of land-use and the distribution of wealth in the English shires in 1086, before the institutions of the Anglo-Saxons (and the Danes) had been much altered by Norman rule; but it was compiled by clerks from Normandy whose everyday language was French and who described what they had seen and heard in Latin. Small wonder that it is not always clear, for example, to what form of land-tenure the term *manerium* (usually 'manor') refers.[11] Nor are our problems solved if we stick to documents written in English. For language itself is a product of history. Old words, especially the more technical ones, pass out of currency, while others acquire a new significance. We have to be on our guard against reading modern meanings into the past. This mutability of language is a central preoccupation for historians of ideas, as will be shown in Chapter 4 (p. 70), but it has implications for all historians except those who deal with the very recent past. Wide reading in the writing of the period is essential, and in some cases familiarity with the work of literary critics on the language of the key texts.

Once historians have become immersed in the sources of their period and have mastered its characteristic turns of phrase and the appropriate technical vocabulary, questions of meaning are unlikely to worry them very often. But the content of a document prompts a further, much more insistent question: is it reliable? No source can be used for historical reconstruction until some estimate of its standing as historical evidence has been made. This question is beyond the scope of any ancillary technique such as palaeography or diplomatic. Answering it calls instead for a knowledge of historical context and an insight into human nature. Here historians come into their own.

Where a document takes the form of a report of what has been seen, heard or said, we need to ask whether the writer was in a position to give a faithful account. Was he or she actually present, and in a tranquil and attentive frame of mind? If the information was learned at second hand, was it anything more than gossip? The reliability of a Medieval monastic chronicler largely depended on how often his cloister was frequented by men of rank and power.[12] Did the writer put pen to paper immediately, or after the sharpness of his or her memory had blurred – a point worth bearing in mind when reading a diary. In reports of oral proceedings, a great deal may turn on the exact form of words used, yet prior to the spread of shorthand in the seventeenth century there was no means of making a verbatim transcript. The earliest mechanical means of recording speech – the phonograph – was not invented until 1877. It is extrordinarily difficult to know exactly what a statesmen said in a given speech: if he wrote it out in advance he may well have departed from his text; and press reporters, usually armed with only pencil and note-pad, are inevitably selective and inaccurate, as can be seen by comparing the reports given by different newspapers of the same speech. In the case of speeches in Parliament a reliable verbatim record can be read, but even this dates back only to the reform of Hansard in 1909.

What most affects the reliability of a source, however, is the intention and prejudices of the writer. Narratives intended for posterity, on which a general impression of the period tends to be based, are particularly suspect. The distortions to which autobiography is subject in this respect are too obvious for comment. Medieval chroniclers were often extremely partisan as between one ruler and another, or as between Church and State: Gerald of Wales's increasing antipathy towards Henry II was due to the king's repeated veto on his promotion to the episcopate; Matthew Paris's treatment of the disputes between Henry III and the English barons was slanted by his identification with virtually all forms of corporate privilege in their dealings with King or Pope.[13] Chroniclers were often influenced too by the prejudices characteristic of educated people of their time – a revulsion against heresy, or a distaste for lawyers and money-lenders. Culture-bound assumptions and stereotypes shared by virtually all literate people of the day call for particularly careful appraisal. For the historian of pre-literate societies such as those of tropical Africa in the nineteenth century, the contemporary accounts of European travellers are a source of major importance, but nearly all of them were coloured by racism and sensationalism: judicial execution (as in Ashanti) appeared as 'human sacrifice', and polygamy was presented as a licence for sexual excess. Nor does creative literature have a special dispensation in this respect. Novelists, playwrights and poets have as many prejudices as anyone else, and these have to be allowed for when citing their work as historical evidence. E. M. Forster's *A Passage to India* (1924) is, among other things, a marvellously convincing and very unflattering portrayal of the British Raj at district level, but some account must surely be taken of Forster's own alienation from the kind of stiff-upper-lip public school man who controlled the administration in India.

The attraction of record sources – of 'witnesses in spite of themselves' (see p. 31) – on the other hand, is that through them the historian can observe or infer the sequence of day-to-day events, free from the controlling purpose of a narrator. But this is merely to eliminate one of the more obvious kinds of distortion. For however spontaneous or authoritative the source, very few forms of writing arise solely from a desire to convey the unvarnished truth. Even in the case of a diary composed without thought of publication the writer may be bolstering his or her self-esteem and rationalizing motives. A document which appears to be a straightforward report of something seen, heard or said may well be slanted – either unconsciously, as an expression of deep-seated prejudice, or deliberately, from a wish to please or influence the recipient. The ambassador in his despatches home may convey a greater impression of bustle and initiative on his own part than is actually the case; and he may censor his impressions of the government to which he is accredited in order to fit them to the policies and preconception of his superiors. Historians today are much more sceptical than they used to be about the claims to objectivity of the great Victorian enquirers into the 'social problem': they recognize that the selection of evidence was often distorted to fit middle-class stereotypes about the poor and to promote the implementation of pet remedies.

Once bias has been detected, however, the offending document need not be consigned to the scrap-heap. The bias itself is likely to be historically significant. In the case of a public figure it may account to a consistent misreading of certain people or situations, with disastrous effects on policy. In published documents with a wide circulation, bias may explain an important shift in public opinion. The reports of nineteenth-century Royal Commissions are a case in point. Newspapers provide other examples: the war reports of the many British dailies which were opposed to Asquith's government in 1915–16 are not a reliable guide to what was happening on the front, but they certainly help to explain why the Prime Minister's reputation at home declined so severely.[14] Even the most tainted sources can assist in the reconstruction of the past.

As described so far, the evaluation of historical evidence may not seem to be unlike the cross-examination of witnesses in a court of law: in both cases the point is to test the reliability of the testimony. But the court-room analogy is misleading if it suggests that primary sources are always evaluated in this way. Public records – traditionally the staple diet of researchers – have most often been studied from one of two standpoints: first, how did the institution which generated the records evolve over time, and what was its function in the body politic? And second, how were specific policies formulated and executed? In this context reliability is hardly the issue, for the records are studied not as *reports* (i.e. testimonies of events 'out there'), but as parts of a *process* (be it administrative, judicial or policy-making) which is itself the subject of enquiry. They are as much the creation of an institution as an individual, and therefore need to be examined in the context of that institution – its vested interests, its administrative routine, and its record-keeping procedures; any records to do with law or public finance call for technical knowledge of a particularly demanding kind. Considered apart from the series to which they belong, the records of public institutions no longer extant are almost certain to be misinterpreted. Thus the records of the Public Record Office should be used in the first instance 'not as a lucky bag that may produce evidence on almost anything, but for what they really are, viz. the systematic record of personal government developing into national government'.[15]

To understand the full significance of these records the historian must if possible study them in their original groupings (a principle on the whole respected in the Public Record Office) rather than in the rearrangement of some tidy-minded archivist. And ideally they should be studied in their entirety. Unfortunately public record-keeping in England before about 1700 was patchy. Medieval Chancery records are basically copies of the government's out-letters, with very few of the letters which it was constantly receiving from its subjects. Conversely, Tudor State Papers are largely confined to incoming correspondence, and only a small proportion of the out-letters survive in private manuscript collections; it is therefore difficult to be sure how policies were executed, or what pressures contributed to their genesis. This deficiency in the record-keeping of the secretaries of state was not rectified until after the Restoration.[16] But, whenever possible, historians try to study the documents in series, and in their entirety, in order to minimize the danger of misinterpreting a particular item out of context.

A knowledge of administrative and archival procedures is also vital if the historian is to be alert to one particularly serious cause of distortion in the surviving record – the deliberate removal of evidence. While the planting of a forgery in the official record presents major difficulties, it may be a comparatively easy matter to suppress an embarrassing or incriminating document. In the State Papers, for example, almost all the letters to and from Lord Chancellor Jeffreys for the reign of James II are missing. Since Jeffreys himself died in the Tower in 1689 after the Revolution, it has been surmised that the papers were removed by some person who had changed sides at the critical moment and stood to gain by suppressing his connection with the infamous judge of the 'Bloody Assize'.[17] In Britain today the centralization of most government record-keeping at the Public Record Office – achieved in the mid-nineteenth century – is an effective check on this kind of tampering, but it is still possible for the responsible official to ensure that a sensitive document never leaves the department in which it was produced. Since total preservation is manifestly impracticable, there is a recognized procedure for destroying ephemeral material judged to be of no historical interest, and this is open to abuse.[18] For example, a number of Colonial Office files relating to Palestine in the late 1940s have been destroyed, presumably in order to cast a veil over British actions during the turbulent last phase of the Mandate administration; it is also likely that crucial British documents relating to the Suez crisis of 1956 were destroyed or removed immediately.[19] No doubt there have been instances of unauthorized censorship which are proof against detection, but the historian familiar with the administrative procedures of the department in question is a great deal less likely to be duped.

While some records have been carefully removed from the historian's reach, others have been pushed into the limelight. In several fields of modern history collections of records published soon after the time of writing can be consulted. It is important that these collections should not be accorded special weight just because they are so accessible. They nearly always represent a selection, whose publication was intended to further some practical end, usually of a short-term political nature. The well-known series of *State Trials* was for a long time accepted as a reliable record of some of the major English criminal proceedings since the sixteenth century. But the first four volumes were promoted in 1719 by a group of propagandists in the Whig cause: as a source for the great political trials of the Stuart period they are therefore distinctly suspect.[20] During the nineteenth century the publication – often on a massive scale – of a politician's correspondence was often considered by his family and followers to be a fitting memorial, but there was usually an element of censorship so that the less savoury episodes were suppressed and the reputation of living persons protected or enhanced. Governments of the same period regarded the publication of select diplomatic correspondence (for example in the British Blue Books) as a legitimate means of building up public support for their policies; some of the 'despatches' were composed for this very purpose. In all these cases the historian will obviously prefer to go to the originals. If these are not available, the published versions must be scrutinized carefully, and as much as possible must be found out from other sources about the circumstances in which they were compiled.

IV

It will be clear, then, that historical research is not a matter of identifying *the* authoritative source and then exploiting it for all it is worth, for the majority of sources are in some way inaccurate, incomplete or tainted by prejudice and self-interest. The procedure is rather to amass as many pieces of evidence as possible from a wide range of sources – preferably from *all* the sources which have a bearing on the problem in hand. In this way the inaccuracies and distortions of particular sources are more likely to be revealed, and the inferences drawn by the historian can be corroborated. Each type of source possesses certain strengths and weaknesses; considered together, and compared one against the other, there is at least a chance that they will reveal the true facts – or something very close to them.

This is why mastery of a variety of sources is one of the hallmarks of historical scholarship – an exacting one which is by no means always attained. One of the reasons why biography is often disparaged by academic historians is that too many biographers have studied only the private papers left by their subject, instead of weighing these against the papers of colleagues and acquaintances and (where relevant) the public records for the period. Ranke himself has been criticized for relying too heavily on the despatches of the Venetian ambassadors in some of his writings on the sixteenth century: observant and conscientious as most of them were, the ambassadors saw matters very much from the point of view of the governing elite, yet with little of the participant's inside knowledge.[21] In this respect standards have become much more rigorous since Ranke's day. In the history of international relations, for example, it is a golden rule that both sides of a diplomatic conversation must be studied before one can be certain what the subject of the conversation was and which side put its case more effectively; this is why the inaccessibility of the Soviet archives is so frustrating for Western historians of the origins of the Second World War. For historians of government policy in twentieth-century Britain, the temptation may be to confine research to the public records, because these survive in such profusion, and their number is increased every year as more records become available for the first time under the thirty-year rule (see p. 44). But this method is hardly conducive to a balanced interpretation. The public records tend to give too much prominence to administrative considerations (thus reflecting the principal interest of the civil servants who wrote most of them), and to reveal much less about the political pressures to which ministers responded; hence the importance of extending the search to the press and Hansard, private letters and diaries, political memoirs, and – for recent history – to first-hand oral evidence.[22]

The examples just discussed – international relations and government policy – are topics for which there exists primary source material in abundance. In each case there is a well-defined body of documents in public custody, with numerous ancillary sources to corroborate and amplify the evidence. But there are many historical topics which are much less well served, either because little evidence has survived, or because what interests us today did not interest contemporaries and was therefore not recorded. If historians are to go beyond the immediate concerns of those who created their sources, they have to learn how to interpret them more obliquely. There are two principal ways of doing so. In the first place, many sources are valued for information which the writers were scarcely aware they were setting down and which was incidental to the purpose of their testimony. This is because people unconsciously convey on paper clues about their attitudes, assumptions and manner of life which may be intensely interesting to historians. A given document may therefore be useful in a variety of ways, depending on the questions asked of it – sometimes questions which would never have occurred to the writer or to people of the time. This, of course, is one reason why beginning research with clearly defined questions rather than simply going where the documents lead can be so rewarding: it may reveal evidence where none was thought to exist. From this point of view, the word 'source' is perhaps somewhat inapposite: if the metaphor is interpreted literally, a 'source' can contribute evidence to only one 'stream' of knowledge. It has even been suggested that the term should be abandoned altogether, in favour of 'trace' or 'track'.[23]

This flair for turning evidence to new uses is one of the distinctive contributions of recent historical method. It has been most fully displayed by historians who have moved beyond the well-lit paths of mainstream political history to fields such as social and cultural history, for which explicit source material is more difficult to come by. A case in point is the religious beliefs of ordinary people in Reformation England. Although the switches of doctrinal allegiance among the elite are relatively well recorded, evidence is very sparse for the rest of the population. But Margaret Spufford in her study of three Cambridgeshire villages has used the unlikely evidence of wills to show how religious affiliation changed. Every will began with a dedicatory clause which allows some inference to be drawn concerning the doctrinal preference of the testator or the scribe. From a study of these clauses, Spufford shows how by the early seventeenth century personal faith in the mediation of Christ – the hallmark of Protestant belief – had made deep inroads among the local people.[24] It was, of course, no part of the testators' intentions to furnish evidence of their religious beliefs; they were concerned only to ensure that their worldly goods were disposed of in accordance with their wishes. But historians alert to the unwitting testimony of the sources can go beyond the intentions of those who created them.

Legal history arouses relatively little interest among historians at present, but court records are probably the single most important source we have for the social history of the Medieval and early modern periods, when the vast majority of the population was illiterate and therefore generated no records of its own. Emmanuel Le Roy Ladurie's *Montaillou* (1978) is a classic illustration of this point. In the Vatican library there survives the greater part of the Register recording an Inquisition carried out between 1318 and 1325 by Jacques Fournier, bishop of Pamiers. Of the 114 people accused of heresy, twenty-five came from Montaillou, a village of the Pyrenees of no more than 250 inhabitants. They were quizzed on their beliefs, their circle of friends (especially the heretical ones) and their moral conduct. The bishop saw to it that the lengthy statements made in his court were meticulously recorded and checked by the witnesses themselves; and since he was also a tireless interrogator and a stickler for detail – 'a sort of compulsive Maigret'[25] – the result is an extraordinarily vivid and revealing document. With the help of supporting evidence, Le Roy Ladurie has been able to reconstruct the everyday life of the peasants of Montaillou – their social relationships, their religious and magical observances, and not just their attitudes to sex but much of their actual sex life. As Le Roy Ladurie puts it, the high concentration of Cathar heretics in Montaillou 'provides an opportunity for the study not of Catharism itself – that is not my subject – but of the mental outlook of the country people'.[26] When historians distance themselves from the contemporary significance of a document in this way, its reliability may be of only marginal significance: what counts is the incidental detail. In eighteenth-century France it was the practice for unmarried pregnant women to make statements to the magistrate in order to pin responsibility on their seducers and salvage something of their reputations. Richard Cobb has carried out a study of fifty-four such statements made at Lyon in 1790–92, and as he points out, the identity of the seducers is a trivial issue compared with the light that is shed on the sexual mores of the urban poor, their conditions of work and leisure, and the popular morality of the day.[27] It is studies like these which demonstrate the full force of Marc Bloch's injunction to his fellow-historians to study 'the evidence of witnesses in spite of themselves' (see p. 31).

The second oblique method of exploiting historical evidence is much more controversial, and it was also propounded by Marc Bloch. Bloch wanted to reconstruct French rural society in the Middle Ages. The documents for the period contain a great deal of information, but little sense of how the details fit together to form an overall picture. Such a picture only emerges in the eighteenth century, when French agrarian life was systematically described by agronomists and by commissions of enquiry, and when accurate local maps began to appear in large numbers. Bloch maintained that only someone familiar with the structure of French rural society as it was revealed in the eighteenth century could make sense of the Medieval data. He did not, of course, assume that nothing had changed in the meantime; his point was rather that in this kind of situation the historian should carefully work back by stages from what is known in order to make sense of the fragmentary and incoherent evidence for earlier periods:

> The historian, especially the agrarian historian, is perpetually at the mercy of his documents; most of the time he must read history backwards if he hopes to break the secret cypher of the past.[28]

This approach, known as the *regressive* method, is much used in African history, where the documentary sources for pre-colonial society are of poor quality. In his book *The Tio Kingdom* (1973), for example, Jan Vansina draws on his own ethnographic fieldwork in the 1960s to shed light on the observations of European visitors to the kingdom in the 1880s who mentioned many indigenous features without understanding their meaning or their place in the social structure. It would otherwise have been quite impossible to make any sense of Tio society as a whole on the eve of the European take-over. The regressive method is certainly a second-best which contravenes the usual rules for evaluating primary sources, but if applied sensitively with an eye for change it produces revealing results.

V

In approaching the sources, the historian is anything but a passive observer. The relevant evidence has to be sought after in fairly out-of-the-way and improbable places. Ingenuity and flair are required to grasp the full range of uses to which a single source may be put. Of each type of evidence the historian has to ask how and why it came into being, and what its real import is. Divergent sources have to be weighed against each other, forgeries and gaps explained. No document, however authoritative, is beyond question; the evidence must, in E. P. Thompson's telling phrase, 'be interrogated by minds trained in a discipline of attentive disbelief'.[29] Perhaps these precepts hardly merit the name of method, if that suggests the deliberate application of a set sequence of scientific procedures for verifying the evidence. Innumerable handbooks of historical method have, it is true, been written for the guidance of research students since Ranke's time;[30] but there is, nevertheless, something to be said for the view that what historians bring to the sources is not so much a method as an attitude of mind – an instinct almost – which can only be acquired by trial and error; certainly experience is all the schooling which many eminent British historians have ever received, in contrast to the more formal instruction in research techniques which is customarily given on the continent and in the United States.

But to argue further, as some recent sceptics have done, that the principles of historical enquiry defy definition altogether is a mystification.[31] In practice, unfavourable notice of a secondary work often turns on the author's failure to apply this or that test to the evidence. Admittedly, the rules cannot be reduced to a formula, and the exact procedures vary according to the type of evidence; but much of what the experienced scholar does almost without thinking can be spelt out – as I have tried to do here – in terms which are comprehensible to the uninitiated. When spelt out in this way, historical method may seem to amount to little more than the obvious lessons of commonsense. But it is commonsense applied very much more systematically and sceptically than is usually the case in everyday life, supported by a secure grasp of historical context and, in many instances, a high degree of technical knowledge. It is by these taxing standards that historical research demands to be judged.

NOTES

1.   Anthony P. Adamthwaite, *The Making of the Second World War*, Allen & Unwin, 1977, p. 20.

2.   Elizabeth M. Hallam and Michael Roper, 'The capital and the records of the nation: seven centuries of housing the public records in London', *The London Journal*, IV, 1978, p. 91.

3.   Richard Cobb, *A Second Identity: Essays on France and French History*, Oxford University Press, 1969, p. 15.

4.   J. H. Hexter, *On Historians*, Allen Lane, 1979, p. 241. The label is rather unfairly pinned on Chistopher Hill.

5.   Emmanuel Le Roy Ladurie, *The Peasants of Languedoc*, llinois University Press, 1974, p. 4.

6.   C. R. Cheney, *Medieval Texts and Studies*, Oxford University Press, 1973, p. 8.

7.   William Camden, Preface to *Britannia* (1586), as quoted in J. R. Hale (ed.) *The Evolution of British Historiography*, Macmillan, 1967, p. 15.

8.   Lord Acton, *Lectures on Modern History*, Fontana, 1960: first published in 1906, p. 22.

9.   Marc Bloch, *The Historian's Craft*, Manchester University Press, 1954, p. 86.

10. Helen Wallis and others, 'The strange case of the Vinland Map: a symposium', *Geographical Journal*, CXL, 1974, pp. 183–214.

11. Bloch, *The Historian's Craft*, p. 165; J. J. Bagley, *Historical Interpretation, Vol. I: Sources of English Medieval History, 1066– 1540*, Penguin, 1965, pp. 24, 29–30.

12. See, for example, the impressive list of informants and contacts in Richard Vaughan, *Matthew Paris*, Cambridge University Press, 1958, pp. 11–18.

13. Antonia Gransden, *Historical Writing in England, c.550 to c.1307*, Routledge & Kegan Paul, 1974, pp. 242–5, 367–72.

14. Stephen Koss, *Asquith*, Allen Lane, 1976, pp. 181–2, 217.

15. V. H. H. Galbraith, *Studies in the Public Records*, Nelson, 1948, p. 6.

16. G. R. Elton, *England, 1200– 1640*, The Sources of History, 1969, pp. 41, 70–3.

17. G. W. Keeton, *Lord Chancellor Jeffreys and the Stuart Cause*, Macdonald, 1965, p. 23.

18. Michael Roper, 'Public records and the policy process in the twentieth century', *Public Administration*, LV, 1977, pp. 153–68.

19. Colin Holmes, 'Government files and privileged access', *Social History*, VI, 1981, p. 342.

20. G. Kitson Clark, *The Critical Historian*, Heinemann, 1967, pp. 92–6, 109–14.

21. Herbert Butterfield, *Man on His Past*, Cambridge University Press, 1955, p. 90.

22. For a fuller discussion, with examples, see Alan Booth and Sean Glynn, 'The public records and recent British economic historiography', *Economic History Review*, 2nd series, XXXII, 1979, pp. 303–15.

23. G.J. Renier, *History: Its Purpose and Method*, Allen & Unwin, 1950, pp. 96–105.

24. Margaret Spufford, *Contrasting Communities: English Villagers in the Sixteenth and Seventeenth Centuries*, Cambridge University Press, 1974, pp. 320–44.

25. Emmanuel Le Roy Ladurie, *Montaillou: Cathars and Catholics in a French Village, 1294–1324*, Penguin, 1980, p. xiii.

26. Ibid., p. 231.
27. Richard Cobb, 'A view on the street', in his *A Sense of Place*, Duckworth, 1975, pp. 79–135.
28. Marc Bloch, *French Rural History*, Routledge & Kegan Paul, 1966, p. xxviii.
29. E. P. Thompson, *The Poverty of Theory*, Merlin Press, 1978, pp. 220–1.
30. The classic work is C. V. Langlois and C. Seignobos, *Introduction to the Study of History*, Greenwood, 1979: first published in 1898. Louis Gottschalk, *Understanding History: A Primer of Historical Method*, Knopf, 1951, and Jacques Barzun and Henry F. Graff, *The Modern Researcher*, Harcourt, Brace Jovanovich, 3rd edn, 1977, are to be preferred as more up-to-date statements.
31. See, for example, Richard Cobb, 'Becoming a historian' in his *A Sense of Place*, pp. 47–8; and Jacques Barzun, *Clio and the Doctors*, Chicago University Press, 1974, p. 90.

Chapter 4

THE MAIN THEMES: POLITICS, BIOGRAPHY, IDEAS

Both the immense variety of primary sources discussed in Chapter 2 and the laborious methods of evaluation outlined in Chapter 3 limit severely the extent to which historians can claim competence in their subject. Their expertise is usually confined to a particular period: scholars are labelled as, for example, 'Medievalists', 'Early Modernists' or 'Contemporary Historians', and in practice the period for which they have a sound grasp of the sources is likely to be limited still further – to a century perhaps in the case of a Medievalist, and often no more than a decade in the case of a specialist in the nineteenth or twentieth centuries. Nearly always, too, these periods are studied in relation to one country or region only. The specialist in the English Revolution of the seventeenth century, for example, would naturally be interested in those countries of western Europe which, like France and the Netherlands, experienced their own crises at the same time, but his or her knowledge of them would probably not be founded on anything more than a reading of the secondary literature – and regrettably in many cases only the literature in English and one other European language. Those historians with first-hand research experience in more than one country or period are a small minority.

In addition to the specialization of time and place, there is also the specialization of theme. Of course in any epoch of the past all aspects of human thought, activity and achievement have a claim on the historian's attention, but they cannot all be studied at once, unless the horizon of research is drastically confined to a single locality (an approach which is discussed below, pp. 90–1). For historians who wish to maintain a national or regional focus, concentration on one theme or strand immediately reduces the volume of essential primary sources to more manageable proportions. Which theme is pursued in research may owe much to personal considerations – a particular enthusiasm or eccentricity. But whereas modern historical scholarship achieves a more or less steady output for all the periods and countries which are reasonably well documented, its choice of theme is much more subject to changing fashion. The claims of social relevance, the development of new techniques of research, and the theoretical insights of the social sciences all influence historians in determining which aspects of the past should enjoy research priority. For these reasons, choice of theme gives a much clearer indication of the actual content of historical enquiry than does choice of period or country. This chapter and the next consider four broad categories which are by now well established – political history, intellectual history, economic history and social history – and one other which is only now winning general acceptance: the history of collective mentalities.

I

Political history is conventionally defined as the study of all those aspects of the past which have to do with the formal organization of power in society, which for the majority of human societies in recorded history means the state. It includes the institutional organization of the state, the competition of factions and parties for control over the state, the policies enforced by the state, and the relations between states. To many people, the scope of history would appear to be exhausted by these topics. The syllabuses taught in British schools until very recently, publishers' lists of best-sellers, and television programmes all convey the impression that if political history is not the only kind of history, it is much the most important. Historians themselves, however, are by no means of one mind on this point. The reason why political history merits its status as the senior branch is not because it is intrinsically more significant than any other – though naturally advocates of political history claim that it is[1] – but because it enjoys much the longest pedigree. While political history has been written and read continuously since ancient times, other branches have developed as permanent additions to the repertory only during the last hundred years.

The reasons for this traditional dominance are clear enough. Historically the state itself has been much more closely associated with the writing of history than with any other literary activity. On the one hand, those who exercised political power or aspired to it looked to the past for guidance as to how best to achieve their ends. At the same time, political elites had an interest in promoting for public consumption a version of history which legitimized their own position in the body politic, either by emphasizing their past achievements, or by demonstrating the antiquity of the constitution under which they held office (see Ch. 1). Moreover, political history has always found an avid lay readership. The rise and fall of statesmen and of nations or empires lends itself to dramatic treatment in the grand manner. Political power is intoxicating, and for those who cannot exercise it themselves, the next best thing is to enjoy it vicariously in the pages of a Clarendon or a Guicciardini. The consequences were bitterly deplored by Arthur Young, the English agronomist famous for his descriptions of the French countryside on the eve of the Revolution:

> To a mind that has the least turn after philosophical inquiry, reading modern history is generally the most tormenting employment that a man can have: one is plagued with the actions of a detestable set of men called conquerors, heroes, and great generals; and we wade through pages loaded with military details; but when you want to know the progress of agriculture, or commerce, and industry, their effect in different ages and nations on each other . . . all is a blank.[2]

In fact during the Enlightenment of the eighteenth century, a 'philosophical' turn of mind was rather more evident than Young allowed for. Voltaire's historical works ranged over the whole field of culture and society, and even Gibbon did not confine himself to the dynastic and military fortunes of the Roman Empire. But the nineteenth-century revolution in historical studies greatly reinforced the traditional preoccupation with statecraft, faction and war. German historicism was closely associated with a school of political thought, best represented by Hegel, which endowed the concept of the state with a moral and spiritual force beyond the material interests of its subjects; it followed that the state was the main agent of historical change. Equally, the nationalism which inspired so much historical writing at this time led to an emphasis on the competition between the great powers and the struggles of submerged nationalities for political self-determination. Few historians would have quarrelled with Ranke when he wrote, 'the spirit of modern times . . . operates only by political means'.[3] The Victorian historian, E. A. Freeman, put it more simply: 'History is past politics.'[4] The new emphasis on the critical study of primary sources merely confirmed the trend since the state archives – the richest and most accessible body of source material – were first and foremost a record of policy-making and institutional growth. The new university professors in the Rankean mould were essentially political historians.

Yet, as the definition given earlier would suggest, political history can mean many different things, and its content has been almost as varied and as subject to fashion as any other branch of history. Ranke himself was chiefly interested in how the great powers of Europe had acquired their strongly individual characters during the period between the Renaissance and the French Revolution. He looked for explanations less to the internal evolution of those states than to the unending struggle for power between them. One of Ranke's legacies, therefore, was a highly professional approach to the study of foreign policy. *Diplomatic history* has been a staple pursuit of the profession ever since, its appeal periodically reinforced as historians have responded to a public demand to understand the origins of the latest war. In the aftermath of the First World War especially, much of this work verged on propaganda and it was too heavily dependent on the archives of a single country. At times diplomatic history has been reduced to scarcely more than a record of what one diplomat or foreign minister said to another, with little awareness of the wider influences which so often shape foreign policy – financial and military factors, the influence of public opinion, and so on. Nowadays the best diplomatic history deals with international relations in the most comprehensive sense, rather than the diplomacy of a particular nation. A fine example is Christopher Thorne's *Allies of a Kind* (1978), a political and strategic study of the Western powers' campaign against Japan between 1941 and 1945, based on official and private documents in the USA, Britain, the Netherlands and Australia.

Many of Ranke's contemporaries and followers emphasized instead the internal evolution of the European nation-states, and *constitutional history* was largely their creation. This emphasis was most pronounced in Britain, where history became an academically respectable subject during the 1860s and 1870s almost entirely on the strength of constitutional history. Its leading proponent, William Stubbs, was at pains to stress the intellectual advance which this approach represented on the kind of history that had gone before:

> The History of Institutions cannot be mastered – can scarcely be approached – without an effort. It affords little of the romantic incident or of the picturesque grouping which constitute the charm of History in general, and holds out small temptation to the mind that requires to be tempted to the study of Truth. But it had a deep value and an abiding interest to those who have the courage to work upon it . . . Constitutional History has a point of view, an insight, a language of its own; it reads the exploits and characters of men by a different light from that shed by the false glare of arms, and interprets positions and facts in words that are voiceless to those who have only listened to the trumpet of fame.[5]

Its central theme was of course the evolution of Parliament, considered by the Victorians to be England's most priceless contribution to civilization, and thus the appropriate focus for a national history. England's constitutional history was seen as a sequence of momentous conflicts of principle, alternating with periods of gradual change, stretching back to the early Middle Ages; it was enshrined in a succession of great state documents (Magna Carta and the like) which required disciplined textual study. For fifty years after the publication of Stubbs's three-volume *Constitutional History of England* (1873–78), constitutional history carried the greatest academic prestige in this country, and major revisionist work continues to be done to this day. In the hands of Stubbs's followers – most of them Medievalists as he was – the subject was diversified to encompass two closely related specialisms: the history of law and administrative history. Legal history attracts relatively little interest today, but administrative history shows every sign of enjoying a new lease of life as historians seek to interpret the massive increase in the functions and personnel of government which has taken place in all Western societies during this century.

II

The third approach inherited from the nineteenth century is more than a dimension of political history and merits consideration as a distinct specialism. This is the *history of ideas*, or intellectual history. Besides political thought, it includes economic and social thought, theology, scientific thought, and the values and assumptions expressed in the writing of history itself (i.e. historiography). At its most ambitious, especially as practised in the United States, the history of ideas amounts to an attempt to capture the intellectual climate of an entire epoch. In spite of this broadening range, however, the majority of work in this field probably continues to be about the history of political thought, and as such is rooted in a tradition which was firmly established during the nineteenth century. Most of the great political historians from Ranke onwards were agreed that what gave history its coherence and continuity was the power of ideas to shape human destiny – ideas about nationhood, the state, constitutional liberties and religion. From this it was a short step to regard the history of ideas as a valid specialism, and to trace the origin of concepts such as natural rights, representative democracy and the national community. To explain their evolution was to explain the process of history itself.

In the twentieth century confidence in this approach has been undermined from two directions at once. On the one hand, the stress on the unconscious by Freud and the popularizers of psycho-analysis has given rise to some scepticism as to whether formal professions of belief or principle bear much relation to what people actually think or do: Namier's fascination with Freudian theory certainly accounted for much of his hostility to the history of ideas.[6] On the other hand, Marx's materialist interpretation of history represents a full-scale attack on the autonomy of intellectual history. Although the different schools of Marxist thought vary in their stance on this issue, the implication usually drawn from Marxism is that ideologies are essentially an expression of the tensions inherent in class-ridden societies (see Ch. 8). The result of these changes in the intellectual climate is that the pretensions of today's historians of ideas are more modest than those of their predecessors, and they do not claim the same autonomy for their field. Their work continues to be significant because, although social and material conditions may place limits on the range of ideas which can gain acceptance in any age, they certainly do not determine the precise form which those ideas take. Much can only be accounted for by the inventiveness of the human mind and by the power of tradition.

Whereas historians of ideas were traditionally concerned to trace the ancestry of particular concepts down the ages, recent work has stressed the dangers inherent in this approach of reading more into a given work than is really there. This is because the meaning of language itself changes subtly from one generation to the next; potent idioms, and sometimes individual words such as 'liberty' or 'authority', shed old associations and acquire fresh nuances. What the great treatises of political theory such as Machiavelli's *The Prince* or Hobbes's *Leviathan* actually meant to their authors and contemporary readers can only be discovered by a careful reconstruction of the context in which they were written – both the personal circumstances of the author and the resources of language that were available at the time. How later ages have reinterpreted those works and dragooned them into service for other ends is a separate question – though an equally valid one.[7]

A much keener awareness is now also shown of the fact that the intellectual landscape of a period is not primarily composed of the handful of great works which have inspired posterity; almost by definition, these were novel and unconventional, and inaccessible to all but a few. The common wisdom of the day against which they were judged (and often condemned) was what contemporaries had retained, often selectively and incoherently, from earlier traditions of thought. For the political historian especially, what counts is the set of ideas within which people with no claims to intellectual originality thought, and from this perspective the diffusion of new ideas through second-rate and ephemeral literature is as important as their genesis in the mind of a great thinker. The intellectual context of periods of revolutionary change when ideas are often particularly potent can be properly understood in no other way. In *The Intellectual Origins of the American Revolution* (1967), for example, Bernard Bailyn reconstructed the political culture of ordinary Americans largely from four hundred or so pamphlets bearing on the Anglo-American conflict which were published in the thirteen colonies between 1750 and 1776. His research revealed the influence of not only the New England Puritan tradition and the thought of the Enlightenment, which had long been taken for granted, but also the anti-authoritarian political thought of the Civil War period in England, kept alive by English radical pamphleteers of the early eighteenth century and transmitted across the Atlantic.

Lastly, the role of ideas remains central to a historical understanding of literature and the arts. At one level, the great artistic achievements of the past demand a critical response in which their stylistic and aesthetic qualities are evaluated. But historians of art and literature go very much further than this: their aim is to understand the arts in the context of the age in which they were produced. The social context is obviously relevant – the position of the artist or writer, his or her relationship with the wider audience of the day, and the role of patronage. But the intellectual context is probably the most crucial to our understanding of what a particular work of art meant or was intended to mean. Through metaphor and symbol art has at different times expressed ideas of theology, philosophy, politics and social morality. One of the first historians to treat the arts in this way was Jacob Burckhardt whose book, *The Civilization of the Renaissance in Italy* (1860) was founded on the premise that the brilliant culture of the period embodied a new and more direct perception by people of themselves and the world round them than anything to be found in the Middle Ages. Few modern historians would venture such bold generalizations.[8] But what they have done is to fathom the often complex and covert allusions which, to the lay person contemplating any work of art created more than a century ago, are likely to be a closed book. Erwin Panofsky demonstrated that in order to understand Gothic or Renaissance iconography (i.e. the meaning of the images) it was necessary to be steeped in the intellectual history of the period. The paintings and sculptures of Michelangelo, for example, express the neo-Platonic ideas which were so fashionable in intellectual circles in Florence and Rome at the beginning of the sixteenth century.[9] Although the history of art clearly amounts to more than the applied history of ideas, this is probably the most formidable weapon in the hands of today's art historians.

III

Implicit in all the approaches discussed so far is an interest in the outstanding individual – the great creative thinkers, the makers of foreign policy, and the statesmen who promoted or resisted constitutional change. Quite apart from the intrinsic importance of such people, political narrative of any kind has always owed much of its broad appeal to the fact that the lives of statesmen are more fully and vividly documented than those of any other category of people in the past. This human curiosity has been indulged by historians in the form of *biography* for as long as history has been written. It has, however, often been overlaid by intentions which are inconsistent with a strict regard for historical truth. During the Middle Ages and the Renaissance many biographies were frankly didactic, designed to present the subject as a model of Christian conduct or public virtue. In Victorian times the characteristic form of biography was commemorative: for the heirs and admirers of a public figure the most fitting memorial was a large-scale 'Life', based almost exclusively on the subject's own papers (many of them carefully preserved for this very purpose) and so taking the writer at his or her own valuation. Figures in the more distant past were treated hardly less reverently. Honest, 'warts-and-all' biography was practised by only a few brave spirits. The Victorian reader of biographies was therefore confronted by a gallery of worthies, whose role was to sustain a respect for the nation's political and intellectual elite.

Although biographies of this kind are still published from time to time, the grosser distortions perpetrated by nineteenth-century biographers largely belong to the past. For historians the essential requirement in a biography is that it understands the subject in his or her historical context. It must be written by someone who is not merely well-grounded in the period in question but who has examined all the major collections of papers which have a bearing on the subject's life – including those of adversaries and subordinates as well as friends and family. A historical biography is, in short, a major undertaking. For her study, *George I: Elector and King* (1978), Ragnhild Hatton spent seven years in a quest which took her to the Royal Archives at Windsor Castle, the Public Record Office, the Hannover archives in West Germany, and the private papers of leading politicians in both England and Hannover. For earlier figures the volume of material is likely to be smaller, but it may be even more scattered; one of the reasons why there is hardly a single satisfactory biography of a Renaissance pope is that both their early careers and their many-sided interests as popes often ranged over the whole of Europe and are reflected in more archives than any one historian can hope to cover.

Yet even biography which meets the requirements of modern scholarship is not without its critics. Many historians believe that it has no serious place in historical study. The problem of bias cannot be lightly disposed of. Although there has been a vogue for debunking biography ever since Lytton Strachey exposed the human frailties of his ironically named *Eminent Victorians* (1918), anyone who devotes years to the study of one individual – something which Strachey never did – can hardly escape some identification with the subject and will inevitably look at the period to some extent through that person's eyes. Furthermore, biographical narrative encourages a simplified, linear interpretation of events. Maurice Cowling, a leading specialist in modern British political history, has argued that political events can only be understood by showing how members of the political establishment reacted on one another. 'For this purpose', he writes:

> biography is almost always misleading. Its refraction is partial in relation to the [political] system. It abstracts a man whose public action should not be

abstracted. It implies linear connections between one situation and the next. In fact connections were not linear. The system was a circular relationship: a shift in one element changed the position of all the others in relation to the rest.[10]

It is hard to deny that, with the best will in the world, biography nearly always entails some distortion, but there are good grounds for not dismissing it altogether. Firstly, Cowling's objection carries much less weight in the case of political systems where power is concentrated in one man: full-scale biographies of Hitler and Stalin are indispensable to an understanding of Nazi Germany or Soviet Russia. Secondly, at the other extreme, biographies of people who were in no way outstanding can sometimes, if the documentation is rich enough, illuminate an otherwise obscure aspect of the past: Iris Origo's *Merchant of Prato* (1957) recreates the domestic world of a fourteenth-century Tuscan merchant who was remarkable only for the pains he took to ensure that his voluminous correspondence should be preserved for posterity (see p. 38). Thirdly, it is sometimes forgotten by the detractors of biography that the critical use of primary sources requires systematic biographical research. What the authors of these sources wrote can be fairly interpreted only if their background and day-to-day circumstances are grasped: for this if for no other reason historians need to have a good biography of Gladstone, whose writings over a period of some fifty years are such an important source for nineteenth-century British political history.[11]

Lastly, and perhaps most important of all, biography is indispensable to the understanding of motive and intention. There is much dispute among historians as to how prominently matters of motive – as distinct from economic and social forces – should feature in historical explanation, and they certainly receive less emphasis now than they did in the nineteenth century; but plainly the motives of individuals have *some* part to play in explaining historical events. Once this much is conceded, the relevance of biography is obvious. The actions of an individual can only be fully understood in the light of his or her emotional make-up, temperament and prejudices. Of course in even the best documented lives a great deal remains a matter of conjecture: the writings of public figures especially are usually coloured by self-deception as well as deliberate calculation. But the biographer who has studied the development of his or her subject from childhood to maturity is much more likely to make the right inferences. It is for this reason that during the present century biographers have increasingly stressed the private or inner lives of their subjects as well as their public careers. From this perspective the personal development of important individuals in the past is a valid subject of historical enquiry in its own right.

It is this conviction which has given rise to the only radical innovation in the recent writing of biography – the application of psycho-analysis to the past. Freud claimed that, as a result of his clinical work with neurotic patients, he had arrived at a theory which placed our understanding of the human mind on an entirely new and more scientific footing. His theory turned on the concept of the unconscious – that part of the mind imprinted by the experience of traumas in infancy (weaning, toilet-training, Oedipal conflict, etc.) which determines the emotional response of the individual to the world around him in later life. For Freud and the many followers who modified or extended his theory, the primary use of psycho-analysis lay in the treatment of psychiatric disorders. But Freud himself believed that his theory also offered a key to the understanding of historical personalities, and in a famous essay on Leonardo da Vinci (written in 1910) he in effect carried out the first exercise in 'psycho-history'. From the 1950s onwards this approach to biography enjoyed a considerable following, especially in the United States where psycho-analysis was more widely accepted than in any other country. Of all the technical and methodological innovations made in the past thirty years, psycho-history has attracted the most curiosity outside the profession, but it is also the most flawed, and for two principal reasons. First, there is the problem of evidence. Whereas the therapist seeks to recover the infantile experience of the patient through the analysis of dreams, verbal slips and other material produced by the subject, the historian has only the documents which are likely to contain very little, if any, material of this mind and very few direct observations about the subject's early infancy. Secondly, even if the claims of psycho-analysis are accepted – and they remain hotly contested among psychologists to this day – there is no reason to assume that they are valid for previous ages. Indeed, the assumption should rather be the reverse: Freud's picture of emotional development is very culture-bound, rooted in the child-bearing practice and mental attitudes (especially towards sex) of late nineteenth-century middle-class urban society. The application of Freud's insights (or those of any other contemporary school of psycho-analysis) to individuals living in any other period or society is anachronistic. As one particularly trenchant critic has put it, psycho-history stands condemned as a determinist form of 'cultural parochialism'.[12]

But if psycho-history is now somewhat discredited, biography continues to be practised by historians for the reasons given earlier, and the popularization of psycho-analytical concepts has at least served to alert historians to the irrational and incoherent in human conduct, and to investigate the bearing of emotional factors on the lives of public figures. In 1956 J. H. Plumb lamented the lack of interest in biography shown by academic historians at that time.[13] That this was only a temporary phase is demonstrated by the intervening years, which have seen the appearance of well-rounded biographies of the calibre of Plumb's own work on Sir Robert Walpole and Robert Blake's *Disraeli* (1966).

IV

It would be very misleading, however, to suggest that the practice of political history remains wedded to the categories marked out in the nineteenth century – diplomatic history, constitutional history, the history of political thought and the lives of 'great men'. In Britain especially reaction against the traditional forms of political history has turned on the contention that none of them confronts directly what ought to be a central issue in any study of politics, namely the acquisition and exercise of political power and the day-to-day management of political systems. From this perspective, the Stubbs tradition, with its emphasis on constitutional principles and the formal institutions of government, seems unhelpful, although the central issues of constitutional history which he raised continue to be vigorously debated.

The most influential spokesman for this reaction was L. B. Namier, whose writings on eighteenth-century England marked something of a turning point. What interested Namier was not primarily the great political issues of the time or the careers of the leading statesmen, but the composition and recruitment of the political elite as revealed by the minutiae of the personal case-histories of ordinary MPs. His method was essentially collective biography (for which the technical term is 'prosopography', although Namier did not use it). In *The Structure of Politics at the Accession of George III* (1929) and later works Namier asked why men sought a seat in the Commons, how they obtained one, and what considerations guided their political conduct in the House. He cut through the ideological pretensions with which politicians clothed their behaviour (aided and abetted by later historians), and neither their motives nor their methods emerged with much credit. As a result, most of the accepted picture of eighteenth-century English politics was demolished – the two-party system, the packing of the Commons with government placemen, and the assault on the constitution by the young George III. Namier's approach was quickly taken up by historians working on other periods, and towards the end of his life he enshrined it in the officially sponsored *History of Parliament*, which will eventually comprise biographies of everyone who sat in the House of Commons between 1485 and 1901.[14]

If Namier's approach to political history seems limited, it at least had the merit of correcting the distorting effects of the 'great man' school of history. It also happened to be rather appropriate to mid-eighteenth-century English politics which were particularly faction-ridden and barren of major issues of principle. In the work of several more recent historians, however, can be found an even narrower focus, applied to other periods in British history when issues of principles were of much greater moment. According to this approach, what really matters is 'High Politics' – that is, the manoeuvring for power and influence among the few dozen individuals who controlled the political system.[15] An extreme instance is the work of A. B. Cooke and John Vincent, who justify their treatment of the Irish Home Rule crisis of 1885–86 – a crisis with extra-parliamentary dimensions if ever there was one – in these terms:

> Explanations of Westminster should centre not on its being at the top of a coherently organized pyramid of power whose bottom layer was the people, but on its character as a highly specialized community, like the City or Whitehall, whose primary interest was inevitably in its own very private institutional life.[16]

Such an approach, in which the analysis of motive and manoeuvre is allowed full play, makes for a fascinating study in the psychology of political conflict. But it illuminates the surface only. As soon as it is conceded that politics is not only about personalities but also about the clash of competing economic interests and rival ideologies, then the wider society outside the rarified atmosphere of court or parliament becomes critically important. This is self-evident in the case of periods of revolutionary change when the political system broke down as a result of changes in the structure of economy or society. In more stable political situations the dimensions of class and ideology may not be so clearly articulated, but they are present nonetheless, and any analysis of political trends beyond the short term demands that they be understood. At the very least, historians have to be aware of the social and economic background of the political elite and the role of public opinion. Namier himself was not as deficient in this respect as has sometimes been supposed. The effect of his obsession with the 'small men' of politics was to reveal the eighteenth-century House of Commons as a microcosm of the landed and monied society of the day; but at the same time he was largely indifferent to the evidence which extra-parliamentary agitation afforded of more deep-seated changes in politics and society. Because of the way in which politics in our own time is habitually presented as an enclosed world with its own rituals and conventions, political historians are particularly prone to apply too narrow a definition to their subject. More than any other branch of history, political history depends for its vitality on a close involvement with its intellectual neighbours, and particularly with the fields of economic and social history which are the subject of the next chapter.

NOTES

1. For example, S. T. Bindoff, 'Political history', in H. P. R. Finberg (ed.), *Approaches to History*, Routledge & Kegan Paul, 1962, and G. R. Elton, *Political History*, Allen Lane, 1970, pp. 57–72.
2. Arthur Young writing from Florence in 1789, quoted in J. R. Hale (ed.) *The Evolution of British Historiography*, Macmillan, 1967, p. 35.

3. Leopold von Ranke, *History of Servia*, 1828, quoted in Theodore H. von Laue, *Leopold Ranke: the Formative Years*, Princeton University Press, 1950, p. 56.

4. Edward A. Freeman, *The Methods of Historical Study*, Macmillan, 1886, p. 44.

5. William Stubbs, *The Constitutional History of England*, Vol. I, Oxford University Press, 1880, p. v.

6. See for example Namier's essay, 'Human nature in politics', 1955, reprinted in Fritz Stern (ed.) *The Varieties of History*, Macmillan, 2nd edn, 1970.

7. See Quentin Skinner, 'Meaning and understanding in the history of ideas', *History and Theory*, VIII, 1969, pp. 3–53, and J. G. A. Pocock, *Politics, Language and Time*, Methuen, 1972, especially Ch. 1.

8. For a sympathetic critique of the ambitious kind of cultural history attempted by Burckhardt and others, see E. H. Gombrich, 'In search of cultural history', 1967, reprinted in his *Ideals and Idols*, Phaidon, 1979.

9. Erwin Panofsky, *Studies in Iconology*, Harper & Row, 1962, Ch. 6.

10. Maurice Cowling, *The Impact of Labour, 1920–1924*, Cambridge University Press, 1971, p. 6.

11. Derek Beales, *History and Biography*, Cambridge University Press, 1981.

12. David E. Stannard, *Shrinking History: On Freud and the Failure of Psychohistory*, Oxford University Press, 1980, p. 30.

13. J. H. Plumb, 'History and biography', 1956, reprinted in his *Men and Places*, Cresset Press, 1963.

14. Sir Lewis Namier and John Brooke, *The House of Commons 1754–1790*, 3 vols, HMSO, 1964, marked the first stage in this massive enterprise.

15. The concept of 'High Politics' is expounded in Cowling, *Impact of Labour*, pp. 3–12.

16. A. B. Cooke and John Vincent, *The Governing Passion: Cabinet Government and Party Politics in Britain, 1885–86*, Harvester, 1974, p. 22.

Chapter 5

THE MAIN THEMES: ECONOMY, SOCIETY, MENTALITY

Each of the three main categories described in the last chapter was already a well-established part of the scholarly scene by the end of the nineteenth century. Modern research in these fields has therefore been built on a solid foundation of inherited methods and inherited findings. But the result of these strengths in nineteenth-century historiography was that the subject was almost exclusively confined to the activities of individuals and narrowly defined elites. During the twentieth century, however, much the most significant enlargement in the scope of historical studies has been the shift of interest from the individual to the mass – from the drama of public events in which individual achievement and failure were most evident to the underlying structural changes which over the centuries have transformed the lot of ordinary men and women.

I

It is hardly an exaggeration to say that economic and social history, which exemplify this shift, did not exist for Ranke's generation. By the late nineteenth century, however, Western Europe and the United States were emerging from a major economic and social transformation which historical study as then practised was manifestly incapable of explaining. Although Marx's thought has been rigorously applied to historical research in the West on a large scale only during the last thirty years (see Ch. 8), his emphasis on the historical significance of the means of production and of relations between classes had already gained wide currency among politically literate people by the early twentieth century. Moreover the effect of the rise of organized labour and the mass socialist parties was to push issues of economic and social reform more insistently onto the centre of the political stage than ever before. Developments in the early twentieth century pointed in the same general direction. For many, the First World War dealt a fatal blow to the ideal of the nation-state, whose rise had been the great theme of nineteenth-century historiography, while the recurrent slumps and depressions in the world economy confirmed the need for a more systematic grasp of economic history.

Around the turn of the century the narrowly political focus of academic history came under increasing attack from historians themselves. Manifestoes calling for a new and broader approach were launched in several countries – most self-consciously in the United States, where it sailed under the flag of the 'New History'. In Britain the connection between historical study and current social issues was particularly evident in the careers of Sidney and Beatrice Webb, social reformers and historians of the British Labour movement; economic history featured from the start in the curriculum of the London School of Economics which they founded in 1895.

It was, however, in France that the implications of broadening history's scope were most fully worked out. This was the achievement of Marc Bloch, a Medievalist, and Lucien Febvre, a specialist in the sixteenth century, whose followers today probably command greater international prestige in the academic world than any other school. In 1929 Bloch and Febvre founded a historical journal called *Annales d'histoire sociale et économique*, usually known simply as *Annales*.[1] In the first issue they demanded of their colleagues not just a broader approach but an awareness of what they could learn from other disciplines, especially the social sciences – economics, sociology, social psychology and geography (a particularly strong enthusiasm of the *Annales* historians). While conceding that the practitioners of these disciplines were primarily concerned with contemporary problems, Bloch and Febvre maintained that only with their help could historians become aware of the full range of significant questions which they could put to their sources. And whereas earlier reformers had called for an inter-disciplinary method, it was systematically put into practice by the *Annales* historians in a formidable corpus of publications, of which Marc Bloch's *Feudal Society* (1940) is probably the best known outside France. From this basic premise, historians of the *Annales* school have continued to broaden and refine the content and methodology of history, with the result that many of the new directions which the discipline has taken in the past thirty years owe much to their contribution. At the same time, the principal apologists of the *Annales* school heaped considerable scorn on the traditional pursuits of political narrative and individual biography – a reaction which was shared by many economic and social historians in Britain: in Tawney's words, politics was 'the squalid scaffolding of more serious matters'.[2]

II

In this new intellectual climate, *economic history* was the first specialism to gain recognition. By 1914 it had emerged as a sharply defined area of study in several countries, including Britain. The relevance of economic history to contemporary problems largely explains its head-start over other contenders; indeed, in many universities, especially in America, economic history was studied not as part of general history, but in conjunction with economics, a discipline whose own claims to academic respectability had only just won general recognition by the end of the nineteenth century. Both in Britain and on the continent, much of the pioneer work concerned the economic policies of the state – an approach which required the minimum adaptation on the part of historians schooled in political history. But this was clearly an inadequate base on which to come to grips with the historical phenomenon of industrialization, which from the start loomed large on the agenda of economic historians everywhere. It resulted in a special emphasis on Britain, the first country to experience an industrial revolution, and attracted continental as much as British historians. Their work was particularly strong on local studies of particular industries, such as Lancashire cotton textiles or Yorkshire woollens, and it highlighted individual initiative and technical innovation. A pale reflection of this approach is still to be seen in those old-fashioned textbooks which chronicle Britain's industrial revolution as a sequence of inventions made in the late eighteenth century.

Today economic historians can fairly claim that their subject matter embraces every aspect of economic life in the past, which is to say all those activities which have to do with production, exchange and consumption. But the character and haphazard distribution of the primary sources place severe limits on the periods and places whose economic history can be reconstructed in the round – far more serious than in the case of political history. The urge to gather information about the contemporary economy, which consumes so much energy and money today, dates back no further than the seventeenth century at the earliest, and it was only during the nineteenth century that either government departments or private bodies pursued their enquiries at all systematically. For their knowledge of earlier periods, historians depend on laboriously collating the records kept by individuals and institutions of their own financial transactions, and the survival of these records is very much a matter of chance. In England's case manorial estate records survive in considerable numbers from the thirteenth century, especially those belonging to the Church, which changed hands less frequently than estates in secular ownership and which commanded higher standards of literacy.[3] But the only major documentary archive of a Medieval English trading firm which has come down to us is the papers of the Cely family, who were prominent in the export of wool to the Low Countries in the 1470s and 1480s.[4] Not until the eighteenth century do commercial records become really plentiful. Public records have, of course, proved more durable, but the government's curiosity about the economic activities of its subjects was almost entirely confined to those which it taxed. Thus, although the main features of England's export trade from the late thirteenth century emerge clearly enough from the customs records,[5] we know frustratingly little about the country's internal trade which went virtually untaxed. For the Middle Ages, and for much of the early modern period too, the range of economic questions which historians can answer with any degree of confidence is drastically limited by the paucity of the evidence.

Two trends stand out in current writing on modern economic history though they do not, of course, define its entire scope. The first one is business history – the systematic study of individual firms on the basis of their business records. The source materials are usually manageable, and firms which allow access to them sometimes foot the bill for research as well. Whether or not the historian identifies with the values of capitalist entrepreneurship, what comes out of the best of these studies is a keener understanding of the mechanisms of economic expansion, often at a critical juncture in the history of an industry. This is certainly true of Charles Wilson's path-breaking *History of Unilever* (1954) which, by tracing the history of the British and Dutch parent companies from the 1850s onwards, showed how the manufacturing of soap and margarine grew to its massive modern proportions. The implications of research in business history can be wider still. How far the beginning of Britain's economic decline in the period 1870–1914 was caused by a failure of entrepreneurship is a major issue on which business historians have much to contribute.[6]

Business history may be regarded as economic history on the ground. The second approach, by contrast, seeks to explain the dynamics of growth or decline for an entire economy. This is quite simply the biggest issue in economics today, both for professional economists and for the lay public; and since it has been present in a recognizably modern form since the onset of industrialization two hundred years ago, it is hardly surprising that historians should be interested too. But in seeking to contribute to a wider debate they have been compelled to sharpen their analytical tools. The older economic histories like J. H. Clapham's *Economic History of Modern Britain* (1926–38) were essentially descriptive: they reconstructed the economic life of a particular period, sometimes in vivid detail, but in explaining how one phase gave way to the next they showed little interest in the actual mechanisms of economic change. The current debates are very largely about those mechanisms, and they are conducted in the context of the highly sophisticated theoretical work on growth which economists have been carrying out since the 1950s. If historians are to do justice to their material in this area, they have to be much more versed in the competing theoretical explanations than they used to be; and since the testing of these theories depends on the accurate measurement of indices of growth, historians must become quantifiers. As will be discussed in Chapter 9, more and more economic historians since the 1960s have been becoming essentially quantitative historians, for whom both questions and methods of research are increasingly set by economic theory rather than history. In this field the breaking down of those inter-disciplinary barriers which the *Annales* school called for half a century ago has been more complete than in any other.

III

Social history is less self-evident in its identity and scope than any of the categories discussed so far. It is only in the last twenty years that any measure of agreement has emerged among social historians as to what their subject is really about. Until that time the term 'social history' was understood in three quite distinct ways, each one marginal to the interests of historians in general, and it was regarded (in Britain at least) as no more than a very junior partner of economic history. There was, firstly, the history of social problems such as poverty, ignorance, insanity and disease. Historians focused less on the experience of people afflicted by these conditions than on the 'problem' which they posed to society as a whole; they studied the reforming efforts of private philanthropy, as seen in charitable institutions like schools, orphanages and hospitals, and the increasingly effective intervention of the state in the social field from the mid-nineteenth century onwards. Social history meant, secondly, the history of everyday life in the home, the work-place and the community. As G. M. Trevelyan put it, 'Social history might be defined negatively as the history of a people with the politics left out'.[7] His *Social History of England* (1944), for long a standard work, took little account of economics either, and much of it reads like a catch-all for the miscellaneous topics which did not fit into his earlier (and largely political) *History of England* (1926); there is much descriptive detail, but little coherence of theme.

Lastly, there was the history of the common people, or working classes, who were almost entirely absent from political history, and who featured in economic history only in an inert and undifferentiated way as 'labour' or 'consumers'. In Britain this kind of social history was from the end of the nineteenth century dominated by historians sympathetic to the labour movement. Although often passionately committed to the workers' cause, their writings were hardly affected by

Marxist influence at all. Their main concern was to furnish the British labour movement with a collective historical identity, and they sought it not through a new theoretical framework (for which Marxism was of course well suited) but in the historical experience of the working class itself during the preceding century – the material and social deprivation, the tradition of self-help, and the struggles for improved wages and conditions of employment. For G. D. H. Cole, the leading British labour historian during the 1930s and 1940s, nothing seemed more important than that 'as the working class grows towards the full exercise of power, it should look back as well as forward, and shape its policy in the light of its own historic experience'.[8] Labour history tended to live in a world of its own, with only a limited impact on those not involved in the labour movement. Yet precisely because of this political context, labour history continues to be written – if under new labels such as 'history from below' or 'people's history'. It represents the strongest strand within the History Workshop movement which emerged during the 1970s as a forum of academic and community historians, based at Ruskin College, Oxford (itself closely associated with the trade union movement) (see above, pp. 6–7). It is today much the most lively of the three approaches described so far.

But none of these approaches explains why social history, for so long the poor relation, now enjoys such prominence. What has happened in recent years is that its subject-matter has been redefined in a much more ambitious manner. Social history now aspires to offer nothing less than the history of social structure. The notion of 'social structure' is a sociological abstraction of a conveniently indeterminate kind which can be – and has been – clothed in any number of theoretical garbs. But what it essentially means is the sum of the social relationships between the many different groups in society. Under the influence of Marxist thought, class has had the lion's share of attention, but it is by no means the only kind of group to be considered: there are also the cross-cutting ties of age, gender, race and occupation.

The notion of social structure may seem to be a static, timeless one, partly because it has been treated in this way in the writings of many sociologists. But it need not be so, and historians tend naturally to adopt a more dynamic approach. As Keith Wrightson, a leading social historian of early modern England, puts it:

> Society is a process. It is never static. Even its most apparently stable structures are the expression of an equilibrium between dynamic forces. For the social historian the most challenging of tasks is that of recapturing that process, while at the same time discerning long-term shifts in social organization, in social relations and in the meanings and evaluations with which social relationships are infused.[9]

Against the background of a durable social structure, those individuals or groups who move up or down are often particularly significant, and social mobility has been much studied by historians. Beyond a certain point, social mobility is incompatible with the maintenance of the existing structure and a new form of society may emerge, as happened most fundamentally during the Industrial Revolution. Urbanization, in particular, needs to be studied not just in its economic aspects, but as a process of social change, including the assimilation of immigrants, the emergence of new forms of social stratification, the hardening distinction between work and leisure, and so on; important work along these lines has been pioneered in America.[10] The analysis of social structure and social change can have major implications for economic and political history, and social historians in recent years have staked out large claims in these areas. The long drawn out 'gentry controversy' was mainly a dispute about the connection between changing social structure and political conflict in England during the hundred years before the Civil War.[11] The origins of the Industrial Revolution are now sought not only in economic and geographical factors, but in the social structure of eighteenth-century England – especially the 'open aristocracy' with a two-way flow of men and wealth into and out of its ranks.[12] At this point, social history begins to approximate to the 'history of society' in its broadest sense which, it has been argued, is its proper domain.[13]

Much of the earlier, less ambitious social history is relevant to this new concern, provided its terms of reference are revised. The new social historians include many who started within the more limited horizons of one or other of the established categories. E. P. Thompson, the best-known social historian in England today, has his roots deep in the labour history tradition, but in *The Making of the English Working Class* (1963) he stepped outside it; the growth of a working-class awareness during the Industrial Revolution is placed in the widest possible context, including religion, leisure and popular culture, as well as the factory system and the origins of trade unionism; and, so far from politics being 'left out', the presence of the state is both constant and menacing, as an instrument of class control.

As social history has raised its sights, so its research techniques have become more demanding. There is probably no other field whose primary sources are so varied, so widely dispersed, and so uneven in quality. The vast majority of extant historical records were, after all, created by large corporate institutions, such as government, church and business. While this suits the political historian well enough, and up to a point the economic historian too, it poses major problems for the social historian. The limited scope of the earlier social history is partly explained by the tendency of historians to take the line of least resistance and follow the trail through the records of institutions with an avowedly 'social' function – schools, hospitals, trade unions and the like: the result was all too often work of a narrowly institutional character. But the new social history demands a great deal more. Social groups do not leave corporate records. Their composition and their place in the social structure have to be reconstructed from a broad range of sources composed for quite different and usually much more mundane reasons. Some idea of the effort required can be grasped from Lawrence Stone's *The Crisis of the Aristocracy, 1558–1641* (1965). His conclusions are based primarily on the estate records and personal correspondence of the families concerned, some of it on public deposit in libraries and county record offices, but much of it still in the muniment rooms of stately homes; in addition he draws on the records of lawsuits and of correspondence with the government in the Public Record Office, contemporary literary sources, and a vast array of local and family histories compiled over the last two centuries or so.

An even greater problem is posed by the vast mass of the population which lived outside the charmed circle of literacy. Their conditions and opinions became the subject of systematic social surveys only during the nineteenth century. Until then the picture which we form of the lower classes is inevitably dominated by those activities which brought down on them the attention of the authorities: litigation, sedition, and – most of all – common crime and offences against church discipline. At times of popular discontent this attention was particularly intrusive, and whole areas of society which normally remain 'invisible' may be illuminated by legal and police records. The riots which periodically broke out in eighteenth-century London are a case in point.[14] Equally, fear of revolution may intensify official surveillance of lower-class activities, as in England during the Napoleonic Wars: 'But for spies, narks and letter-copiers, the history of the English working class would be unknown', writes E. P. Thompson with only a little overstatement.[15] Such opportunities are all the more precious because at other times information about the common people is usually much thinner. Court records are still useful, but in more settled conditions judicial activity was less intense, and it is therefore much more difficult to build up the profile of a local community. Before any generalization can be made with confidence, a vast quantity of court records has to be sifted, usually in conjunction with other sources such as manorial records, tax registers, wills and the records of charitable institutions. In Britain, as in other countries, there is almost limitless scope for further work along these lines.

IV

One of the reasons why the study of social structure and social change appeals to historians is that it offers a means of getting to grips with the historical experience of whole societies instead of restricted elites. But it is not the only means of doing so, or necessarily the most effective. The approaches to social history just described entail a high degree of abstraction from that experience. Most of the structures detected by historians were probably not perceived at the time, and certainly not by the illiterate and untravelled who at any period before the nineteenth century constituted the majority of the population in all societies It is one thing to categorize people according to their place in a given ,tructure by indicating their occupation, status and wealth. It is quite another to enter into their assumptions and attitudes, to see them as 'sentient reflecting beings'.[16] Of course historians have for a long time taken pains to see the prominent personalities of the past in this way; the study of an individual's private papers is important because it allows the historian to see the world through his or her eyes. But it is only quite recently that historians have faced up to the need to make a comparable effort in the case of people in the mass. How, in any given society in the past, did people apprehend their daily experience? What were their attitudes to time and space, pain and death, family relationships, and religious observance? How should we characterize their ambitions and anxieties? What were their common values? All this is subsumed in a new and flourishing branch of historical enquiry, usually referred to as the *history of collective mentality*, or states of mind. There is obviously a connection with the history of ideas, considered in the previous chapter; but while the history of ideas deals with formally articulated principles and ideologies, the history of mentality is concerned with the emotional, the instinctive and the implicit – areas of thought which have often found no direct expression at all. And it is social historians rather than intellectual historians who have made the running in this new field.

The first scholar to approach the history of mentality in any systematic way was Lucien Febvre, co-founder of *Annales*. He made the point that the worst kind of historical anachronism is psychological anachronism – the unthinking assumption that the mental framework with which people interpreted their experience in earlier periods was the same as our own. What, he asked, were the psychological implications of the differences between night and day and between winter and summer which were experienced much more harshly by Medieval men and women than they are today? Febvre called for a 'historical psychology', developed by historians and psychologists working together.[17] But for recent historians who have taken up Febvre's challenge, the most fertile source of ideas has not been psychology but anthropology.

Although the relevance to history of the study of exotic small-scale societies of the present day may not be readily apparent, there are several reasons why historians should be alert to the findings of anthropology. These reasons are most insistent for those historians who are themselves specializing in some area of Third World history, but they

86

apply also to their colleagues in more conventional fields. For example, certain long-lost features of our own society such as the blood-feud or witchcraft accusations still persist in some parts of the world today and are far more fully documented: direct observation of the modern variant prompts a fuller grasp of the relevant questions to be asked about comparable features in our own past for which the direct evidence may be very sparse or uneven. But it is in the sphere of mentality that anthropology has made the greatest impact so far. Because anthropologists study their subject by combining the roles of participant and observer, they can hardly fail to register the vastly different mental assumptions which operate in pre-literate, technologically simple societies. Much recent anthropology has been concerned to identify patterns of thought as revealed in ritual and symbol, and to see how they mould collective and individual behaviour – that is, as the anthropologists themselves would put it, to study 'culture' in its broadest sense. Underlying the notion of 'culture' is the belief – well supported by anthropological case-studies – that seemingly bizarre and irrational features in fact reflect a coherence of thought and behaviour which in the last resort is what holds society together. No other discipline has produced insights of comparable value into the thought processes of societies other than our own. The findings of anthropology suggest something of the range of mentalities to be found among people who are acutely vulnerable to the vagaries of climate and disease, who lack 'scientific' control of their environment, and who are tied to their own localities – conditions which obtained in the West during most of the Medieval and early modern periods. For historians encountering a past society through the medium of documentary sources there is – or ought to be – the same sense of 'culture shock' that the modern investigator experiences in an exotic or 'primitive' community.

Unlike the anthropologist, however, the historian is for the most part thrown back on oblique evidence of what went on in the minds of ordinary people. Two types of evidence have been found particularly useful. There is first of all the source material on which social historians of all kinds are so dependent – the records of legal proceedings. For the researcher prepared to work through enough of them, the cumulative effect of court records is to expose much of the popular attitude towards family and neighbourhood relationships, sexual conduct, religion and many other topics. For most periods before the eighteenth century this is particularly true of the church courts which took such an inquisitive interest in the moral peccadilloes of both clergy and laity. Emmanuel Le Roy Ladurie's *Montaillou* (1976), not unfairly described by a friendly critic as a book which 'rambles around inside people's heads',[18] is a striking example of what can be gleaned from court records (see above, p. 60). The second type of evidence is art forms: not the 'high' art which art historians write about so much as popular art, created by the people themselves or designed by others to appeal to popular taste. As anthropologists have demonstrated, artefacts and performances often express in symbolic or ritual form deeply held collective attitudes. In his *Popular Culture of Early Modern Europe* (1978), Peter Burke draws on the evidence of broadsheets and woodcuts, ballads and folklore, carnivals and street theatre to advance some tentative generalizations about the mentality of peasants and craftsmen in pre-industrial society. Much more work of this kind is likely to follow.

It should not be supposed from these examples that the study of mentality is necessarily confined to the remote past. In his massive work, *France 1848–1945* (2 vols, 1973 and 1977), Theodore Zeldin measures the self-image of the French – as well as Anglo-Saxon stereotypes of the French – against the diversity of values and aspirations which animated French men and women during this period, and finds that self-image to have been very largely the creation of intellectuals who enjoyed exceptional public esteem in France. But it remains true that most attention has been directed to earlier periods in order to chart the transition to a number of characteristically modern attitudes. Important areas include the decline of belief in magic in seventeenth-century England[19] and the spread of a precise notion of clock-time during the Industrial Revolution.[20] Above all, there is currently an upsurge of interest in emotional aspects of the history of the family. Most historians are agreed that during the last three hundred years or so the nuclear family in Western society has become a more self-contained unit, while relations within it have come to depend more on sentiment than on the distance and deference which previously marked relations both between husbands and wives and between parents and children. When and why this transition to what Stone has called 'affective individualism'[21] took place are matters of intense debate which are only now being assessed against systematically assembled evidence.[22] What is clear is that here, as in their other spheres of interest, historians of collective mentality are not content to reconstruct states of mind for their own sake, or as a means of entering more fully into the experience of people in the past. Their argument is that mentality is an independent variable not determined – or at any rate not entirely – by economic and demographic conditions, and that our grasp of historical change will remain partial and distorted unless the autonomy of this branch of history is conceded.

V

Historians and their writings are commonly classified according to one of the categories described in this chapter and the previous one. It is probably inevitable that this should be so. In all branches of knowledge most advances are made by specialists working on a narrow front, and the fivefold division of political, intellectual, economic, social and mental history at least corresponds to recognizable areas of thought and behaviour. The problem is that no human activity can be pigeon-holed in this way without denying some of its dimensions: political conflict is often an expression of fundamental ideological or material differences, the pace of economic change is likely to be conditioned by the rigidity or suppleness of the social structure, and so on. Historians who specialize in one branch of history risk attributing too much to one kind of factor in their explanations of historical change. Economic history which does not look beyond the factors of production, political history confined to a Namierite perspective, international history which reflects only the small change of diplomacy – all these are instances of what J. H. Hexter has aptly termed 'tunnel vision'.[23] It is an occupational disease of historians (as of other scholars) and it is intensified among those who are set on applying the theories and techniques of the social sciences – usually economics or sociology.

One might expect that these deficiencies would be made good by survey works – those general syntheses which seek to draw together the research findings of a large number of specialists into a coherent whole. The performance of historians in this respect has often been woefully inadequate. Traditionally the writing of such works was placed in the hands of political historians on the grounds that political history constituted the 'core' of the subject. The results were some-times bizarre. As recently as 1960, the volume in the Oxford History of England series for the period 1760–1815 was almost entirely composed of political narrative; less than one tenth of the book was devoted to economic change, although no theme during the period had greater significance than the onset of the Industrial Revolution.[24] Nowadays a much more even-handed coverage is usually found in survey works, and political historians no longer hog the show. But surveys which achieve a real integration are very much the exception, and it is still rare to find one which incorporates the history of collective menta-lity.[25] The conventional division between 'politics', 'economics', 'society' and 'ideas' is often rigidly adhered to in the structure of these books, because historians who approach their own research with 'tunnel vision' are conditioned to think in this way when they attempt a bird's eye view.

In historical research there are therefore compelling reasons in favour of avoiding thematic specialization. The influence of the *Annales* historians has been particularly salutary here. The appeal of the founders was not so much for new specialisms – although they were certainly attacking the excessive ascendancy of political history in France at the time – as for an end to compartmentalization: the direction of research must be determined not by the label attached to the historian or by the character of the chosen body of sources, but by the intellectual requirements of a specified historical problem. The ultimate aim of the historian was to recapture human life in all its variety or – in the phrase which has since become the rallying-cry of the *Annales* school – to write 'total history' *(histoire totale* or *histoire intégrale)*. The fulfilment of this ideal has often been credited to Fernand Braudel, Febvre's successor as editor of *Annales* and *doyen* of the historical profession in France. In *The Mediterranean and the Mediterranean World in the Age of Philip II* (1947) Braudel treated every dimension of his vast subject in brilliantly evocative detail: the physical and human geography of the region, its economic and social life, its political structures, and the Mediteranean policies of Philip II and his rivals. The book is probably the finest achievement of the *Annales* school, but it still falls short of 'total history' because – as many critics have pointed out[26] – the different approaches are not integrated with each other: the political narrative which forms the third and concluding section of the book is largely detached from the geographical and economic panorama in the first two parts.

Braudel's experience suggests that the ideal of 'total history' cannot be realized on so vast a stage as the Mediterranean. It is scarcely more practicable for a single country. If all the sources are to be mastered and a full integration of theme to be achieved, the geographical limits of the enquiry must be drastically narrowed down. Paradoxically, therefore, 'total history' turns out in practice to mean *local history*. Traditionally local history was the preserve of amateurs whose horizons were limited by their local loyalties and their social position in the community (usually squire or parson); their work was much stronger on antiquarian detail than on interpretation, and was largely ignored in academic circles. In the last twenty years, however, local history has been increasingly taken up by professional historians because of the opportunity it offers of straddling the conventional demarcations between specialisms. The *Annales* historians were among the first to practise the new kind of local history. Le Roy Ladurie's work on rural Languedoc between the fifteenth and eighteenth centuries exemplifies the strengths of the *Annales* approach; he summed up the subject of his first book, *The Peasants of Languedoc* (1966), as

> the long-term movements of an economy and of a society – base and superstructure, material life and cultural life, sociological evolution and collective psychology, the whole within the framework of a rural world which remained very largely traditional in nature.[27]

In Britain the emphasis has been not so much on regions as on individual towns and villages, where the historian can become familiar with every inch of the ground as well as every page of documentation. But the aspiration towards 'total history' is comparable. As W. G. Hoskins put it,

> The local historian is in a way like the old-fashioned G.P. of English medical history, now a fading memory confined to the more elderly among us, who treated Man as a whole.[28]

Even at the local level, the attainment of a true 'total history' still presents immense difficulties, and only a handful of works have brought it off. But the many local histories which have travelled some way along this road have nevertheless acted as a powerful solvent of the rigidities to which conventional specialists working on a larger canvass are so prone. For political historians particularly, local history serves as a reminder that their subject is about not only the central institutions of the state but also the assertion of authority over ordinary people; politics is likely to be interpreted less as an enclosed arena than as the sphere in which conflicts between opposing interests in society are fought out. Thus, as a result of the many county studies undertaken in recent years, historians now have a more sophisticated understanding of the inter-relationship between religious, economic and political factors in the origins of the English Civil War.[29] That local history enjoys such high standing among present-day historians probably offers the best assurance that the traditional boundaries between specialisms will not be permitted to stand in the way of a thematically integrated view of the past.

NOTES

1. The journal was renamed *Annales: économies, sociétés, civilisations* in 1946.
2. R. H. Tawney, obituary of George Unwin (1925), quoted in N. B. Harte (ed.) *The Study of Economic History*, Frank Cass, 1971, p. xxvi.
3. See the helpful discussion in J. Z. Titow, *English Rural Society, 1200–1350*, Allen & Unwin, 1969.
4. Alison Hanham (ed.) *The Cely Letters 1472–1488*, Oxford University Press, 1975.
5. See, for example, E. M. Carus-Wilson and O. P. Coleman, *England's Export Trade 1275–1547*, Oxford University Press, 1963.
6. For a review of the literature, see P. L. Payne, *British Entrepreneurship in the Nineteenth Century*, Macmillan, 1974.
7. G. M. Trevelyan, *English Social History*, Longman, 1944, p. vii. An almost identical definition is given in G. J. Renier, *History: Its Purpose and Method*, Allen & Unwin, 1950, p. 72.
8. G. D. H. Cole, *A Short History of the British Working-Class Movement, 1789–1947*, Allen & Unwin, 1948, pp. v–vi.
9. Keith Wrightson, *English Society 1580–1680*, Hutchinson, 1982, p. 12.

10. See Stephan Thernstrom, 'Reflections on the new urban history', *Daedalus* C, 1971, pp. 359–75.

11. For a review of the literature, see Lawrence Stone, *The Causes of the English Revolution, 1529–1642*, Routledge & Kegan Paul, 1972.

12. Harold Perkin, *The Origins of Modern English Society, 1780–1880*, Routledge & Kegan Paul, 1969.

13. E. J. Hobsbawm, 'From social history to the history of society', *Daedalus* C, 1971, pp. 20–45.

14. See, for example, George Rudé, *Paris and London in the Eighteenth Century: Studies in Popular Protest*, Fontana, 1970.

15. E. P. Thompson, *Writing by Candlelight*, Merlin Press, 1980, p. 126.

16. I have taken this phrase from Margaret Spufford, *Contrasting Communities: English Villagers in the Sixteenth and Seventeenth Centuries*, Cambridge University Press, 1974, p. xxiii.

17. Lucien Febvre, 'History and psychology', 1938, reprinted in Peter Burke (ed.), *A New Kind of History*, Routledge & Kegan Paul, 1973.

18. Lawrence Stone, *The Past and the Present*, Routledge & Kegan Paul, 1981, p. 90.

19. Keith Thomas, *Religion and the Decline of Magic*, Weidenfeld & Nicolson, 1971.

20. E. P. Thompson, 'Time, work-discipline and industrial capitalism', *Past & Present*, XXXVIII, 1967, pp. 56–97.

21. Lawrence Stone, *The Family, Sex and Marriage in England, 1500–1800*, Weidenfeld & Nicolson, 1977.

22. The debates are reviewed in Michael Anderson, *Approaches to the History of the Western Family, 1500–1914*, Macmillan, 1980.

23. J. H. Hexter, *Reappraisals in History*, Longman, 1961, pp. 194–5.

24. 58 out of 573 pages in J. Steven Watson, *The Reign of George III, 1760–1815*, Oxford University Press, 1960.

25. A striking exception is J. R. Hale, *Renaissance Europe, 1480–1520*, Fontana, 1971.

26. See, most recently, J. H. Hexter, *On Historians*, Collins, 1979, pp. 132–40.

27. Emmanuel Le Roy Ladurie, *The Peasants of Languedoc*, University of Illinois Press, 1974, p. 289.

28. W. G. Hoskins, *English Local History: the Past and the Future*, Leicester University Press, 1966, p. 21.

29. For a fuller discussion of this point, see R. C. Richardson, *The Debate on the English Revolution*, Methuen, 1977, Ch. 7.

Chapter 6

HISTORICAL WRITING

The previous two chapters were intended in the first instance to indicate the main categories of enquiry which confine the task of original research to manageable proportions; but inevitably they strayed into a consideration of the contribution which each approach has made to historical knowledge, and in so doing glanced over a vital intervening stage in the historian's work – the ordering of the material in written form. The application of critical method to the primary sources along the lines described in Chapter 3 generally results in the validation of a large number of facts about the past with a bearing on one particular issue, or a group of related issues, but the significance of this material can only be fully grasped when the individual items are related to each other in a coherent exposition. There is nothing obvious or predetermined about the way in which the pieces fit together, and the feat is usually accomplished only as a result of much trial and error. Many historians who have a flair for working on primary sources find the process of composition excruciatingly laborious and frustrating. The temptation is to continue amassing material so that the time of reckoning can be put off indefinitely.

I

One school of opinion maintains that historical writing is of no real significance anyway. The intense excitement which they experience in contemplating the original documents has led these historians to the position that the only historical education worth the name is the study of primary sources – preferably in their original state, but failing that in reliable editions. One of the austerest proponents of this view was V. H. Galbraith, a distinguished Medievalist who was Regius Professor at Oxford in the 1950s. Almost all his published work was devoted to elucidating particular documents and placing them in their historical context – notably Domesday Book and the chronicles of St Albans Abbey; he never wrote the broad interpretative work on fourteenth-century England for which he was uniquely qualified. As he put it:

> What really matters in the long run is not so much what we write about history now, or what others have written, as the original sources themselves . . . The power of unlimited inspiration to successive generations lies in the original sources.[1]

There is a certain logic about this purist position. It will evoke a sympathetic response in all those historians whose research is source-oriented rather than problem-oriented (see above pp. 48–9), many of whom find it extraordinarily difficult to determine when, if ever, the time for synthesis has arrived. In history, more than most other disciplines, undirected immersion in the raw materials has an intellectual justification. Exposure to original sources ought to feature in any programme of historical study, and it is entirely proper that scholarly reputations should continue to be founded on the editing of these materials. But as a general prescription Galbraith's rejection of conventional historical writing is completely misplaced. It would of course entail an abdication from all history's claims to social relevance, which require that historians communicate what they have learned to a wider audience. But it would be hardly less disastrous even supposing that these claims to relevance could be refuted. For it is in the act of writing that historians make sense of their research experience and bring into focus whatever insights into the past they have gained. Much scientific writing takes the form of a report expressing findings which are entirely clear in the scientist's mind before he or she puts pen to paper. It is highly doubtful whether any historical writing proceeds in the same way. The reality of any historical conjuncture as revealed in the sources is so complex, and sometimes so contradictory, that only the discipline of seeking to express it in continuous prose with a beginning and an end enables the researcher to grasp the connections between one area of historical experience and another. Many historians have remarked on this creative aspect of historical writing, which is what can make it no less exhilarating than the detective-work in the archives.[2] Historical writing is essential to historical understanding, and those who shrink from undertaking it are something less than historians.

II

Historical writing is characterized by a wide range of literary forms. The three basic techniques of description, narrative and analysis can be combined in many different ways, and every project poses afresh the problem of how they should be deployed. This lack of clear guide-lines is partly a reflection of the great diversity of the historian's subject-matter: there could not possibly be one literary form suited to the presentation of every aspect of the human past. But it is much more the result of the different and sometimes contradictory purposes behind historical writing, and above all of the tension which lies at the heart of all historical enquiry between the desire to *re-create* the past and the urge to *interpret* it (see Ch. 1). A rough and ready explanation for the variety of historical writing is that narrative and description address the first requirement, while analysis attempts to grapple with the second.

That the re-creation of the past – 'the reconstruction of the historical moment in all its fulness, concreteness and complexity'[3] – is more than a purely intellectual task is plain to see from its most characteristic literary form – *description*. Here historians are striving to create in their readers the illusion of direct experience, by evoking an atmosphere or setting a scene. A great many run-of-the-mill historical works testify to the fact that this effect is not achieved by mastery of the sources alone. It requires imaginative powers and an eye for detail not unlike those of the novelist or poet. This analogy would have been taken for granted by the great nineteenth-century masters of historical description such as Macaulay and Carlyle, who were much influenced by contemporary creative writers and took immense pains with their style. Modern historians are less self-consciously 'literary', but they too are capable of remarkably evocative descriptive writing – witness Braudel's panorama of the Mediterranean environment in the sixteenth century.[4] Whatever else they may be, such historians are artists, and there are too few of them.

Braudel's work is unusual today for the prominence which it accords to description. For effective – indeed indispensable – as such writing is, it cannot express the historian's primary concern with the passage of time. Its role has therefore always been subordinated to the main technique of the re-creative historian – *narrative*. In most European languages the word for 'history' is the same as that used for 'story' (French: *histoire*; Italian: *storia*; German: *Geschichte*). Narrative too is a form which the historian shares with the creative writer – especially the novelist and the epic poet – and it explains much of the appeal which history has traditionally enjoyed with the reading public. Like other forms of story-telling, historical narrative can entertain through its ability to create suspense and arouse powerful emotions. But narrative is also the historian's basic technique for conveying what it felt like to observe or participate in past events. The forms of narrative which achieve the effect of re-creation most successfully are those which approximate most nearly to the sense of time which we experience in our own lives: whether from hour to hour, as in an account of a battle, or from day to day, as in an account of a political crisis, or over a natural lifespan, as in a biography. The great exponents of re-creative history have always been masters of dramatic and vividly evocative narrative. Modern classics of narrative history include Steven Runciman's *History of the Crusades* (3 vols, 1951–54) and C. V. Wedgwood's two works on the reign of Charles I, *The King's Peace* (1955) and *The King's War* (1958).

The re-creation of the past requires one thing more – that we should be able to enter into the minds of the historical actors – to see events 'from the inside'. Individual motives are, however, seldom as patent as the course of events; they have to be inferred from fragmentary and usually conflicting evidence and understood in the context of the range of options available at the time. The flow of the traditional historical narrative is thus interrupted not only by the atmospheric set-piece description, but by more analytical passages in which the state of mind of the participants is explored. In each instance the intention is the same: to deepen our sense of immersion in the lives of people in the past – 'to restore their immediacy of experience' as C. V. Wedgwood puts it.[5]

But the historian is of course engaged in very much more than an exercise in resurrection. It would be entirely consistent with this objective to treat events in the past as isolated and arbitrary, but the historian does not in fact treat them in this way. Historical writing is based on the presupposition that particular events are connected with what happened before, with contemporary developments in other fields, and with what came afterwards; they are conceived, in short, as part of a historical process.   The questions 'What happened?' and 'What were conditions like at such-and-such a time?' are preliminary — if indispensable — to asking 'Why did it happen?' and 'What were its results?'.   Historical explanation is fundamentally to do with causation and consequences, and the more pregnant the consequences of an event, the greater the attention devoted to unravelling its causes.

Asking the question 'Why?' may simply mean asking why an individual took a particular decision. Historians have always given close attention to the study of motive, both because of the traditional prominence of biography in historical studies and because the motives of the great are at least partially reflected in their surviving papers. Diplomatic history is particularly prone to dwell on the intentions and tactics of ministers and diplomats. But even in this limited setting the question 'Why?' is less simple than it looks. The actions taken by individuals, however honest and coherent their expressed intentions may be, are influenced by subconscious motives, by the mental outlook common to people of their time, nationality and class, and by external factors which determine what alternatives are open to them. Besides, the really significant questions in history do not turn on the conduct of individuals but concern major events and collective transitions which cannot possibly be explained by the sum total of human intentions. To attempt to account for, say, the overseas expansion of

Europe in the fifteenth and sixteenth centuries or the Industrial Revolution in these terms would be absurd. The actions of individuals or groups usually have unintended consequences, and one of the main reasons why this is so is that they cannot possibly have a full grasp of the structural constraints under which they are operating, nor can they know how those who are actually affected by their actions will respond. This is where hindsight tells, and for historians to confine themselves to the reconstruction of motive would be to throw away some of the best cards in their hand.

Narrative has frequently been employed for the purpose of historical explanation. It was the characteristic mode of Ranke and the great academic historians of the nineteenth century who in practice were certainly interested in more than 'how things actually were'. And the most widely read (and readable) professional historian in Britain today – A. J. P. Taylor – has hardly written anything else. But this traditional literary technique in fact imposes severe limitations on any systematic attempt at historical explanation. The placing of events in their correct temporal sequence does not settle the relationship between them. As Tawney put it:

> Time, and the order of occurrences in time, is a clue, but no more; part of the historian's business is to substitute more significant connections for those of chronology.[6]

The problem is twofold: in the first place, narrative can take the reader up a blind alley. Because B came after A does not mean that A *caused* B, but the flow of the narrative may easily convey the impression that it did. (Logicians call this the *post hoc propter hoc* fallacy.) Secondly, and much more importantly, narrative imposes a drastic simplification on the treatment of cause. The only uncontroversial generalization which can be made about causation in history is that it is always multiple and many-layered; it embraces situational or background causes and direct or immediate causes, and the complexity arises from the manner in which different areas of human experience constantly obtrude on one another. The historical understanding of a particular occurrence proceeds by enlarging the inventory of causes, while at the same time trying to place them in some sort of pecking order. Narrative is entirely inimical to this pattern of enquiry. It can keep only two or three threads going at once, so that only a few causes or results will be made apparent. Moreover, these are not likely to be the most significant ones, being associated with the sequence of day-to-day events rather than long-term structural factors. This is true of the political sphere which appears to lend itself so well to narrative and has always been the principal theme of the great narrative historians. In the case of revolutions or wars, for example, narrative historians emphasize the precipitating causes of conflict at the expense of those factors which predisposed the societies concerned to conflict. But this limitation applies still more to institutional and economic change, and is clearest of all in the case of the 'silent changes' in history[7] – those gradual transformations in mental and social experience which were reflected on the surface of events in only the most oblique manner. As the scope of historical studies has broadened in the twentieth century to include these topics, so the hold of narrative on historical writing has weakened. Few intellectual rallying-cries have proved more effective than the attack by the *Annales* school on *l'histoire événementielle*.[8]

The result of these misgivings is that historical writing is now very much more analytical than it was a hundred years ago. In historical analysis the main outline of events tends to be taken for granted; what is at issue is their significance and their relationship with each other. These issues are generally tackled in one of two ways. Analysis can serve firstly to elucidate the connectedness of events and processes occurring at the same time, and especially to lay bare the workings of an institution or a specific area of historical experience. In British historiography the classic instance is Namier's *Structure of Politics at the Accession of George III* (1929), a sequence of analytical essays on the various influences which determined the composition and working of the House of Commons around 1760. Structural studies of this kind are most prevalent in social and economic history, where some grasp of the totality of the social or economic system is required if the significance of particular changes is to be fairly assessed.

The second and much more challenging type of analysis is the systematic assessment of causes (and results). The multiple nature of causation in history demands that the narrative be suspended and that each of the relevant factors be assessed in turn, without losing sight of their connectedness and the likelihood that the configuration of each factor shifted over time. This is a task which calls for high powers of organization and abstraction, of the kind displayed by Lawrence Stone in his hundred-page essay, 'The causes of the English revolution' (1970): by considering in turn the 'preconditions' which came into being in the century before 1629, the 'precipitants' (1629–39) and the 'triggers' (1640–42), Stone is able to show the interplay between long-term factors, such as the rise of the gentry, the spread of Puritanism and the failure of the Crown to acquire the instruments of autocracy, with the role of individual personalities and fortuitous events.[9]

But consequences are important too. Indeed, there are some grounds for arguing, as Barraclough does, that from the perspective of posterity they are *more* important than causes, and that historians too easily forget this. If we ask what the meaning of an event was, we are primarily concerned with its results in the context of the broader processes of history.[10] The Anglo-Boer War of 1899–1902 is only one of the many examples which could be cited in this connection. An immense amount of scholarly work has been devoted to the origins of the war, most of it on the intentions and actions of Chamberlain, Milner and Kruger, who were the main political leaders involved. But historically the real significance of the Boer War was that it cleared the way not just for the political unification of the four colonies but for the remodelling of South African society in line with the needs of mining capital. This is a topic which is surely fundamental to an understanding of modern South Africa, but which has only begun to receive the attention it deserves in the past ten years.[11] Like the treatment of causes, the unravelling of consequences calls for analytical skills of a high order. Indispensable though narrative continues to be, major advances in historical understanding are generally achieved by analytical thought and writing.

III

These problems of presentation are usually confronted for the first time by the practising historian in the form of the monograph – that is, the writing up of a piece of original research, initially as a thesis for a higher degree and then as a book or an article in one of the learned journals. In this kind of writing the complexities of the evidence are likely to be displayed in the text, and the statements made there validated by meticulous footnote references to the appropriate documents. Many monographs are highly technical and are hardly accessible to anyone but fellow specialists. And, since the essence of the monograph is that it is based on primary rather than secondary sources, its scope is likely to be very restricted. This is particularly so in the case of a young scholar presenting the results of three or four years' Ph.D. research. Although in a technical sense such works are 'an original contribution to knowledge' (as required under the regulations for higher degrees), their significance is often slight. The pressure to complete an acceptable thesis within a few years in order to secure an academic job often causes the researcher to play safe by focusing on a well-defined body of sources never previously studied – or at any rate not with the same historical problem in mind. Lucien Febvre caustically observed the tendency for most historical works to be written by people who 'simply set out to show that they know and respect the rules of their profession'.[12] That is doubtless an unavoidable consequence of the professionalization of history. At the same time, arresting results do from time to time emerge from postgraduate research: one thinks, for example, of J. R. Vincent's *The Formation of the British Liberal Party* (1966), a major revisionist interpretation of British politics in the 1860s. The prospects for the apprentice are best in new fields of research: the progress of African history during the past twenty-five years has been marked by a string of major Ph.D. theses which have mapped out entirely new terrain.[13] At the very least, the Ph.D. provides an apprenticeship in the conduct of research and the writing of monographs, and it is by these means that the stock of properly validated historical knowledge is extended.

Yet if historians confined their writings to those topics for which they have mastered the primary sources, historical knowledge would be so fragmented as to be meaningless. Making sense of the past means explaining those events and processes which appear significant with the passage of time, and which are inevitably defined in terms that are broader than any researcher can encompass by his or her own unaided efforts: the origins of the English Civil War rather than the policies of Archbishop Laud, the social consequences of the Industrial Revolution rather than the decline of the handloom weavers of the West Riding, the Scramble for Africa rather than the Fashoda crisis. It must be obvious that an understanding of topics of this complexity is not attained by the mere accumulation of detailed researches. In Marc Bloch's words, 'The microscope is a marvellous instrument for research; but a heap of microscopic slides does not constitute a work of art.'[14] When historians step back to take an overview of one of these topics, they face much more acute problems of interpretation – of combining many strands into a coherent account, of determining the weight of this factor or that. And even after a lifetime of research in the relevant primary sources which may allow them to be discriminating in the use they make of other scholars, they will still have to take much of their work on trust.

These difficulties are compounded when the historian steps still further away from the moorings of his or her firsthand research and attempts a comprehensive survey of an entire epoch. If a monograph is a secondary source, the survey can fairly be described as a 'tertiary' source, since the writer is inevitably placed in the position of making emphatic statements about topics based on no more than a reading of the standard secondary authorities. Nitpicking criticism by the specialists whose fields have been trespassed upon is the inevitable result. Works of this kind will be much more vulnerable to the vagaries of fashion, and their judgements will be overtaken by new research much more quickly than those of the narrowly conceived monograph. The academic standing of the synthesis by a single hand is further compromised by the sad truth that many are not true syntheses at all, but textbooks which for ease of reference summarize the state of knowledge in a rigidly compartmentalized and mechanical fashion. Some historians, conscious that their claims to professional expertise are most convincingly demonstrated in the evaluation of primary sources, feel instinctively that this is no work for 'real scholars'.[15] Others have sought to meet the demand for surveys by participating in collaborative histories. The prototype was the *Cambridge Modern*

History, planned under the supervision of Lord Acton in 1896, and covering European history since the mid-fifteenth century in twelve volumes, each composed of national and thematic chapters by the leading authorities. Since then collaborative histories have pro-liferated. Yet, invaluable though they may be as concise statements of specialist knowlege, such compilations evade the issue. However like-minded the contributors and however forceful the editor, a consistency of approach cannot be attained, and the themes which cut across the specialist concerns of the contributors are completely omitted.

The wide-ranging survey by a single historian fulfils several vital functions. First, it is at its best a fertile source of new questions. Unremitting primary research, with its necessary but obsessive atten-tion to detail, can lead to a certain intellectual blinkering: 'the dust of archives blots out ideas', as Acton rather unkindly put it.[16] The his-torian who takes time off from the records to survey an extended period is much more likely to detect new patterns and new correlations which can later be tested in detailed research. E. J. Hobsbawm's *Age of Revolution* (1962), still unsurpassed as a survey of Europe from 1789 to 1848 under the twin impact of the French Revolution and the Industrial Revolution, positively bristles with arresting juxtapositions which no historian confined to a single country could have entertained. In a new field where major issues of interpretation have scarcely been formulated, this kind of stock-taking can yield particularly rich divi-dends; for ten years the questions thrown up by A. G. Hopkins in his pioneering *Economic History of West Africa* (1973) have influenced the direction of research in that region.

Secondly, the grand survey is the principal means by which his-torians fulfil their obligations to the wider public. Popular interest in the writings of academic historians is by no means confined to survey works – witness the success of Garrett Mattingly's *The Defeat of the Spanish Armada* (1959) or more recently Emmanuel Le Roy Ladurie's *Montaillou* (1976). But the appeal of these two books is primarily of a re-creative kind. If historians are to succeed in communicating their understanding of historical change and of the connectedness of past and present, then it is through the ambitious overview that they will do it. Many historians, intent on preserving their academic standing at all costs, are unduly oppressed by the dangers of superficiality and out-right error, and there is much snobbish disparagement of those who write for the general reader. But it is not impossible to combine sound scholarship with a lay appeal. *Haute vulgarisation*, as Hobsbawm describes his own highly distinguished ventures in this field,[17] is a necessary skill of the historian.

Lastly, the large-scale synthesis raises questions of historical expla-nation which are profoundly important in their own right and which are beyond the scope of anything less ambitious. History is a 'progres-sive' subject in the sense that few people contemplating the past with the benefit of hindsight can fail to ask themselves in what direction events were moving. This question is not a matter of metaphysical speculation, but rather a recognition that fundamental areas of human experience are subject to cumulative change over time. The issue may be evaded in studies confined to a short timespan, but it is central to any attempt to make sense of a whole era: can one detect increasing occupational specialization, or enlargement of social scale, or an expansion in the scope of government, or greater freedom of belief and expression – or any of these trends in reverse? In other words, consideration of an extended period raises problems of historical interpretation of a different – and surely more significant – order than those which crop up in the study of a well-defined episode.

The historian's perspective is equally enriched by syntheses which range widely over space as well as time, because these open up the possibility of the comparative method. No society in the past should be viewed in isolation, not only because hardly any of the societies which historians have studied were isolated in reality, but also because many of their most significant features prevailed over a wide area at the same time: think of feudal tenure in early Medieval Europe, or plantation slavery in the New World in the seventeenth and eighteenth centuries, or absolute monarchy in eighteenth-century Europe. A comparison between the countries involved enables us to separate the essential from the particular and to weight our explanations accordingly. In *White Supremacy* (1981), for example, George M. Fredrickson compares the development of race relations in America and South Africa from the arrival of the first white settlers in the seventeenth century until the ascendancy of the ideology of segregation in the twentieth century. In so doing he exposes the particularities of each society more clearly; white supremacy turns out to be not a 'seed planted by the first settlers that was destined to grow at a steady rate into a particular kind of tree', but 'a fluid, variable, and open-ended process'.[18] Why analogous societies differ in their historical experience is a problem of perennial interest which is accessible only to the synthesizer standing outside the confines of primary research.

One consequence of the immense expansion in the scope of historical enquiry which has taken place in the past hundred years is that our definition of a 'comprehensive' survey is much more demanding than that of the great nineteenth-century masters: it includes both the giddy passage of 'events' and the material and mental conditions of life which in many periods – and certainly in the pre-industrial world – changed very slowly if at all, and yet constrained what people could do or think. G. R. Elton's affirmation that 'history deals in events, not states; it investigates things that happen and not things that are'[19] is a questionable half-truth. How surface and background – or events and 'structure' – are related is central to any understanding of historical process. The recent upsurge of writing inspired by the Marxist tradition can be interpreted as one manifestation of this concern (see Ch.8), but it is the *Annales* school which has confronted the problem most directly, and Fernand Braudel more than anyone else. 'Is it possible', he asks,

> somehow to convey simultaneously both that conspicuous history which holds our attention by its continual and dramatic changes – and that other, submerged history, almost silent and always discreet, virtually unsuspected either by its observers or its participants, which is little touched by the obstinate erosion of time?[20]

For Braudel the root of the difficulty lies in the conventional historian's idea of unilinear time – that is, a single time-scale characterized by continuity of historical development. Because of the historian's emphasis on the documents and the aspiration to get inside the minds of those who wrote them, this time-scale can hardly be other than a short-term one which registers the sequence of events to the exclusion of structure. Braudel's solution is to jettison unilinear time altogether, and to introduce instead the 'plurality of social time'[21] – the notion that history moves on different planes or registers, which can for practical purposes be reduced to three: the long term (*la longue durée*), which reveals the fundamental conditions of material life, states of mind and above all the impact of the natural environment; the medium term in which the forms of social, economic and political organization have their lifespan; and the short term, the time of the individual and of *l'histoire événementielle*. The problem, which Braudel himself did not solve in *The Mediterranean*, is how to convey the co-existence of these different levels in a single moment of historical time – how to elucidate their interaction in a coherent exposition which incorporates different levels of narrative, description and analysis. This is an issue about which contemporary historians are much more keenly aware than their predecessors; it is perhaps the most fundamental which they face.

IV

What qualities does the successful practice of history call for? Outside observers have often taken an unflattering view. Probably the most famous put-down of the profession ever written was Dr Johnson's:

> Great abilities are not requisite for an Historian; for in historical composition, all the greatest powers of the human mind are quiescent. He has the facts ready to hand so there is no exercise of invention. Imagination is not required in any high degree; only about as much as is used in the lower forms of poetry.[22]

This was hardly fair comment even in Johnson's day, and in the light of the development of the profession since the eighteenth century it seems even less apt. For the truth is that the facts do *not* lie ready to hand. New facts continue to be added to the body of historical knowledge, while at the same time the credentials of established facts are subject to constant reassessment; and, as Chapters 2 and 3 showed, the defective condition of the sources renders this dual enterprise far more difficult than might appear at first sight. The training of academic historians instituted in the nineteenth century was – and still is – primarily intended to disabuse them of any notion that the facts can be apprehended without effort. The qualities most emphasized in manuals of historical method are accordingly mastery of the primary sources and critical acumen in evaluating them.

But these skills can only take the historian one stage along the road. The process of interpretation and composition suggests a number of other equally essential qualities. First of all, the historian has to be able to perceive the relatedness of events and to abstract from the mountains of detail those patterns which make best sense of the past: patterns of cause and effect, patterns of periodization which justify such labels as 'Renaissance' or 'Medieval', and patterns of grouping which make it meaningful to speak of a petit-bourgeoisie in nineteenth-century France or 'rising gentry' in early seventeenth-century England. The more ambitious the scope of the enquiry the greater the powers of abstraction and conceptualization required. The small number of really satisfying syntheses on the grand scale is a measure of how rare a generous endowment of these intellectual qualities is.

But as well as an intellectual cutting edge, the historian also requires imagination. This term can easily lead to confusion in the context of historical writing. It is not intended to convey the idea of sustained creative invention, though it was evidently against this yardstick that Dr Johnson found historians wanting. The point is rather that any attempt to reconstruct the past presupposes an exercise of imagination, because the past is never completely captured in the documents which it left behind. Again and again historians encounter gaps in the record which they can fill only by being so thoroughly exposed to the surviving sources that they have a 'feel' or instinct for what might have happened. Matters of motive and mentality frequently fall into this category, and the more alien and remote the culture the greater the imaginative leap required to understand it. Those books condemned as 'dry-as-dust' are usually the ones in which the accumulation of detail has not been brought to life by the play of the writer's imagination.

How is the historical imagination nurtured? It helps, of course, to keep your eyes and ears (and nostrils) open to the world around you. As Richard Cobb found:

A great deal of Paris eighteenth-century history, of Lyon nineteenth-century history can be walked, seen, and above all heard, in small restaurants, on the platform at the back of a bus, in cafés, or on the park bench.[23]

The ability to empathize with people in the past presupposes a certain self-awareness, and some historians have gone so far as to suggest that psycho-analysis might form part of the apprentice's training.[24] Breadth of experience, however, is a much more promising foundation. In the days when history-writing was largely confined to political narrative, experience of public life was widely regarded as the best training for historians: as Gibbon said of his short career as an MP:

The eight sessions that I sat in parliament were a school of civil prudence, the first and most essential virtue of an historian.[25]

Wartime service probably deepened the insights of many twentieth-century historians of politics, diplomacy and war. But it is *variety* of experience that really tells – experience of different countries, classes and temperaments – so that the range of imaginative possibilities in the historian's mind bears some relation to the range of conditions and mentalities in the past. Unfortunately the usual career-pattern of academic historians nowadays makes little allowance for this requirement. A recent suggestion that the best training for a historian is a trip round the world and several jobs in different walks of life may have been impracticable, but it was not meant to be flippant.[26]

It is one thing, however, to have an imaginative insight into the past, and quite another to be able to convey this to the reader. Verbal or literary skills are of considerable importance to the historian. At any time prior to the nineteenth century this would have been taken for granted. Since classical times the profession of historian had been considered by its leading exponents to be above all a literary accomplishment. History had its presiding Muse (Clio), a secure place in the culture of the reading public, and a range of rhetorical and stylistic conventions which it was the principal task of the aspirant historian to master. All this changed with the rise of academic history. The problems which exercised the professional historians who followed in Ranke's footsteps were those of method rather than presentation. Command of the sources or 'scholarship' has often been counterposed to 'writing', to the detriment of the latter; 'Clio, once a Muse, is now more commonly seen, with a reader's ticket, verifying her references at the Public Record Office.'[27] As a result a great deal of unreadable history has been written in the last hundred years.

But good writing is more than an optional extra or a lucky bonus. It is central to the re-creative aspect of history. The insights derived from the exercise of historical imagination cannot be shared at all without a good deal of literary flair – an eye for detail, the power to evoke mood, temperament and ambience, and an illusion of suspense – qualities which are most fully developed in creative writing. History of the explanatory kind does not share so much common ground with creative literature, which may be one reason why those historians who set most store by the literary claims of their discipline – G. M. Trevelyan or C. V. Wedgwood for example – have contributed relatively little to this sphere. Close argument and the need to hedge so many statements about with qualifications and caveats are not conducive to 'literary' expression. Neverthless, the problem of combining narrative with analysis which attends any venture in historical explanation is essentially a problem of literary form. Its solution is hardly ever dictated by the material.

Set out in this way, it may be that none of the qualities or skills required of the historian seems particularly demanding. But it is rare to find all of them combined in sufficient measure in the same person. Very few historians are equally endowed in the technical, intellectual, imaginative and stylistic spheres, and despite the immense expansion of professional scholarship in recent decades, the number of fully satisfying historical works in any branch of study remains small. At the same time, the varied nature of the historian's equipment serves to reiterate another point – that history is essentially a *hybrid* discipline, combining the technical and analytical procedures of a science with the imaginative and stylistic qualities of an art.

NOTES

1. V. H. Galbraith, *An Introduction to the Study of History*, C. Watts, 1964, p. 80.
2. See for example, E. H. Carr, *What is History?*, Penguin, 1964, pp. 28–9, and J. G. A. Pocock, 'Working on ideas in time', in L. P. Curtis (ed.) *The Historian's Workshop*, Knopf, 1970, pp. 161, 175.
3. H. Butterfield, *History and Human Relations*, Collins, 1951, p. 237.
4. Fernand Braudel, *The Mediterranean and the Mediterranean World in the Age of Philip II*, Collins, 1972.
5. C. V. Wedgwood, *The King's Peace 1637–1641*, Collins, 1955, p. 16.
6. R. H. Tawney, *History and Society*, Routledge & Kegan Paul, 1978, p. 54.
7. R. W. Southern, *The Making of the Middle Ages*, Hutchinson, 1953, pp. 14–15.
8. The generalization remains valid, notwithstanding Stone's claim to have detected a 'revival of narrative' in the last few years. Lawrence Stone, *The Past and the Present*, Routledge & Kegan Paul, 1981, Ch. 3.
9. Reprinted as Chapter 3 of Lawrence Stone, *The Causes of the English Revolution, 1529–1642*, Routledge & Kegan Paul, 1972.

10. Geoffrey Barraclough, *History and the Common Man*, Historical Association, 1966, pp. 12–14.

11. For some stimulating observations along these lines see Shula Marks and Stanley Trapido, 'Lord Milner and the South African state', *History Workshop Journal*, VIII, 1979, pp. 50–80.

12. Lucien Febvre, 'A new kind of history', 1949, translated in Peter Burke (ed.), *A New Kind of History*, Routledge & Kegan Paul, 1973, p. 38.

13. For example, Andrew Roberts, *A History of the Bemba*, Longman, 1973; Jeff Guy, *The Destruction of the Zulu Kingdom*, Longman, 1979.

14. Marc Bloch in *Annales*, 1932, quoted in R. R. Davies, 'Marc Bloch', *History*, LII, 1967, p. 273.

15. See for example F. M. Powicke, *Modern Historians and the Study of History*, Odhams, 1955, p. 202.

16. Quoted in H. Butterfield, *Man on His Past*, Cambridge University Press, 1955, p. 91.

17. E. J. Hobsbawm, *The Age of Revolution: Europe 1789–1848*, Cardinal, 1973, p. 11.

18. George M. Fredrickson, *White Supremacy: a Comparative Study in American and South African History*, Oxford University Press, 1981, p. xviii.

19. G. R. Elton, *The Practice of History*, Fontana, 1969, p. 22.

20. Braudel, *The Mediterranean*, Vol. I, p. 16.

21. Fernand Braudel, 'History and the social sciences: the *longue durée*', 1958, reprinted in Braudel's *On History*, Weidenfeld & Nicolson, 1980, p. 26.

22. R. W. Chapman (ed.) *Boswell's Life of Johnson*, Oxford University Press, 1953, p. 304.

23. Richard Cobb, *A Second Identity*, Oxford University Press, 1969, pp. 19–20.

24. H. Stuart Hughes, *History as Art and as Science*, Chicago University Press, 1964, pp. 65–6.

25. M. M. Reese (ed.) *Gibbon's Autobiography*, Routledge & Kegan Paul, 1970, p. 99.

26. Theodore Zeldin, 'After Braudel', *The Listener*, 5 November 1981, p. 542.

27. Galbraith, *Introduction*, p. 4.

Chapter 7

THE LIMITS OF HISTORICAL KNOWLEDGE

The earlier chapters of this book were essentially descriptive. They were intended to show how historians go about their work – their guiding assumptions, their handling of the evidence, and their presentation of conclusions. The point has now been reached where some fundamental questions about the nature of historical enquiry can be posed: how securely based is our knowledge of the past? Can the facts of history be taken as given? What authority should be attached to attempts at historical explanation? Can historians be objective? Answers to these questions have taken widely divergent forms and have occasioned intense debate. But the battle-lines are not drawn up, as might be expected, between historians trumpeting their own professionalism and objectivity on the one hand and sceptics outside the fold on the other. The profession itself is deeply divided about the status of its findings. At one extreme there are those like G. R. Elton who maintain that humility in the face of the evidence and training in the technicalities of research have steadily enlarged the stock of certain historical knowledge; notwithstanding the arguments which the professionals take such delight in, history is a cumulative discipline.[1] At the other extreme, Theodore Zeldin holds that all he (or any historian) can offer his readers is his personal vision of the past, and the materials out of which they in turn can fashion a personal vision which corresponds to their own aspirations and sympathies: 'everyone has the right to find his own perspective'.[2] Although the weight of opinion among academic historians inclines strongly towards Elton's position, every viewpoint between the two extremes finds adherents within the profession. Historians are in a state of confusion about what exactly they are up to – a confusion not usually apparent in the confident manner with which they often pronounce on major problems of interpretation.

I

To ask such questions about history or any other branch of learning is
to enter the terrain of philosophy, since what is at issue is the nature of
knowledge itself; and the status of historical knowledge has been hotly
contested among philosophers since the Renaissance. Most working
historians – even those disposed to reflect on the nature of their craft –
take little account of these debates, believing with some justification
that they often obscure rather than clarify the issues.[3] But the intense
disagreement which divides historians reflects a keen debate among
philosophers, and in particular two sharply opposed positions which
came into open confrontation during the nineteenth century.

Essentially the debate is about whether man should be studied in the
same way as other natural phenomena – whether, in short, history is a
science. The first position is committed to the methodological unity of
all forms of disciplined enquiry into the human and natural order. Its
proponents argue that history employs the same procedures as the
natural sciences and that its findings should be judged by scientific
standards. They may differ as to how far history has in fact fulfilled
these requirements, but they are agreed that historical knowledge is
valid only in so far as it conforms to scientific method. During the
twentieth century conceptions of the nature of science have been
radically modified, but the nineteenth-century view was straightforward enough. The basis of all scientific knowledge was the meticulous
observation of reality by the disinterested, 'passive' observer, and the
outcome of repeated observations of the same phenomenon was a
generalization or 'law' which fitted all the known facts and explained
the regularity observed. The assumption of this, the 'inductive'
method was that generalizations flowed logically from the data, and
that scientists approached their task without preconceptions and without moral involvement. As a result of its immense strides in both pure
and applied work, science enjoyed unrivalled prestige during the
nineteenth century. If its methods unlocked the secrets of the natural
world, might they not prove the key to understanding society and
culture? *Positivism* is the name given to the philosophy of knowledge
which expresses this approach in its classic, nineteenth-century form.
Its implications for the practice of history are clear. The historian's first
duty is to accumulate factual knowledge about the past – facts which
are verified by applying critical method to the primary sources; those
facts will in turn determine how the past should be explained or
interpreted. In this process the beliefs and values of historians are
irrelevant; their sole concern is with the facts and the generalizations
to which they logically lead. Auguste Comte, the most influential
Positivist philosopher of the nineteenth century, believed that historians would in due course uncover the 'laws' of historical develop-

ment. Full-blown professions of positivist faith are still made occasionally,[4] but nowadays a watered-down version is preferred. Latter-day Positivists maintain that the study of history cannot generate its own laws; rather, the essence of historical explanation lies in the correct application of generalizations derived from other disciplines supposedly based on scientific method such as economics, sociology and psychology.

The second position, which corresponds to the school of philosophy known as *Idealism*, rejects the fundamental assumption of Positivism. According to this view, human events must be carefully distinguished from natural events because the identity between the enquirer and his or her subject-matter opens the way to a fuller understanding than anything which the natural scientist can aspire to. Whereas natural events can only be understood from the outside, human events have an essential 'inside' dimension composed of the intentions, feelings and mentality of the actors. Once the enquirer strays into this realm the inductive method is of limited use. The reality of past events must instead be apprehended by an imaginative identification with the people of the past, which depends on intuition and empathy – qualities which have no place in the classical view of scientific method. According to Idealists, therefore, historical knowledge is inherently subjective, and the truths which it uncovers are more akin to truth in the artist's sense than the scientist's. Furthermore, historians are concerned with the individual, unique event. The generalizations of the social sciences are not applicable to the study of the past, nor does history yield any generalizations or laws of its own.

This outlook came naturally to the nineteenth-century proponents of historicism (see Ch. 1) with their demand that every age be understood in its own terms and their practical emphasis on political narrative made up of the actions and intentions of 'great men'. Ranke's fame as the champion of rigorous source criticism has sometimes been allowed to obscure the emphasis which he laid on contemplation and intuition. In the English-speaking world the most original and sophisticated exponent of the Idealist position has been the philosopher and historian R. G. Collingwood. In his posthumously published *The Idea of History* (1946), he maintained that all history is essentially the history of thought, and that the historian's task is to re-enact in his or her own mind the thoughts and intentions of individuals in the past. Collingwood's influence is evident in the case of present-day opponents of 'scientific' theory like Zeldin, who deplores the tendency for history to become 'a coffee-house in which to discuss the findings of other disciplines in time perspective' and pleads for a history concerned with individuals and their emotions.[5] Conversely history's scientific pretensions tend to be taken much more seriously by historians of collective behaviour – voting or consumption for example – because in these spheres regularities are evident which can sometimes form the basis of firm and significant generalizations.

But the implications of the unresolved clash between Positivism and Idealism go much further than the distinction between traditional political history and the more recent fields of economic and social history. It helps to explain why there is so much disagreement among historians about the nature of virtually every aspect of their work from primary source evaluation through to the finished work of interpretation.

II

Much of the professional self-esteem of the new breed of academic historians in the nineteenth century as based on the rigorous techniques which they had perfected for the location and criticism of primary sources. The canons which they established have governed the practice of historians ever since, so that the whole edifice of modern historical knowledge is founded on the painstaking evaluation of original documents. But the injunction 'Be true to your sources' is less straightforward than it looks, and sceptics have seized on a number of problem areas. Firstly, the primary sources available to the historian are an *incomplete* record, not only because so much has perished by accident or design, but in a more fundamental sense because a great deal that happened left no material trace whatever. This is particularly true of mental processes, both conscious and unconscious. No historical character, however prominent and articulate, has ever set down more than a tiny proportion of his or her thoughts and assumptions. In the second place, the sources are *tainted* by the less than pure intentions of their authors and – more insidiously – by their confinement within the assumptions of men and women in that time and place. 'The so-called "sources" of history record only such facts as appeared sufficiently interesting to record';[6] or, more polemically, the historical record is forever rigged in favour of the ruling class which at all times has created the vast majority of the surviving sources. In some Marxist circles this contention has led to an absolute scepticism about the possibility of knowledge of the past, and history has been put on the intellectual scrap-heap (see p. 147).

There is an element of truth in both these criticisms, but those who push them to extremes betray an ignorance of how historians actually work. What a researcher can learn from a set of documents is not confined to their explicit meaning; that meaning is first of all scrutinized for bias and then used as the basis for inference. When properly applied, the critical method enables the historian to make allowances for both deliberate distortion and the unthinking reflexes of the writer.

Much of the criticism rests on the common misconception that primary sources are the testimonies of witnesses – who like all witnesses are fallible but in this instance are not available for cross-examination. Yet, as was shown in Chapter 3, a great deal of the historian's documentation is made up of record sources which themselves constitute the event or process under investigation: historians interested, say, in the character of Gladstone or the administrative machinery of the Medieval Chancery are not dependent on contemporary reports and impressions (interesting though these may be); they can base their accounts on the private correspondence and diaries of Gladstone himself, or on the records generated in the course of the Chancery's day-to-day business. Moreover, much of the importance attached to primary sources derives not from the intentions of the writer but from information which was incidental to his or her purpose and yet may provide a flash of insight into an otherwise inaccessible aspect of the past. The historian, in short, is not confined by the categories of thought in which the documents were composed.[7]

But there is a third and more formidable difficulty in the notion that historians simply follow where the documents lead, and this turns on the *profusion* of the available sources. These sources may, it is true, represent a very incomplete record; yet for all but very remote periods and places they survive in completely unmanageable quantities. This is a problem which has been confronted only during the present century. Nineteenth-century historians, especially those of a Positivist turn of mind like Lord Acton, believed that finality in historical writing would be attained when primary research had brought to light a complete assemblage of the facts; many of these facts might seem obscure and trivial, but they would all tell in the end. These writers were blinded to the limitations of their method by the very narrow way in which they conceived both the content of history and a primary source: when Acton at the end of the century wrote, 'nearly all the evidence that will ever appear is accessible now',[8] he was referring only to the great collections of state records. Since Acton's day the subject-matter of history has been vastly enlarged, and the significance of whole bodies of source material whose existence nineteenth-century historians were scarcely aware of has been established. Faced with the virtually limitless content which history could in theory embrace, modern historians have been compelled to subject the notion of historical 'fact' to severe scrutiny.

Objection is sometimes made to the idea of 'facts' in history on the grounds that they rest on inadequate standards of proof: most of what pass for the 'facts' of history actually depend on inference. Historians read between the lines, or they work out what really happened from several contradictory indications, or they may do no more than establish that the writer was probably telling the truth. But in none of these cases can the historian observe the facts, in the way that a physicist can.

Historians generally have little time for this kind of critique. Formal proof may be beyond their reach; what matters is the validity of the inferences. In practice historians spend a good deal of time disputing and refining the inferences which can be legitimately drawn from the sources, and the facts of history can be said to rest on inferences whose validity is widely accepted by expert opinion. Who, they ask with some justice, could reasonably ask for more?

Historians are much more troubled by the implications of the apparently limitless number of facts about the past which can be verified in this way. If the entire past of mankind falls within the historian's scope, then every fact about that past may be said to have some claim on our attention. But historians do not proceed on this assumption – not even the specialist in some limited aspect of a well-defined period. There is in practice no limit to the number of facts which have a bearing on such a problem, and the historian who resolved to be guided solely by the facts would never reach any conclusion. The commonsense idea (and the central tenet of Positivism) that historians efface themselves in front of the facts 'out there' is therefore an illusion. The facts are not given, they are selected. Despite appearances they are never left to speak for themselves. However detailed a historical narrative may be, and however committed its author to the re-creation of the past, it never springs from the sources ready-made; many events are omitted as trivial, and those which do find a place in the narrative tend to be seen through the eyes of one particular participant or a small group. Analytical history, in which the writer's intention is to abstract the factors with greatest explanatory power, is more obviously selective. Historical writing of all kinds is determined as much by what it leaves out as by what it puts in. That is why it makes sense to distinguish with E. H. Carr between the facts of the past and the facts of history. The former are limitless and in their entirety unknowable; the latter represent a selection made by successive historians for the purpose of historical reconstruction and explanation:

> The facts of history cannot be purely objective, since they become facts of history only in virtue of the significance attached to them by the historian.[9]

If historical facts are selected, it is important to identify the criteria employed in selecting them. Are there commonly shared principles, or is it a matter of personal whim? One answer, much favoured since Ranke's day, is that historians are concerned to reveal the essence of the events under consideration. Namier expressed this idea metaphorically:

> The function of the historian is akin to that of the painter and not of the photographic camera; to discover and set forth, to single out and stress that which is of the nature of the thing, and not to reproduce indiscriminately all that meets the eye.[10]

But this amounts to little more than a restatement of the original question, for how is the 'nature of the thing' to be determined? It makes for less confusion if it is admitted outright that the standards of significance applied by the historian are defined by the nature of the historical problem which he or she is seeking to solve. As M. M. Postan put it:

> The facts of history, even those which in historical parlance figure as 'hard and fast', are no more than relevances: facets of past phenomena which happen to relate to the preoccupations of historical inquirers at the time of their inquiries.[11]

As new historical facts are accepted into the canon, so old ones pass out of currency except, as Postan mischievously remarks, in text-books which are full of 'ex-facts'.[12]

There is an element of rhetorical exaggeration about this view. Historical knowledge abounds in facts like the Great Fire of London or the execution of Charles I whose status is for all practical purposes unassailable, and critics like Elton have seized on this point to discredit the distinction between the facts of the past and the facts of history, which they feel introduces a dangerous element of subjectivity.[13] But, as anyone who has sampled the work of professional historians knows, historical writing is never composed entirely, or even principally, of these unassailable facts. The decision whether to include this set of facts rather than that, is closely affected by the purpose which informs the historian's work.

Clearly, then, much depends on the kind of questions which the historian has in mind at the outset of research. As was discussed in Chapter 3, there is something to be said for selecting a rich and previously untapped vein of source material and being guided by whatever questions it throws up (see above, pp. 48-9). The difficulty with this approach is that nobody actually approaches the sources with a completely open mind – the grounding in the standard secondary literature that precedes any research will see to that. Even if no specific questions have been formulated, the researcher will study the sources with certain assumptions which are only too likely to be an unthinking reflection of current orthodoxy, and the result will be merely a clarification of detail or a modification of emphasis within the prevailing framework of interpretation.

Significant advances in historical understanding are more likely to be achieved when a historian puts forward a clearly formulated hypothesis which can be tested against the evidence. The answers may not correspond to the hypothesis which must then be discarded or modified, but merely to ask new questions has the important effect of altering historians to unfamiliar aspects of familiar problems and to unsuspected data in well-worked sources. Consider, for example, the origins of the English Civil War. Nineteenth-century historians approached this as a problem of competing political and religious ideologies, and they selected accordingly from the great mass of surviving information about early seventeenth-century England. From the 1930s onwards an increasing number of scholars sought to test a Marxist approach to the conflict, and as a result new material which related to the economic fortunes of the gentry, the aristocracy and the urban bourgeoisie became critically important. In the last few years several historians have been employing a 'Namierite' approach in which the constitutional and military conflicts are seen as the expression of rivalry between political factions: hence the networks of patronage and the intrigues at court are now coming more into play.[14] The point is not that the Marxist or Namierite position amounts to a rounded explanation of the War, but rather that each hypothesis has brought into focus certain previously neglected factors which will have a bearing on any future interpretation. Marc Bloch, whose own work proceeded on the basis of hypotheses, put the issue clearly:

> Every historical research supposes that the inquiry has a direction at the very first step. In the beginning, there must be the guiding spirit. Mere passive observation, even supposing such a thing were possible, has never contributed anything productive to any science.[15]

Significantly, scientists today would themselves mostly agree. The Positivist theory still dominates the lay person's view of science, but it no longer carries much conviction among the scientific profession. Inductive thought and passive observation have ceased to be regarded as the hallmarks of scientific method. Rather, all observation whether of the natural or the human world is selective and therefore presupposes a hypothesis or theory, however incoherent it may be. In Karl Popper's influential view, scientific knowledge consists not of laws but the best available hypotheses; it is provisional rather than certain knowledge. Our understanding advances through the formulation of new hypotheses which go beyond the evidence currently available and must be tested against further observation which will either refute or corroborate the hypothesis. And because hypotheses go beyond the evidence, they necessarily involve a flash of insight or an imaginative leap, often the bolder the better. Scientific method, then, is a dialogue between hypothesis and attempted refutation, or between creative and critical thought.[16] To historians this is a much more congenial definition of science than the one it has replaced.

But although history and the natural sciences may converge in their fundamental methodological assumptions, important differences remain. In the first place, far greater play is allowed to the imagination in history. It is by no means confined to the formulation of hypotheses, but permeates the historian's thinking. Historians are not, after all, only concerned to explain the past; they also seek to reconstruct or re-create it – to show how life was experienced as well as how it may be understood – and this requires an imaginative engagement with the mentality and atmosphere of the past. In maintaining that all history is the history of thought, Collingwood unduly confined the scope of the subject. But it is certainly true that the evaulation of documentary sources depends on a reconstruction of the thought behind them; before anything else can be achieved, the historian must first try to enter the mental world of those who created the sources.

Furthermore, although Idealists from Ranke to Collingwood have placed an exaggerated emphasis on 'unique' events, individuals are certainly a legitimate and necessary object of historical study, and the variety and unpredictability of individual behaviour (as opposed to the regularities of mass behaviour) demands qualities of empathy and intuition in the enquirer as well as logical and critical skills. And whereas scientists can often create their own data by experiment, historians are time and again confronted by gaps in the evidence which they can make good only by developing a sensitivity as to what might have happened, derived from an imagined picture which has taken shape in the course of becoming immersed in the surviving documentation. In all these ways imagination is vital to the historian. It not only generates fruitful hypotheses; it is also deployed in the reconstruction of past events and situations by which those hypotheses are tested.

The second and even more critical distinction to be made between history and the natural sciences is that the standing of explanations put forward by historians is very much inferior to that of scientific explanation. It may be that scientific explanations are no more than provisional hypotheses, but they are for the most part hypotheses on which all people qualified to judge are in agreement; they may be superseded one day, but for the time being they represent the nearest possible approximation to the truth, and are commonly recognized as such. In matters of historical explanation, on the other hand, a scholarly consensus scarcely exists. The known facts may not be in doubt, but how to interpret or explain them is a matter of endless debate, as my example of the English Civil War illustrated. The 'faction hypothesis' has not superseded the 'class-conflict hypothesis' or the 'ideology hypothesis'; all are very much alive and receive varying emphasis from different historians.

The reason for this diversity of opinion lies in the complex texture of historical change. Both in their individual and collective behaviour human beings can be influenced by such an immense variety of factors that no comprehensive theory of historical causation is possible: each situation has to be interpreted afresh. The problem is that the evidence is never sufficiently full and unambiguous to place a casual interpretation beyond doubt. Very often the sources do not directly address the central issues of historical explanation at all. Some of the influences on human conduct like the natural environment or the neurotic and irrational are apprehended subconsciously; others may be experienced directly but not disclosed in the sources. Questions of historical explanation cannot, therefore, be resolved solely by reference to the evidence. Historians are also guided by their intuitive sense of what was possible in a given historical context, by their reading of human nature, and by the claims of intellectual coherence. In each of these areas they are unlikely to concur. As a result several different hypotheses can hold the field at any one time. Burckhardt frankly acknowledged the problem in the Preface of his *Civilization of the Renaissance in Italy* (1860):

> In the wide ocean upon which we venture, the possible ways and directions are many; and the same studies which have served for this work might easily, in other hands, not only receive a wholly different treatment and application, but lead also to essentially different conclusions.[17]

The area of knowledge beyond dispute is both smaller and much less significant in history than it is in the natural sciences. This is a crucial limitation which is not properly confronted by present-day champions of 'objectivity' in history.[18]

III

This comparison between history and natural sciences is perhaps somewhat contrived, given that the assumptions which most people make about the standing of scientific knowledge are an outdated residue of nineteenth-century Positivism; scientific knowledge is in reality less certain and less objective than is commonly supposed. But what the comparison does bring out is the extent to which our knowledge of the past depends on choices freely exercised by the historian. The commonsense notion that the business of historians is simply to uncover the past and display what they have found will not stand up. The essence of historical enquiry is *selection* – of 'relevant' sources, of 'historical' facts and of 'significant' interpretations. At every stage both the direction and the destination of the enquiry are determined as much by the enquirer as by the data. Clearly, the rigid segregation of fact and value demanded by the Positivists is unworkable in history. In this sense, historical knowledge is not, and cannot be 'objective' (that is, empirically derived in its entirety from the object of the enquiry). This does not mean, as sceptics might suppose, that it is therefore arbitrary or illusory. But it does follow that the assumptions and attitudes of historians themselves have to be carefully assessed before we can come to any conclusion about the real status of historical knowledge.

Up to a point those standards can be seen as the property of the individual historian. The experience of research is a personal and often very private one, and no two historians will share the same imaginative response to their material. As Richard Cobb puts it, 'the writing of history is one of the fullest and most rewarding expressions of an individual personality'.[19] But however rarefied the atmosphere which historians breathe, they are, like everyone else, affected by the assumptions and values of their own society. It is more illuminating to see historical interpretation as moulded by social rather than individual experience. And because social values change, it follows that historical interpretation is subject to constant revision. What one age finds worthy of note in the past may well be different from what previous ages found worthy. This principle can be illustrated many times over within the relatively short span of time since the emergence of the academic profession of history. For Ranke and his contemporaries the sovereign nation-states which dominated the Europe of their day seemed the climax of the historical process; the state was the principal agent of historical change and human destiny was largely determined by the shifting balance of power between states. This world-view was seriously eroded by the First World War: after 1919, against the background of optimism engendered by the League of Nations, history-teaching in Britain tended to stress rather the growth of internationalism over the centuries. More recently, the way in which historians study the world beyond Europe and the United States has been transformed in the light of the changes which they have lived through. Thirty years ago the history of Africa was still treated as an aspect of the expansion of Europe, in which the indigenous peoples scarcely featured except as the object of white policies and attitudes. Today the perspective is very different. African history exists in its own right, embracing both the pre-colonial past and the African experience of – and response to – colonial rule, and stressing the continuities of African historical development which had previously been completely obscured by the stress on the European occupation. And those continuities have already been reassessed: whereas in the 1960s historians of Africa were mainly concerned with placing African nationalism in a historical perspective of pre-colonial state formation and resistance to colonial rule, they are now, after twenty years' disillusionment with the fruits of independence, preoccupied with the historical antecedents of Africa's deepening poverty. Twice in the course of a single generation the standards of significance applied by historians to the African past have been substantially revised.

To say, however, that history is rewritten by each generation (or decade) is only part of the truth – and positively misleading if it suggests the replacement of one consensus by another. In the case of history written during the High Middle Ages or the Renaissance it might be appropriate to speak of a scholarly consensus, since historians and their audience were drawn from a very restricted sector of society, and at this distance in time the differences between historians seem much less significant than the values which they held in common. But the attainment of universal literacy and the extension of education in Western society in this century mean that historical writing now reflects a much wider range of values and assumptions. The towering political personalities of the past like Oliver Cromwell or Napoleon Bonaparte are interpreted in widely divergent ways by professional historians as well as lay people, partly according to their own political values.[20] Liberal or conservative historians like Peter Laslett tend to conceive of social relations in pre-industrial England as reciprocal, while radically inclined historians like E. P. Thompson see them as exploitative.[21] Michael Howard has recently made public confession of a bias which is widely shared – a bias in favour of a liberal political order in which alone the historian has been permitted to work without censorship.[22] Many other historians, however, would set a higher value on material progress or equality in social relations than on freedom of thought and expression. Historical interpretation is a matter of value judgements, moulded to a greater or lesser degree by moral and political attitudes. At the turn of the century Acton's successor at Cambridge, J.B. Bury, looked forward to the dawn of scientific history with these words: 'Though there be many schools of political philosophy, there will no longer be divers schools of history.'[23] It would be nearer the truth to say that for as long as there are many schools of political philosophy there will be divers schools of history. Paradoxically there is an element of present-mindedness about all historical enquiry.

The problem, of course, is to determine at what point present-mindedness conflicts with the historian's aspiration to be true to the past. The conflict is clearest in the case of those writers who ransack the past for material to fuel a particular ideology, or falsify it in support of a political programme, as Nazi historians did under the Third Reich and Stalinist historians in the Soviet Union. Such works are propaganda, not history, and are usually clearly recognizable. Among historians themselves the most common manifestation of present-mindedness is an interest in the historical origins of the modern world, or some particularly salient feature of it – say the nuclear family household or parliamentary democracy. In itself this is a positive response to the claims of social relevance, and it has the merit of providing a clear principle of selection leading to an intelligible picture of the past. But it also carries risks of superficiality and distortion. The problem with seeking the historical antecedents of some characteristically 'modern' feature is that the outcome can so easily seem to be pre-determined, instead of being the result of complex historical processes. Abstracting one strand of development to be traced back to its origins too often means an indifference to historical context; the further back the enquiry proceeds, the more likely will a stress on

linear descent obscure the contemporary significance of the institution
or convention in question. Thus the Whig historians of the nineteenth-
century completely misunderstood the structure of medieval English
government because of their obsessive interest in the origins of Parliament. A comparable criticism has been levelled at recent work on the
Medieval and early modern history of family relations and sexuality.[24]
As Butterfield put it in *The Whig Interpretation of History* (1931) –
probably the most influential polemic ever written against present-
minded history:

> The study of the past with one eye, so to speak, upon the present is the
> source of all sins and sophistries in history, starting with the simplest of
> them, the anachronism.[25]

Present-minded history exhibits a tendency to underestimate the differences between past and present – to project modern ways of thought
backwards in time and to discount those aspects of past experience
which are alien to modern ideas. In this way it reduces history's social
value, which derives largely from its being a storehouse of past experiences contrasted to our own. Nowadays the charge of 'present-
mindedness' (or 'presentism') is often levelled at left-wing exponents
of people's history or women's history. Butterfield's book is a useful
reminder that goal-oriented or teleological history has been prevalent
among establishment historians of every persuasion.

Yet if the outcome of historical enquiry is so heavily conditioned by
the preferences of the enquirer and can so easily be altered by the
intervention of another enquirer, how can it merit any credibility as a
serious contribution to knowledge? If fact and value are inextricably
tied together, how can a distinction be drawn between sound and
unsound history? Between the wars it was the fashion in some quarters
to concede most, if not all of the sceptics' case. Historical interpretation, these historians averred, should be considered true only in relation to the needs of the age in which it was written. With the phrase
'Everyman his own historian',[26] the American scholar Carl M. Becker
renounced the aspirations to definitive history which had characterized the profession since Ranke. More recently the case has been
succinctly put by Gordon Connell-Smith and Howell Lloyd:

> History is not 'the past', nor yet the surviving past. It is a reconstruction of
> certain parts of the past (from surviving evidence) which in some way have
> had relevance for the present circumstances of the historian who recon-
> structed them.[27]

The implications of this position are disturbing. Not surprisingly
historians are reluctant to allow their discipline's claim to academic
respectability to be so lightly abandoned. In opposition to relativism
they have generally adopted one of two positions. The first and more
orthodox is essentially a restatement of historicism. Historians, the

argument goes, must renounce any standards or priorities external to the age they are studying. Their aim is to understand the past in its own terms, or in Elton's words 'to understand a given problem from the inside'.[28] Historians should be steeped in the values of the age and should attempt to see events from the standpoint of those who participated in them. Only then will they be true to their material and their vocation. But this claim to speak with the voice of the past will not bear inspection. On the face of it, historians may appear to be strikingly successful in assimilating the values of those they write about: diplomatic historians usually accept the ethics of *raison d'état* which have governed the conduct of international relations in Europe since the Renaissance, and the historian of a political movement may well be able to achieve an empathy with the outlook and aspirations of its members. However, as soon as the historians cast their net more widely to embrace an entire society, 'the standards of the age' becomes a question-begging phrase. Whose standards should be adopted? – those of the rich or the poor, the colonized or the colonizers, Protestant or Catholic? It is a fallacy to suppose that historians who renounce all claim to 'relevance' thereby ensure the objectivity of their work. In practice their writing is exposed to two dangers. On the one hand they may find themselves confined by the priorities and assumptions of those who created the sources; on the other, the end-product is quite likely to be influenced – if only unconsciously – by their own values which are difficult to make allowances for because they are undeclared. Elton's work illustrates both these tendencies: his Tudor England is seen through the spectacles of the authoritarian paternalist bureaucracy whose records Elton knows so intimately and whose outlook is evidently congenial to his own conservative convictions.[29] Re-creative history is a legitimate pursuit, but it is a mistake to suppose that it can ever be completely realized, or that it carries the promise of objective knowledge about the past.

There is another serious difficulty encountered by the strictly historicist approach. We can never recapture the authentic flavour of a historical moment as it was experienced by people at the time because we, unlike them, know what happened next; and the significance which we accord to a particular incident is inescapably conditioned by that knowledge. This is one of the most telling objections which can be made against Collingwood's idea that historians re-enact the thought of individuals in the past. Like it or not, the historian approaches the past with a superior insight conferred by hindsight. But should not hindsight be viewed as an asset to be exploited, rather than a disability to be overcome? It is precisely our position in time relative to the subject of our enquiry which enables us to make sense of the past – to identify conditioning factors of which the historical participants were unaware, and to see consequences for what they were, rather than what they were intended to be. Strictly interpreted, 'history for its own sake' would entail surrendering most of what makes the subject worth pursuing at all. Yet a surprising amount of professional history-writing has been characterized by this form of self-denial, especially in Britain where Butterfield's scathing indictment of the excesses of Whig history has been credited with deterring a generation of scholars from 'explanatory' history.[30] Even today there are many historians who feel most at ease when confined to a few years or even months of history for which they can give a blow-by-blow account with a minimum of selection or interpretation. History of this kind is not only less objective than it appears; it also confines the scope of the subject to the point where its claim on the attention of non-historians is practically nil.

The second response to the charge of relativism, by contrast, makes a virtue of selection and hindsight. E. H. Carr, its frankest exponent, regarded the effort to reconstruct the past 'from the inside' as futile and misconceived. The objective historian, according to Carr, is one who applies the *right* standard of significance to the past. That standard is not a matter of morality, nor merely a reflection of the pre-occupations of the moment; it is rather based on a sense of direction in history, an ability to identify the trajectory along which events are moving here and now. 'The historian of the past can make an approach towards objectivity only as he approaches towards the understanding of the future.'[31] To mean anything at all, history must be relevant to an end in view, and historical developments are judged as 'progressive' or 'reactionary' according to the fulfilment of that end. As time unfolds, the definition of the goal will shift, and with it the standard of significance applied to the past, but at any given conjuncture there is only one correct interpretation of the past.

Since this redefinition of the concept of objectivity would appear to open the way to a major social role for the historian, it may seem odd that so few historians have subscribed to it. But there are major difficulties. Nothing is likely to be so subjective and value-laden as the projection of historical trends into the future, and Carr's attempt to do so with authority seems self-confident to the point of arrogance. In practice Carr's programme would produce not one standard of significance, but several opposed standards, leading to a more dogmatic variant of present-minded history than already exists. Indeed the subordination of historical understanding to an evolving goal would seem to lead to the same distortions as the discredited Whig interpretation of history – that is, a commitment to the 'winning side' and an indifference to those events and experiences which lay outside the assumed trajectory of historical development. Carr's own writing on the history of the Soviet Union has been criticized in precisely these terms.[32] Although intended partly as a rebuttal of historical relativism, Carr's solution merely strengthens the hand of the sceptics.

IV

The problems of historical objectivity can be evaded neither by a retreat into the past for the past's sake, nor by invoking the future to legitimize assumptions and aspirations which are rooted in the present. Historical scepticism is better countered by recognizing the main difficulties and seeing how far they can be overcome in practice. Those difficulties are chiefly two: the need to *select* not only which aspects of the past merit attention but the interpretative framework which will make the evidence most intelligible; and the exercise of *imagination* required to re-create the world of the past and to plug the many gaps in the surviving evidence. Together these two salient features of historical enquiry give historians immense scope to express their personal preferences, their political and social beliefs, and the unthinking assumptions common to people of their particular background. How far can or should these tendencies be checked?

In so far as differences of outlook and temperament lead to the exploration of different facets of the past, they must surely be counted an asset. The alternative is not 'universal history' which is a manifest impossibility, but the perpetuation of one principle of selection – something which has all too often impoverished the practice of history in the past, and which today still afflicts the mass audience for royal biographies and military history. We need to be constantly reminded of the many-faceted nature of the past and the range of themes which would be excluded from view if we were confined to what 'mainstream' history puts on offer. For this reason alone, the proliferation of 'new' histories, 'oppositional' history, radical history and the rest is to be welcomed. The principles of selection on which they are based are no less valid than other longer established means of reducing the past to manageable proportions. Indeed in one sense they are *more* valid; for whereas the heavy traditional emphasis on political history too easily conveyed the impression that 'real history' consisted of nothing else, the branches of history that are currently so fashionable tend to be less exclusive in their pretensions. Their proponents do not as a rule claim that theirs is the only meaningful way to make sense of the past, but merely that the scope of historical enquiry should be broadened to encompass all areas of human experience.

In relation to the debate on objectivity in history, the problems arise less from the necessity of selection itself than from the fact that the values which lead historians to choose a particular theme may also distort their interpretation of the relevant evidence. This charge is often levelled at those specialisms like women's history or black history which are closely associated with current liberation ideologies; it is said that their purpose is not just to uncover what was previously 'hidden from history'[33] but to demonstrate historical experience of a

123

predetermined kind – in this case oppression and resistance – to the exclusion of material which fits less neatly with the preference of the writer. Obviously political commitment *may* lead to bad history. The error lies in supposing that it necessarily does so, or that the distortions to which present-mindedness is liable are confined to 'oppositional' or radical historiography. All historians reflect in some measure the outlook of their own age. In E. H. Carr's words, 'The historian is part of history. The point in the procession at which he finds himself determines his angle of vision over the past.'[34] But what historians *can* do is to ensure that within the area of the past which they find significant they are as true as they can be to the reality of the past.

Three requirements stand out in this respect. First, the historian should scrutinize his or her own assumptions and values in order to see how they relate to the enquiry in hand. This is particularly important in the case of those historians who have no particular axe to grind but can all too easily be the unconscious vector of values taken for granted by people of their own background. Secondly, the risk of assimilating findings to expectations is reduced if the direction imparted to the enquiry is cast in the form of an explicit hypothesis, to be accepted, rejected or modified in the light of the evidence – and the author should always be the first to try to pick holes in his or her interpretation. The appropriate conduct for historians, then, is not to avoid social relevance, but to be fully aware of why they are attracted to their particular slice of history and to show as much respect for contrary as for supporting evidence. Thirdly and above all, historians must submit their work to the discipline of historical context. Butterfield's complaint against present-minded history was that it removed events and personalities from their real time and place and forced them into a conceptual framework which would have meant nothing to the age in question. But anachronism does not follow inescapably from present-mindedness. In fact historians have much less excuse for falling into this trap than they used to. The enlargement of the scope of historical studies during the past fifty years and the way in which the best historical syntheses reflect this enlargement mean that historians today should have a much better developed sense of context than their predecessors did.

Respect for these three injunctions does much to limit the amount of distortion in historical writing. It does not, however, put an end to debate and disagreement. It would be wrong to suppose that if all historians could only attain a high degree of self-awareness, make their working hypotheses explicit and maintain a scrupulous respect for historical context they would then concur in their historical judgements. Nobody can become completely dispassionate about his or her own assumptions or those of earlier ages; the evidence can usually be read in support of conflicting hypotheses; and, since the sources never recapture a past situation in its entirety, the sense of historical context depends also on an imaginative flair which will vary according to the insight and experience of the individual scholar. The nature of historical enquiry is such that, however rigorously professional the approach, there will always be a plurality of interpretation. Our knowledge of the past will be broadened and in many particulars corrected by future research. But it will never be placed beyond controversy. 'History', in the words of the great Dutch historian Pieter Geyl, 'is indeed an argument without end.'[35]

NOTES

1. G. R. Elton, *The Practice of History*, Fontana, 1969.
2. Theodore Zeldin, 'Ourselves as we see us', *Times Literary Supplement*, 31 December 1982. See also his article, 'After Braudel', *The Listener*, 5 November 1981.
3. See, for example, Elton, *Practice of History*, pp. vii–viii.
4. Lee Benson, *Toward the Scientific Study of History*, J. B. Lippincott, 1972.
5. Zeldin, 'After Braudel'. See also his article, 'Social and total history', *Journal of Social History*, X, 1976, pp. 237–45.
6. K. R. Popper, *The Open Society and its Enemies*, Vol. 2, 5th edn, Routledge & Kegan Paul, 1966. p. 265.
7. E. H. Carr, *What is History?*, Penguin, 1964, p. 16, rather surprisingly falls into this error.
8. Lord Acton, letter to the contributors to the *Cambridge Modern History*, 1896, reprinted in Fritz Stern (ed.) *Varieties of History*, 2nd edn, 1970, p. 247.
9. Carr, *What is History?*, p. 120.
10. L. B. Namier, *Avenues of History*, Hamish Hamilton, 1952, p. 8.
11. M. M. Postan, *Fact and Relevance*, Cambridge University Press, 1970, p. 51.
12. Ibid, p. 54.
13. Elton, *Practice of History*, pp. 74–82.
14. See R. C. Richardson, *The Debate on the English Revolution*, Methuen, 1977.
15. Marc Bloch, *The Historian's Craft*, Manchester University Press, 1954, p. 65.
16. Popper's views are lucidly expounded in Bryan Magee, *Popper*, Fontana, 1973.
17. Jakob Burckhardt, *The Civilization of the Renaissance in Italy*, Phaidon, 1960, p. 1.
18. This is particularly true of Elton, *Practice of History*.
19. Richard Cobb, *A Second Identity*, Oxford University Press, 1969, p. 47. See also Zeldin's comments in the same vein in *France 1848–1945*, Vol. I, Oxford University Press, 1973, p. 7.

20. See, for example, Pieter Geyl, *Napoleon: For and Against*, 2nd edn.
     Cape, 1964.
21. Compare, for example, Peter Laslett, *The World we have Lost*, 2nd edn.
     Methuen, 1971, with E. P. Thompson, *Whigs and Hunters*, Penguin,
     1977.
22. Michael Howard, *The Lessons of History*, Oxford University Press,
     1981, p. 21.
23. J. B. Bury, 'The science of history', 1902, reprinted in Stern, *Varieties of
     History*, p. 215.
24. Adrian Wilson, 'The infancy of the history of childhood: an appraisal of
     Philippe Ariès', *History and Theory*, XIX, 1980, pp. 132–53.
25. H. Butterfield, *The Whig Interpretation of History*, Penguin, 1973, p. 30.
26. Cited in J. H. Hexter, *On Historians*, Collins, 1979, p. 15.
27. Gordon Connell-Smith and Howell A. Lloyd, *The Relevance of History*,
     Heinemann, 1972, p. 41.
28. Elton, *Practice of History*, p. 31.
29. Elton's conservative convictions are most clearly set out in his inaugural
     lecture, *The Future of the Past*, Cambridge University Press, 1969.
30. R. H. C. Davies, 'The content of history', *History*, LXVI, 1981, p. 364.
     One of the strongest repudiations of 'explanatory' history is to be found
     in G. J. Renier, *History: Its Purpose and Method*, Allen & Unwin, 1950,
     pp. 175, 181.
31. Carr, *What is History?*, p. 123.
32. Norman Stone, 'Grim eminence', *London Review of Books*, 20 January
     1983.
33. Cf. Sheila Rowbotham, *Hidden from History*, Pluto Press, 1973.
34. Carr, *What is History?*, p. 36.
35. Geyl, *Napoleon: For and Against*, p. 16.

Chapter 8

HISTORY AND THEORY

In the last chapter it made sense to counterpose history and the natural sciences because the lay person's conception of the natural sciences provides a convenient and fairly straightforward yardstick by which to measure how far historical enquiry can yield objective knowledge of the past. However the comparison was pursued at the cost of somewhat misrepresenting the current state of discussion about the position of history relative to other disciplines. There can be few historians alive today who would subscribe to J. B. Bury's famous dictum that history is 'simply a science, no less and no more'.[1] The real debate for the present generation concerns whether history should be treated as a *social* science.

This is not at all the same thing as asking whether history is a science *tout court* (in the commonly accepted sense of sharing the methods and standing of the natural sciences). For, although the aspiration of social scientists for their discipline to be recognized as being on the same footing as the natural sciences has been extremely pronounced, the arguments against have been hardly less persuasive than they have in the case of history, and for many of the same reasons. However much social scientists may strive to confine themselves to social behaviour externally observed, they too cannot produce explanations without reference to what goes on in the mind of the actors – their wants and their knowledge of the world which moulds their strategies for achieving those wants – and this introduces an inescapable subjectivity into all social enquiry. Moreover, 'social facts', no less than 'historical facts', have a relative quality because the enquirer is usually compelled to select from the vast compass of relevant evidence. And explanation in the social sciences is more often than not a matter of acute disagreement among the experts, reflecting passing intellectual fashions rather than the cumulative wisdom of the profession. For these and other reasons which need not detain us here, the social sciences are to be clearly demarcated from the natural sciences.[2]

For all that, the debate about whether or not history should be counted among the social sciences raises several important issues. The first and most fundamental one, already discussed, is whether history should share the aspiration of the social sciences to have social relevance. In Chapter 1 I gave a qualified affirmative: historical knowledge can have important practical implications, of which historians should display a much keener awareness than they generally do, but at the same time the kind of enquiry whose sole object is to re-create a particular conjuncture in the past remains valid and important in its own right. The second issue concerns the place of theory in historical explanation. Should historians apply social theory to their work and participate in the development of new theory, or would this amount to a surrender of the essence of historical consciousness and a denial of the autonomy of history? And thirdly, can historians take a leaf out of the social scientists' book in the way they define and exploit their source materials? The last two chapters will address the third issue, looking in turn at the contribution of quantitative methods and the growth of oral techniques. Here I am concerned to evaluate the role of theory in history.

I

I suggested in the previous chapter that one of the ways in which historians can guard against unconsciously assimilating their interpretations of the past to their own bias is by formulating hypotheses to be tested against the available evidence (see pp. 114–15). Such a hypothesis may be no more than a provisional explanation suggested to the historian by a reading of the relevant secondary authorities and exclusive to the historical problem in hand. But a closer inspection as often as not reveals a more elevated parentage. A hypothesis is not just a preliminary assessment of a particular historical conjuncture in its own terms; it usually reflects certain assumptions about the nature of society and of the historical process as a whole; in other words, historical hypotheses amount to an application of *theory*. One of the most striking developments in the writing of history in the past generation is that historians are now much more self-conscious about their use of theory than they used to be. But predictably there are a great many historians – probably a majority in Britain – for whom this new trend is suspect, not least because so much of the theory currently employed is derived from the Marxist tradition. As a result, there is intense debate within the profession about whether or not historians should avail themselves of theory, and if so on what terms. In this chapter I first review the general debate, and then assess in some detail the impact of Marxism on the writing of history.

Broadly speaking, theories of history arise from the problems presented by three aspects of historical explanation. There is first the difficulty of grasping the inter-relatedness of every dimension of human experience at a given time. For most historians up to the end of the nineteenth century this was not in practice a major problem since their interest tended to be confined to political and constitutional history; accordingly some notion of the body politic was all the conceptual equipment they required. But during the present century the enlargement in the scope of historical enquiry and in the volume of evidence, together with the pressures towards thematic specialization, have demanded an ever greater capacity to think in terms of abstractions. We saw in Chapter 5 how easily historians fall into the trap of seeing the past as compartmentalized into 'political', 'economic', 'intellectual' and 'social' history, and how the idea of 'total history' arose as a corrective (see pp. 89–90). But total history is unattainable without some concept of how the component aspects of human experience are linked together to form a whole – some theory of the structure of human society in its widest sense. Most concepts of this kind depend heavily on analogies with the physical world. Society has been variously conceived as an organism, a mechanism and a structure. Each of these metaphors represents an attempt to go beyond the crude notion that any one sphere determines the rest, and to express the reciprocal or mutually reinforcing relationship between the main categories of human action and thought.

The second problem which invites the application of theory is that of historical change. Historians spend most of their time explaining change – or its absence. This dominant preoccupation inevitably raises the question of whether the major transitions in history display common characteristics. Is historical change driven by a motor, and if so what does the motor consist of? More specifically, does industrialization require adherence to one particular path of economic development? Can one identify in history the essential components of a revolutionary situation? In framing their hypotheses in particular instances historians are often influenced by the attractions of this kind of theory – for example the idea that demography holds the key[3] or that the most durable changes in society arise from the gradualist reforms conceded by paternalistic ruling classes rather than from revolutionary demands articulated from below.[4]

Thirdly, and most ambitiously, there are the theories which seek to explain not merely *how* historical change takes place but the direction in which all change is moving; these theories are concerned to interpret the destiny of mankind by ascribing a meaning to history. Medieval writers conceived history as a linear transition from the Creation to the Last Judgement, controlled by divine providence. By the eighteenth century that view had been secularized as the idea of progress: history was interpreted as a story of material and intellectual improvement whose outcome in the future would be the triumph of reason and human happiness. Modified versions of that outlook continued to have a powerful hold in the nineteenth century: on the continent history meant the rise of national identities and their political expression in the nation state; for the Whig historians of England it meant the growth of constitutional liberties. Full-blown professions of faith in progress may be rare today,[5] given the trail of destruction which has marked the history of the present century, and the prospect of nuclear war; but theories of progressive change still underpin many historical interpretations in the economic and social sphere, as is shown by the frequency with which historians reach for words like 'industrialization' and 'modernization'.

Although these three types of historical theory are analytically distinct, they all share an interest in moving from the particular to the general in an effort to make sense of the subject as a whole. It might be supposed that this is a natural progression, shared by all branches of knowledge. A great many historians, however, reject the use of theory completely. They see two possible grounds for doing so. The first argument concedes that there may be patterns and regularities in history, but maintains that they are not accessible to disciplined enquiry. It is hard enough to provide an entirely convincing explanation of any one event in history, but to link them in a series or within an overarching category places the enquirer at an intolerable distance from the verifiable facts. As Peter Mathias (here acting as devil's advocate) concedes:

> The bounty of the past provides individual instances in plenty to support virtually any general proposition. It is only too easy to beat history over the head with the blunt instrument of a hypothesis and leave an impression.[6]

On this view, theoretical history is speculative history and should be left to philosophers and prophets.[7]

The possibility that theory will 'take over' from the facts is certainly not to be made light of. The gaps in the surviving historical record, and especially the lack of clinching evidence on matters of causation, leave a great deal of scope for mere supposition and wishful thinking (see pp. 116–17). At the same time, the range of evidence bearing on many historical problems is so large that selection is unavoidable – and the principles governing that selection may prejudice the result of the enquiry. The record of recent centuries is so voluminous and varied that contradictory results can be obtained simply by asking different questions. In the context of American history Aileen Kraditor puts this point as follows:

> If one historian asks, 'Do the sources provide evidence of militant struggles among workers and slaves?' the sources will reply, 'Certainly'. And if another asks, 'Do the sources provide evidence of widespread acquiescence in the established order among the American population throughout the

past two centuries?' the sources will reply, 'Of course'.[8]

Almost any theory can be 'proved' by marshalling an impressive collection of individual instances to fit the desired pattern.

Theory-oriented history is certainly prone to these dangers – but so too, it must be recognized, is the work of many historians who reject theory and remain blissfully unaware of the assumptions and values which inform their own selection and interpretation of evidence. The way forward is not to retreat into an untenable empiricism, but to apply much higher standards to the testing of theory. Wishful thinking is more likely to be controlled by historians who approach their enquiries with explicit hypotheses than by those who try to follow where the sources lead. When selection of the evidence cannot be avoided, it must be a representative selection which will reveal both contrary and supporting indicators. A given theory may account for *part* of the evidence relating to the problem in hand, but that is not enough; it must be compatible with the weight of the evidence overall. In Kraditor's words, 'the data omitted must not be essential to the understanding of the data included'.[9] All this assumes a certain detachment on the part of historians towards their theories, and a readiness to change tack in the light of the evidence. But where these controls are neglected, the profession as a whole is vigilant in their defence. Historians are seldom happier than when citing contrary evidence and alternative interpretations to cast doubt on the work of their colleagues – especially those who seem to have a bee in their bonnet. Moreover a great deal of historical synthesis consists in comparing the merits of competing theories in order to determine which, if any, illuminates the problem under discussion. The speculative tendencies in theoretical history do not go unchecked for long.

II

The second and more challenging line of attack questions the legitimacy of theory-making in history on the grounds that it denies the very essence of the discipline. Human culture, the argument goes, is so richly diverse that we can only understand man in specific epochs and locations: 'He remains an irreducible subject, the one nonobject in the world.'[10] Models of human behaviour are therefore a delusion. The business of the historian is to reconstruct events and situations in their unique individuality, and on their own terms; their interpretations apply only to particular sets of circumstances. Nothing is to be gained from comparing historical situations separated by time or space – indeed a great deal will be lost since the result can only be to obscure the essentials of each. In David Thomson's words, 'The historical attitude, by definition, is hostile to system-making.'[11] This view has a distinguished pedigree. It captures the essence of historicism as expounded in the nineteenth century. Ranke's injunction that historians should study the past 'to show how things actually were' was intended primarily as an antidote to the great evolutionary schemes of the Enlightenment historians and the followers of Hegel. His narrative style was hostile to abstraction and generalization, and well suited to conveying the particularity of events. The classical historicist position is inimical both to comprehensive theories of social structure and to theories of social change, while its demand that every age should be evaluated in its own terms is difficult to reconcile with any view of history as progress towards a desirable goal.

These grounds for rejecting theories of history are closely related to another argument which has often been given heavy emphasis: that theory denies not only the 'uniqueness' of events but also the dignity of the individual and the power of human agency. Traditional narrative shorn of any explanatory framework gives maximum scope to the play of personality, whereas a concern with recurrent or typical aspects of social structure and social change elevates abstraction at the expense of real living individuals. Worst of all from this viewpoint are theories of the third kind whose insidious effect is to confer an inevitability on the historical process which individuals are powerless to change, now or in the future; all theories of history, the argument goes, have determinist elements, and determinism is a denial of human freedom.[12] The polar opposite of determinism is the rejection of any meaning in history beyond the play of the contingent and the unforeseen – a view held by many historians in the mainstream of the discipline. A. J. P. Taylor delights in informing his readers that the only lesson taught by the study of the past is the incoherence and unpredictability of human affairs: history is a chapter of accidents and blunders.[13]

Lastly, the traditionalists recoil from one of the main practical consequences of writing theory-oriented history which is to place history in a dependent relationship with the social sciences. Theory-minded historians, they maintain, do not develop their own models but apply the theoretical findings of sociology, social anthropology and economics – disciplines whose focus is on the present not the past, and which are interested in history only as a testing-ground for their own theories. Theoretical historians simply play into their hands and undermine the autonomy of their own discipline. Historians ought to be vigilant about threats to the distinctiveness of their calling, whether from within or without. Elton goes further: in its undiluted form, history offers the surest antidote against the system-builders among the social scientists who proffer pat solutions to complex human problems.[14]

Elton's view suggests one explanation as to why the historical profession has been so strongly averse to theory, and that is its conservatism. As we have seen (p. 20) the study of history has attracted more than its fair share of conservatives concerned to invoke the sanction of the past in defence of institutions threatened by radical reform, or quite simply to find a mental escape from the disorienting impact of rapid social change around them. The true conservative, lacking a vision of progress, distrusts theories of the meaning of history as the rhetoric of the Utopian left, and is alarmed by the notion of a general model of social change which might be employed to push through undesirable projects of social engineering in the future. But the research methods of historians themselves have also acted as a strong antidote to theory. As M. M. Postan put it, the

> critical attitude to minutiae has become in the end a powerful agent of selection. It now attracts to history persons of a cautious and painstaking disposition, not necessarily endowed with any aptitude for theoretical synthesis.[15]

In fact a great deal of the opposition to theory is born of prejudice. The negative tendencies which the traditionalists have identified are certainly there and if allowed free rein would lead to the damaging consequences which alarm them so much; but as any examination of the better examples of theoretical history will show, these tendencies do not go unchecked, and the outcome is an enrichment rather than an impoverishment of historical understanding.

Consider, first of all, the contention that theory detracts from the uniqueness of historical events. Historians have in fact never written of events as though they were entirely unique because it is impossible to do so. The very language which historians employ imposes a classification on their material and implies comparisons beyond their immediate field of interest. The only reason why scholars can use the phrase 'feudal tenure' of a particular relationship between lord and tenant, or the word 'revolution' of a major political upheaval, is because they share with their readers a common notion of what those words mean, based on a recognition that the world would be incomprehensible if we did not all the time subsume particular instances into general categories. The point was clearly made by E. E. Evans-Pritchard, the leading figure in the last generation of British social anthropologists, who advocated a cordial relationship between history and the social sciences:

> Events lose much, even all, of their meaning if they are not seen as having some degree of regularity and constancy, as belonging to a certain type of event, all instances of which have many features in common. King John's struggle with his barons is meaningful only when the relations of the barons to Henry I, Stephen, Henry II, and Richard are also known; and also when the relations between the kings and barons in other countries with feudal instititions are known; in other words, where the struggle is seen as a phenomenon typical of, or common to, societies of a certain kind.[16]

But if the use of generalizing concepts alerts us to regularities in the material, it also exposes those aspects which resist categorization and which give the event or situation its unique qualities. The contention of the theoretical historian is that if these comparisons are implicit in any historical analysis worth the name, then there is everything to be gained in clarity of thought by making them explicit – by constructing, for example, a model of feudal society or of revolutionary change.

Equally, the claim that history is the rightful province of the individual looks dangerously misleading on closer inspection. Historians are compelled at every turn to classify people into groups, whether by nationality, religion, occupation or class. This is because it is these larger identities which confer significance on them as social beings. And what these groups have in common is a tendency to think and act in certain ways, to the point where their response can be predicted. No two individuals are ever entirely alike, but how they behave in certain roles (e.g. as consumers of foodstuffs or as adherents of a particular creed) may follow a highly regular pattern. The emphasis which historians place on group activity is not, therefore, a denial of human individuality but simply a recognition that what the individual does in common with others usually has far greater impact, historically, than anything else he or she does. Furthermore, the cumulative effect of the actions which a particular group takes in pursuit of its objectives is to *institutionalize* that behaviour – that is, to entrench it in such a way that the options open to individuals thereafter are constrained or (to use a useful sociological term) *structured*. This is not the same as saying that people's actions are determined: certain patterns of behaviour may be strongly indicated, but they can be rejected or modified by the resolve of a new generation to break out of the mould. No-one has expressed the tension between human agency and social structuring more lucidly than Philip Abrams who significantly combined the professions of historian and sociologist:

> The two-sidedness of society, the fact that social action is both something we choose to do and something we have to do, is inseparably bound up with the further fact that whatever reality society has is an historical reality, a reality in time. When we refer to the two-sidedness of society we are referring to the ways in which, in time, actions become institutions and institutions are in turn changed by action. Taking and selling prisoners becomes the institution of slavery. Offering one's services to a soldier in return for his protection becomes feudalism. Organising the control of an enlarged labour force on the basis of standardised rules becomes bureaucracy. And slavery, feudalism and bureaucracy become the fixed, external settings in which struggles for prosperity or survival or freedom are then pursued. By substituting cash payments for labour services the lord and peasant jointly embark on the dismantling of the feudal order their great-grandparents had constructed.[17]

The best theories – and I will argue shortly that Marxism is one of these – owe their appeal precisely to the fact that they acknowledge and seek to elucidate the reciprocal relationship of action and structure. Theory does not devalue the individual; it seeks rather to explain the constraints which limit people's freedom and frustrate their intentions, and in doing so it uncovers patterns in history. By contrast, the historian who maintains an exclusive focus on the thoughts and actions of individuals (as diplomatic historians all too often do) is likely to find no shape, and to see instead only a chaotic sequence of accident and blunder.

As for the threatened submergence of history by the social sciences, there are strong reasons why historians should – in the first instance at least – avail themselves of imported theory. The social sciences are by definition concerned with what people do in aggregates rather than as individuals; and since their range embraces entire societies, social scientists have from the outset needed theory in order to engage with their subject-matter at all. Economists since Adam Smith in the late eighteenth century and sociologists since Auguste Comte in the mid-nineteenth century have regarded explicit theory as a prerequisite for interpreting their data, and as a result a body of sophisticated theoretical knowledge has been built up in both disciplines, and latterly in social anthropology too. The use made by historians of these theories is simply an acknowledgement that the social sciences have a head start. In fact history has always been influenced by theorists from without, Smith and Comte being cases in point. But it is only in the past thirty years that historians have begun to take the measure of the full range and versatility of social science theory.

There are two real problems here. One is that much social science theory, especially in economics, is intended to explain quite restricted fields of activity, often in a somewhat artificially detached way, and the result of applying this theory to historical work may be to intensify the 'tunnel vision' to which historians specializing in a particlar branch are anyway so prone (see p. 89). The other problem concerns the alleged indifference to history of the social sciences. This charge is not without foundation. Many theories, for example that of the free market economy, are based on the premise of equilibrium which strikes historians as a profoundly ahistorical way of conceiving society – a denial of the trajectories of change and adjustment which are present in every case; and other theories (like the modernization theory so prevalent in America sociology) which purport to embrace a historical dimension are based on a naïve antithesis between 'traditional' and 'modern' at odds with any sense of process in history. Certainly much of the borrowing by historians from the social sciences has been shallow and uncritical, and it has too readily assumed that theory is somehow value-free and objective, whereas it is the subject of sharp ideological differences among social scientists themselves.[18] But neither of these objections is a reason for avoiding theory; they suggest only that historians should be discriminating about what they take on board. In fact the theories whose influence on recent historians has been particularly pervasive are those which seek to encompass social structure or social change as a whole, and of these theories the most influential are derived from the great social thinkers of the last century who had a profound sense of history – Max Weber and above all Karl Marx. But the real answer to the traditionalists' fear of absorption by the social sciences is that these theories are not tablets from Heaven to be inscribed on the historical record. They should be seen rather as a point of departure. The result of historical work will be to modify them, probably quite drastically, and to erect in their place theories which represent a genuine cross-fertilization between history and social science. Both sides can only benefit from that outcome.

III

The way is now open for a discussion in which the Marxist interpretation of history can be assessed in the context of the dangers and opportunities which attend any venture in theoretical history. The dangers in this case are familiar enough: Marx's detractors have made such play with some of the less attractive tendencies in his thought that, to all except the fairly restricted number of people who have read Marx himself or academic commentaries on his writings, he is associated with a bleak determinism and an utter cynicism about human nature. On this reading, the central tenets of Marxism go something like this. 'History is subject to the inexorable control of economic forces which move all human societies along the road to socialism through the same stages, capitalism being the stage currently occupied by most of mankind. At all times material self-interest has been the mainspring of human behaviour, regardless of the motives which people have actually professed. Classes represent the collective expression of this self-interest, and all history is therefore nothing more than the history of class conflict. Ideology, art and culture are merely a mirror of this fundamental identification, having no historical dynamic of their own. The individual is the product of his or her own age and class and however talented and forceful is powerless to affect the course of history; it is the masses who make history, but even they only do so according to a predetermined pattern.' At one time or another in the hundred years that have elapsed since Marx's death, each of these propositions has been subscribed to by Marxists, but all of them represent a crude simplification of what he actually wrote. Marx's thought was developed over some thirty years of research and reflection, and the resulting corpus of theory is far more complex and subtle than the shibboleths of 'vulgar' Marxism allow.

Marx began with the fundamental premise that what distinguishes people from animals is their ability to produce their means of subsistence. In the struggle to satisfy their physiological and material needs, men and women have developed progressively more efficient means of exploiting their environment (or mastering nature, as Marx would have put it). To the question 'what is history about?' Marx answered that it was about the growth of human productive power, and he looked forward to the time when the basic needs of all people would be amply satisfied: only then would humanity find self-fulfilment and achieve its full potential in every sphere. In maintaining that the only true, objective view of the historical process was rooted in the material conditions of life, Marx sharply distinguished himself from the main currents of nineteenth-century historiography with their choice of nationalism, freedom or religion as the defining themes of history. It is entirely appropriate that Marx's view should be referred to as 'historical materialism', a term coined by his lifelong collaborator and intellectual heir, Friedrich Engels. From this basic perspective, first sketched in *The German Ideology* (1846), Marx never wavered. For the rest of his life much of his effort was devoted to working out its implications for the interpretation of social structure, the stages of social evolution, and the nature of social change.

Marx conceived of society as comprising three constituent levels. Underlying all else are the *forces of production* (or productive forces): that is, the tools, techniques and raw materials together with the labour power which realizes their productive potential. The forces of production have certain implications for the *relations of production* (or productive relations) by which Marx meant the division of labour and the forms of cooperation and subordination required to sustain production – in other words the economic structure of society. This structure in turn forms a base or foundation on which is built the *superstructure*, composed of legal and political institutions and their supporting ideology. The most succinct summary of Marx's view of social structure appears in the Preface to his *Contribution to the Critique of Political Economy* (1859):

> In the social production of their existence, men inevitably enter into definite relations, which are independent of their will, namely relations of production appropriate to a given stage in the development of their material forces of production. The totality of these relations of production constitutes the economic structure of society, the real foundation, on which arises a legal and political superstructure and to which correspond definite forms of social consciousness. The mode of production of material life conditions the general process of social, political and intellectual life. It is not the consciousness of men that determines their existence, but their social existence that determines their consciousness.[19]

However, this is not the crudely deterministic model which it has so often been taken to be. In the first place, the forces of production are by no means confined to the instruments of production and the brawn of the workers. Technical ingenuity and scientific knowledge (on which the further development of the forces of production so clearly depended by Marx's day) are also included: full allowance is made for human creativity without which we would remain slaves of the natural world around us. Secondly, although it clearly follows from Marx's view that politics and ideology – the traditional preoccupations of the historians – can only be understood in relation to the economic base, Marx allowed also for influences in the opposite direction. For example, no system of economic relations can become established without a prior framework of property rights and legal obligations; that is to say, the superstructure does not just reflect the relations of production but has an enabling function as well. The three-tier model thus allows for reciprocal influences.[20] And thirdly, Marx did not suggest that all non-economic activities were determined by the base. It is arguable whether artistic creation should be included in the superstructure at all. But even those spheres which belong un-equivocally to the superstructure are not *exclusively* determined by the base. Both political institutions and religion have their own dynamic, as Marx and Engels acknowledged in their own historical writings, and in the short term especially economic factors may be of subsidiary importance in accounting for events; as Braudel observes, Marx was essentially a theorist of *la longue durée* (see p. 103).[21] It is probably closer to the spirit of Marx's thought to see the economic structure as setting limiting conditions rather than determining the elements of the superstructure in all their particularity. Engels was most emphatic on this point. As he wrote to a correspondent some years after Marx's death:

> According to the materialistic conception of history, the *ultimately* determining element in history is the production and reproduction of real life. More than this neither Marx nor I has ever asserted. Hence if somebody twists this into saying that the economic element is the *only* determining one he transforms that proposition into a meaningless, abstract, senseless phrase. The economic situation is the basis, but the various elements of the superstructure . . . also exercise their influence upon the course of the historical struggles and in many cases preponderate in determining their *form*.[22]

Clearly the base/superstructure metaphor lends itself to a deter-ministic interpretation, and several of Marx's utterances can be so interpreted, but his *oeuvre* as a whole does not suggest that he saw it in such stark terms.

One of the best known features of Marx's thought is his periodiza-tion of history. He distinguished three historical epochs down to his own day, each moulded by a progressively more advanced mode of production. These were: Ancient Society (Greece and Rome), Feudal

Society, which emerged after the fall of the Roman Empire, and Capitalist (or 'modern bourgeois') Society which had first come into being in England in the seventeenth century and had since triumphed elsewhere in Europe, particularly as a consequence of the French Revolution. What gave political edge to the periodization was Marx's conviction that Capitalist Society must in due course give way to Socialist Society and the complete self-fulfilment of mankind; indeed when he first sketched the scheme in 1846 he believed the advent of socialism to be imminent. Marx maintained that his periodization was the outcome of his historical enquiries rather than of dogmatic theorizing, and that is born out by the changes and qualifications he made in the light of fuller research. He later posited an additional mode of production in the form of Germanic Society, contemporaneous with Ancient Society and one of the sources of Feudal Society.[23] He placed Asia in a distinct category from Europe: according to Marx, the Asiatic mode of production had an inadequate internal dynamic of historical change, and capitalism (and thus ultimately socialism) could be established in the Orient only as a result of colonialism. And in the Russian case, he retreated from his earlier view that full-scale capitalism was the indispensable prerequisite of socialism, forty years before the Russian Revolution. Marx reproved those critics who

> must metamorphose my historical sketch of the genesis of capitalism in Western Europe into a historic-philosophic theory of the general path every people is fated to tread, whatever the historical circumstances in which it finds itself.[24]

In short, Marx did not lay down a single evolutionary path which all human societies are predetermined to follow exactly.

Such a rigid periodization would have ill consorted with Marx's view of social change, the richest and most suggestive part of his theory of history. Marx summed up his interpretation in the passage which immediately follows the extract from the 1859 Preface quoted earlier:

> At a certain stage of development, the material productive forces of society come into conflict with the existing relations of production or – this merely expresses the same thing in legal terms – with the property relations within the framework of which they have operated hitherto. From forms of development of the productive forces these relations turn into their fetters. Then begins an era of social revolution. The changes in the economic foundation lead sooner or later to the transformation of the whole immense superstructure.[25]

Marx believed that the contradiction or *dialectic* between the forces of production and the relations of production was the principal determinant of long-term historical change: each mode of production contains within it the seeds of its successor. Thus, to take an example on which he held emphatic views, the English Revolution of the seven-

teenth century occurred because the forces of production characteristic of capitalism had reached the point where their further
development was held back by the feudal property relations sanc-
tioned by the early Stuart monarchy; the outcome of the revolution
was a remodelling of the relations of production which cleared the way
for the Industrial Revolution a hundred years later.

This rather abstract conception of historical change is made visible
in the form of *class conflict*. Marx identified classes not according to
wealth, status or education – the usual criteria employed in his day –
but quite specifically in terms of their role in the productive process.
The division of labour which has characterized every mode of production since Ancient Society results in the creation of classes whose true
interests are mutually antagonistic. Each successive stage has had its
dominent class, and has also harboured the class destined to overthrow
it. Thus Marx ascribed the English Revolution to the urban bourgeoisie who were developing the new capitalist forces of production,
just as he expected socialism to be achieved in his own day by the new
factory proletariat spawned by industrial capitalism. It is class conflict
expressing the contradictions within society which drives history in a
forward direction. This is not to say that the masses are the makers of
history. Although Marx believed that humanity's prospects for a better
future lay in the hands of the proletariat, his interpretation confined
the masses to an ancillary role in earlier history; he was only too well
aware that the world in which he lived was essentially the creation of
the bourgeoisie whom Marx both admired and reviled for what they
had achieved.

Marx's conception of class is the point at which his view of the role of
human agency in history can be assessed. Class is defined in structural
terms according to its relation to the means of production, but Marx
knew that for a class to be effective politically requires a *consciousness*
of their class in its members. The long-term trajectory of change may
be determined by the dialectic between the forces and relations of
production, but the timing and the precise form of the transition from
one stage to the next depend on the awareness and capacity for action
of real human beings. Indeed, Marx's entire career was devoted to
equipping the proletariat of his time with an understanding of the
material forces at work in their own society so that they would know
when and how to act against the capitalist system. People are the
victims of material forces, but in the right conditions they have the
opportunity to be agents of historical change. That paradox lies at the
centre of Marx's view of history. As he wrote in his finest piece of
contemporary history, *The Eighteenth Brumaire of Louis Bonaparte*
(1852):

> Men make their own history, but they do not make it just as they please;
> they do not make it under circumstances chosen by themselves, but under
> circumstances directly encountered, given, and transmitted from the past.[26]

How Marx understood the reciprocal relationship of action and circumstances is never made clear, but what he claimed to have done was to reveal the long-term structural factors which render certain historical developments inevitable in the long run. These are, so to speak, the defining limits within which the actions of men and women, whether as individuals or as groups, have their scope.

IV

What were the implications of Marx's theories for the actual writing of history? As we have seen, these theories lend themselves to a simplified rigid schema, and this was the form in which they were expounded by many of the first Marxists whose primary interest was in the political struggle and who were content with an unequivocal determinism which pointed towards a proletarian revolution in the near future. The founders of historical materialism were not in sympathy with this approach. As Engels remarked in 1890:

> Too many of the younger Germans simply make use of the phrase 'historical materialism' (and *everything* can be turned into a phrase) only in order to get their own relatively scanty historical knowledge – for economic history is still in its swaddling clothes! – constructed into a neat system as quickly as possible, and they then deem themselves something very tremendous.[27]

Marx was emphatic that his theory was a guide to study, not a substitute for it:

> Viewed apart from real history, these abstractions have in themselves no value whatsoever. They can only serve to facilitate the arrangement of historical material, to indicate the sequence of its separate strata. But they by no means afford a recipe or schema, as does philosophy, for neatly trimming the epochs of history. On the contrary, our difficulties begin only when we set about the observation and the arrangement – the real depiction – of our historical material, whether of a past epoch or of the present.[28]

What Marx rejected was not historical study as such, but the method employed by the leading historians of his day. Their error, he maintained, lay in taking at face value what the historical actors said about their motives and aspirations; in so doing, Ranke and his imitators imprisoned themselves within the dominant ideology of the age in question which was merely a cloak for the real material interests of the dominant class. 'Objective' history – that is, the dialectic of forces and relations of production – was accessible through research into the economic structure of past societies without reference to the subjective utterances of historical personalities:

> Just as one does not judge an individual by what he thinks about himself, so

one cannot judge such a period of transformation [i.e. a social revolution] by its consciousness, but, on the contrary, this consciousness must be explained from the contradictions of material life, from the conflict existing between the social forces of production and the relations of production.[29]

At the same time, Marx never developed a clear methodology of history. His own historical writings veered from the compelling political narrative of *The Eighteenth Brumaire* (1852) to the abstract economic analysis of the first volume of *Capital* (1867). And there remain ambiguities in his conception of both the forces and the relations of production, as well as the connection between base and superstructure. So historians working within the Marxist tradition have had plenty of interpretative work to do.

During the generation after Marx's death in 1883, historical materialism began to have a pervasive though somewhat blurred effect on the climate of intellectual opinion, as his major writings were translated into other European languages and socialist parties of a Marxist persuasion sprang up. Marxism was certainly one of the main currents contributing to the emergence of economic history as a distinct field of enquiry (see pp. 78–80). As J. H. Clapham – no friend of socialism – conceded in 1929, 'Marxism, by attraction and repulsion, has perhaps done more to make men think about economic history and inquire into it than any other teaching'.[30] But the content and method of the Marxist interpretation took longer to make an impact. It first affected the practise of professional historians on a significant scale in the Soviet Union, where from the Bolshevik take-over until Stalin's clamp-down in 1931–32 historical research and debate within a Marxist framework were very lively.[31] The subjection of historical work to a strict Party line in Russia coincided with the emergence of Marxism as a powerful intellectual stimulus in the West. This was prompted by the obvious crisis in capitalism as a result of the Great Crash of 1929 and the apparent bankruptcy of liberal democracy in the face of Fascism. But although important pioneer work in Marxist history was done in Britain and elsewhere during the 1930s, it was mostly achieved by active members of the Communist Party who were viewed with suspicion by most historians and received little academic preferment. Since the 1950s, however, Marxist approaches to history have been much more widely influential – and with historians who have no connection with the Communist Party and in many cases are not politically active at all. Many of the acknowledged leaders of the profession like Christopher Hill and E. J. Hobsbawm write from a Marxist perspective. Hobsbawm himself (still a member of the Communist Party) put the case fairly in 1978 when he wrote:

It is probably impossible today for any non-Marxist historian not to discuss either Marx or the work of some Marxist historian in the course of his or her normal business as a historian.[32]

Why is it that a historical interpretation which originated as a revolutionary critique of contemporary society and which is open to dogmatic abuse now commands so much attention among scholars? The reason can hardly be any longer the central role accorded by Marxism to economic history, since the majority of economic historians (particularly in Britain and the USA) are non-Marxist. Nor can the appeal of Marxism be attributed to the attractions of an 'underdog' view of history: although the Marxist approach gives great weight to the role of the masses at certain historical conjunctures, it does not offer a worm's eye view of history, nor is it concerned to celebrate the heroism of earlier generations of proletarians. The real reason for Marxism's strong appeal is that it answers so well to the historian's need for theory – and in all three of the areas where theory is least dispensable.

Through the base/superstructure model Marxism offers a particularly useful way of conceiving the totality of social relations in any given society. It is not just that the political, social, economic and technological all have their place; in a full-scale Marxist analysis these familiar distinctions lose their force. Social and economic history become inseparable and the study of politics is saved from becoming the minute reconstruction of the antics of professional politicians in their own arena, to which it can so easily be restricted by the specialist (see pp. 75–6). The appeal of 'total history' as practised by the *Annales* school also rests on its opposition to compartmentalization, but Braudel and his followers have conspicuously failed to develop a satisfactory model for integrating political history with the environmental and demographic studies which provide the backbone of their work (see pp. 90 & 103). In this respect at least, it must be counted as inferior to Marxist history with its emphasis on the reciprocal interaction between the productive forces, the relations of production and the superstructure. It is no accident that Hobsbawm, one of the finest writers of the broad historical survey today, is a Marxist with a profound grasp of the master's own writings.[33]

It is the same reciprocal interaction which saves Marxism from the ahistorical error so common in other theories of regarding social equilibrium as the norm. Marxist historians hold as a fundamental premise that all societies contain both stabilizing elements and disruptive elements (or contradictions), and that historical change occurs when the latter burst out of the existing social framework and through a process of struggle achieve a new order. Historians have found the notion of the dialectic to be an invaluable tool in analysing social change of varying intensity, from the barely perceptible movement within a stable social formation to periods of revolutionary ferment.

Marxism's claim to find a direction in the whole historical process is the most difficult part of its appeal to assess. Marxist historians today are certainly not much given to writing in terms of grand evolutionary schemes, and it is likely that only a minority are interested in the light which their enquiries might shed on the Utopian prospect of a classless society mapped out by Marx for the future. But there can be little doubt that Marxism is today the principal legatee of the view of history as progress. The notion that the major social conflicts in history issue in change for the better exerts a powerful appeal, clearly present in one of Christopher Hill's most unequivocally Marxist statements on the English Civil War:

> A victory for Charles I and his gang could only have meant the economic stagnation of England, the stabilisation of a backward feudal society in a commercial age, and have necessitated an even bloodier struggle for liberation later. The Parliamentarians thought they were fighting God's battles. They were certainly fighting those of posterity, throwing off an intolerable incubus to further advance.[34]

Adherence to the Marxist framework can have the effect of conferring on quite limited enquiries a significance which arises from their place in a grand historical process.

Response to the strong pull exerted by Marxism's theoretical range does not, however, mean that historians practising in the Marxist tradition are confined within an orthodoxy. What is striking about the growth of Marxist historiography during the past thirty years or so, especially in Britain, is its diversity. As familiarity with Marx's writing has spread, so historians have responded to the different and quite contradictory strands in his *oeuvre*, reflected in a major divide in recent Marxist scholarship between what insiders call 'culturalism' and 'economism'. This divide is best illustrated by reaction to the most widely-read work of Marxist history ever written in this country – E. P. Thompson's *The Making of the English Working Class* (see above, p. 84). The central theme of the book is how, in reaction to proletarianization and political repression, the English labouring classes developed a new consciousness so that by 1830 they had achieved a collective identity as a working class and the capacity for collective political action: that consciousness was not the automatic by-product of the factory system but was the outcome of reflection on experience in the light of a vigorous native radical tradition. The book is thus 'a study in an active process, which owes as much to agency as to conditioning'.[35] Thompson himself would maintain that his book is true to Marx's recognition that men do, in some measure, 'make their own history'. His critics argue that Thompson has underestimated the force of the qualification added by Marx to that statement. They point out that in omitting any detailed discussion of the transition from one mode of production to another, Thompson fails to acknowledge the rootedness of class in economic relations and therefore exaggerates the role of collective agency; because Thompson is lax in his theory, they say, he has become trapped within the subjective experience of his protagonists.[36] Thompson is unrepentant; he has reaffirmed the need to hold theory and experience in some kind of balance and to interpret Marxism as an evolving and flexible tradition, rather than a closed system,[37] and such is the power of his own historical writing that 'culturalism' – or 'socialist humanism' as Thompson would prefer to call it [38] – is likely to co-exist with 'economism' within the Marxist fold for the foreseeable future.

The Making of the English Working Class expresses another marked tendency within British Marxist historiography, and that is its interest in the history of popular movements, almost regardless of their efficacy. One of the criticisms which can be made of Marxism, as of other goal-oriented interpretations of history, is that it distorts our understanding of the past by concentrating unduly on those people and movements which were on the side of 'progress' (see p. 122). But Thompson's emphasis falls less on the new factory work-force who were the nucleus of the organized working class of the future, than on the casualties of the Industrial Revolution – people like the handloom weavers whose means of livelihood was destroyed by the factory system. This tendency is even more pronounced in the work of Christopher Hill on the seventeenth century. In recent years, in works like *The World Turned Upside Down* (1972), his attention has shifted more and more from the 'bourgeois' revolution which succeeded to the 'revolt within the Revolution'[39] – to the socialism and libertarianism of sects like the Diggers and Ranters which were born before their time and were completely suppressed by the victors in the Civil War. But this emphasis is no antiquarian indulgence on Hill's part. His contention is that today we are living in a society in which the radical ideas of the sects have a practical socialist relevance – that by rediscovering a lost tradition we can learn from their ideas and experience; at the end of *The World Turned Upside Down* we are urged to be 'doers not talkers only'.[40] In the same spirit – though less plausibly – Thompson suggests that the lost popular causes of the English Industrial Revolution may yield insights which can be acted upon today, if not in England then in the Third World where industrialization is still in its infancy.[41]

Yet for all the fascination held by popular movements, Marxist history is not just 'history from below' (and neither Thompson nor Hill has ever suggested that it is). Struggles between classes are ultimately resolved at the political level, and it is through control of the state that new dispositions of class power are sustained. In fact it can be argued, though it is not very fashionable to do so, that 'history from above' is just as important a perspective for Marxist historians. The results are more interesting than might seem likely at first sight. For the state cannot just be written off as the political arm of whichever class happens to enjoy hegemony at the time: that is a 'vulgar' Marxist simplification. The interpretation most favoured today is that the

state's historic role is to defend the common and long-term interests of
the dominant class – and more particularly to promote the conditions
in which the mode of production on which that hegemony is based can
be reproduced into the next generation. In doing this the state may
often find itself in conflict with the urgent short-term interests of
particular sections within the ruling class. Thus Perry Anderson argues
in his *Lineages of the Absolute State* (1974) that the antagonism often
shown towards sections of the aristocracy by the absolutist monarchies
of seventeenth- and eighteenth-century Europe must not obscure the
fact that these regimes were deeply committed to the maintenance of
feudal relations, and especially private landed property. A further
development of the same idea is the notion that state power depends
not only on control of the instruments of coercion but on a certain
legitimacy in the minds of the ruled; since that legitimacy will not be
acknowledged if the state acts exclusively and nakedly in the interests
of one class, there has to be some sensitivity to the common good and
to principles of natural justice; the likely alternatives would be class
conflict and sedition on a scale which might imperil the continuance of
the dominant mode of production. For this reason the state has usually
displayed a certain autonomy *vis-à-vis* the class which it primarily
represents, but how much autonomy should in practice be allowed to
the state is understandably a source of considerable tension in class-
dominated societies. Far from making political history redundant,
then, a Marxist perspective requires a very careful analysis of the
pressures to which the state has responded and which have often
resulted in the implementation of varied and contradictory policies
within the lifespan of a single social formation. Thus in the area of
history most burdened by the weight of conventional scholarship
Marxist historiography contributes fresh and stimulating insights.

V

A fair assessment of the Marxist theory of history is not made easier by
the inflated claims made by Marx himself. The successive transformations of the mode of production could, he asserted, be 'determined
with the precision of natural science',[42] and this view has been fully
endorsed by official historiography in the Soviet bloc. Like so many
students of society in the nineteenth century, Marx was dazzled by the
apparent successes of natural science. In directing attention at the
material forces in history – rather than ideology or motive – Marx
believed that he could overcome the subjectivity inherent in all mainstream history-writing. Yet even if it is accepted that long-term historical change *does* arise from the development of the productive

process, scientific precision remains an illusory goal, for that process must necessarily be studied by reference to the records and other writings of people whose perceptions of the material world around them were distorted by non-materialist considerations. Penetration beyond the professed meaning of the sources to their 'real' meaning is very much a matter of flair and judgement rather than watertight logical demonstration. Confining the search for causes to materialist factors does not free the Marxist from the difficulties which attend any venture in historical explanation – the gaps in the record and the failure of the evidence to yield clear and unequivocal connections of cause and consequence.

For the Marxist there are two possible responses to this unsatisfactory state of affairs. The first is to place theory on an elevated pedestal where it is untouched by the mundane world of empirical evidence: the deeper structures which underlie both the past and the present cannot be grasped by assembling all the facts but can be apprehended only by those in possession of the correct theory. This is the position adopted by the influential 'structuralist' school of Marxism, led by the French philosopher Louis Althusser. Correct theory is derived from a correct reading of Marx's mature works, especially *Capital*, in a form which practically amounts to a denial of human agency in history. A renunciation of the empirical method is defended (in the teeth of Marx's statements to the contrary) on the grounds that all historical documentation is tainted by the structure of thought and language prevalent at the time of writing: the 'real' facts of history are beyond our reach, and the distorted images we have of the past are an irrelevance.[43] Naturally enough historians react strongly against this dismissal of the premises on which their discipline is founded, and it is not difficult to puncture Althusser's case. Historians do not rely exclusively on written texts; they also exploit material artefacts which yield evidence about the past independently of language and its associations. And – more centrally – the whole critical apparatus deployed by historians on written sources is designed to penetrate the mental categories of the writer and the culture in which he or she wrote, and by piecing together widely disparate evidence to arrive at a perception of the period which was beyond the reach of any contemporary.[44] Even among Marxist ideologues the Althusserian fashion is probably already on the wane. It has had very little influence on the practice of history or on the view taken of it by the wider public.

The second response is to acknowledge, without overstating, the limitations which the nature of historical enquiry imposes on the aspiration to be 'scientific', and to participate in a common enterprise with historians of other persuasions. Broadly speaking this is the course pursued by Hill, Hobsbawm, Thompson and most Marxist historians writing in Britain today. This entails engaging seriously with the criticism most often levelled at theory-oriented history, and

Marxism especially, that it is 'reductionist'. By reductionism is meant the *a priori* selection of one level of reality as fundamental, and the interpretation of everything else in terms of that one level. Perhaps the biggest weakness of Marxist theory is that it does not recognize the strength of associations which men and women enter into for reasons that have nothing to do with production It is not difficult to argue that identification by religion, race or nationality has been at least as important over the long term as identification by class. These loyalties cannot simply be dismissed as 'false consciousness' promoted by the ruling class to blind the lower orders to their real condition of exploitation; it is much more likely that they satisfy a fundamental social need. Like other social theorists Marx could not help being unduly influenced by what was observable in his own day when advancing his universalist claims. Class identification and class conflict were characteristic features of the industrializing societies of Germany, France and Britain in which Marx passed all his life, but they were much less pronounced in earlier periods, and historians of pre-industrial societies have great difficulty in applying Marxist theory in a comprehensive fashion. Significantly Hill's work on seventeenth-century England has shown a progressively stronger tendency to treat religious persuasion as an independent variable.[45] Marxism holds many insights for the history of the Middle Ages and the early modern period, but it is not an adequate vehicle for a 'total history' of pre-industrial societies in Europe – and still less in Asia and Africa.

It is a common opinion among non-Marxist historians that the attempt to apply theory with real commitment to particular situations in the past results in a one-dimensional interpretation which distorts the true complexity of the historical process. But all historians, unless they are diehard traditionalists, concede that theory has been very productive of stimulating hypotheses. Its value, they claim, lies not in its explanatory power but in its capacity to raise interesting questions and alert scholars to fresh source material – in a word, it has merit as a *heuristic* device. Historical research usually demonstrates that a given theory does not hold when confronted by the richness of actual experience, but in the process a new area of historical enquiry may be opened up. From this angle Marxist theory has a very good track record as a source of 'fertile error'[46]: whatever its failings it has generated a great deal of historical knowledge about the connections between political process and the socio-economic structure. Equally it might be argued that the attempt to write comparative history has proved its worth less in revealing common patterns than in sharpening our awareness of the fundamental differences between the periods or places under discussion.

This might be termed the minimalist justification of the use of theory by historians. What it overlooks is that historical knowledge consists of more than specific conjunctures and processes in the past. Historians with their professional commitment to primary research all too easily forget that there are large-scale problems of historical interpretation which cry out for treatment: how to explain long-term processes like the growth of industrialization or bureaucracy, and the recurrence of institutions like feudalism or plantation slavery in widely separated societies. The broader the scope of the enquiry, the greater the need for theory which does not simply alert the historian to fresh evidence, but which actually attempts to *explain* the process or pattern in question. Marxist historiography, if it has done nothing else, has at least brought some of the 'big questions' of history more insistently to the centre of the scholarly arena, and has served to expose to scrutiny the unconscious models which so often inform the work of historians most resolute in their rejection of theory.

The conscious application of theory by historians to these broad questions is still in its infancy. It has given rise to a great deal of reductionist history by second-rate scholars anxious to prove their theoretical credentials. But in the hands of the best historians – and it is by their efforts that the enterprise should surely be judged – the awareness of context and the command of the sources ensure a proper relationship between theory and evidence. As Thompson puts it, historical understanding advances by means of 'a delicate equilibrium between the synthesising and the empiric modes, a quarrel between the model and the actuality'.[47] It is to be expected that, submitted to this discipline, theories should be tried and found wanting, but that is no reason for renouncing the use of theory. The business of historians is to apply theory, to refine it, and to develop new theory, always in the light of the evidence most broadly conceived. And they do so not in pursuit of the ultimate theory or 'law' which will 'solve' this or that problem of explanation, but because without theory they cannot come to grips with the really significant questions in history at all.

NOTES

1. J. B. Bury, 'The science of history', 1902, reprinted in Fritz Stern (ed.) *The Varieties of History*, 2nd edn. Macmillan, 1970, p. 223.
2. These issues are lucidly expounded in Alan Ryan, 'Is the study of society a science?', in David Potter *et al.* (eds.) *Society and the Social Sciences*, Routledge & Kegan Paul, 1981.
3. See Emmanuel Le Roy Ladurie, *The Mind and the Method of the Historian*, Harvester, 1981, Ch. 1.
4. Some such theory evidently underlies much of G. R. Elton's work, and also the 'high politics' school of historiography, discussed above, pp. 75–6.

5.   A major exception is E. H. Carr, *What is History?*, Penguin, 1964.
6.   Peter Mathias, 'Living with the neighbours: the role of economic history', 1970, reprinted in N. B. Harte, (ed.) *The Study of Economic History*, Cass, 1971, p. 380.
7.   For this view, see Jacques Barzun, *Clio and the Doctors*, Chicago University Press, 1974.
8.   Aileen S. Kraditor, 'American radical historians on their heritage', *Past and Present*, LVI, 1972, p. 137.
9.   Ibid., p. 137.
10. Paul K. Conkin, 'Intellectual history', in Charles F. Delzell (ed.), *The Future of History*, Vanderbilt University Press, 1977, pp. 129–30.
11. David Thomson, *The Aims of History*, Thames & Hudson, 1969, p. 105.
12. Isaiah Berlin, 'Historical inevitability', 1954, reprinted in Patrick Gardiner (ed.) *The Philosophy of History*, Oxford University Press, 1974.
13. Comments in this vein recur in Taylor's *Bismarck*, Hamish Hamilton, 1955, and *The Origins of the Second World War*, Penguin, 1964.
14. G. R. Elton, *The Practice of History*, Fontana, 1969, pp. 55–56.
15. M. M. Postan, *Fact and Relevance*, Cambridge University Press, 1971, p. 16.
16. E. E. Evans-Pritchard, 'Anthropology and history', 1961, reprinted in his *Essays in Social Anthropology*, Faber, 1962, p. 49.
17. Philip Abrams, *Historical Sociology*, Open Books, 1982, pp. 2–3.
18. See the criticism of Gareth Stedman Jones, 'From historical sociology to theoretical history', *British Journal of Sociology*, XXVII, 1976, pp. 295–305, and Tony Judt, 'A clown in regal purple: social history and the historians', *History Workshop Journal*, VII, 1979, pp. 66–94.
19. Karl Marx, *A Contribution to the Critique of Political Economy*, Lawrence & Wishart, 1971, pp. 20–21.
20. This interpretation is convincingly argued in Melvin Rader, *Marx's Interpretation of History*, Oxford University Press, 1979. For a contrary view, see G. A. Cohen, *Karl Marx's Theory of History: A Defence*, Oxford University Press, 1978.
21. Fernand Braudel, 'History and the social sciences: the *longue durée*', 1958, reprinted in his *On History*, Weidenfeld & Nicolson, 1980, p. 51.
22. Engels to J. Bloch, 21 September 1890, reprinted in Karl Marx and Friedrich Engels, *Basic Writings on Politics and Philosophy*, ed. L. S. Feuer, Fontana, 1969, pp. 436–7.
23. Karl Marx, *Pre-Capitalist Economic Formations*, Lawrence & Wishart, 1964, especially Introduction by E. J. Hobsbawm.
24. Marx to the editorial board of *Otechestvennive Zapiski*, November 1877, reprinted in Marx and Engels, *Basic Writings*, p. 478.
25. Marx, *Contribution*, p. 21.
26. Marx, 'The eighteenth Brumaire of Louis Bonaparte', 1852, reprinted in Marx and Engels, *Basic Writings*, p. 360.
27. Engels to C. Schmidt, 5 August 1890, reprinted in Marx and Engels, *Basic Writings*, p. 436.
28. Marx and Engels, 'The German ideology', 1846, in *Basic Writings*, p. 289.

29. Marx, *Contribution*, p. 21.
30. J.H. Clapham, 'The study of economic history', 1929, reprinted in Harte, *Study of Economic History*, pp. 64–65.
31. John Barber, *Soviet Historians in Crisis, 1928–30*, Macmillan, 1981.
32. Eric Hobsbawm, 'The Historians' Group of the Communist Party', in Maurice Cornforth (ed.) *Rebels and their Causes*, Lawrence and Wishart, 1978, p. 39.
33. See his *Age of Revolution*, Weidenfeld and Nicolson, 1962, and his *Age of Capital*, Weidenfeld & Nicolson, 1976.
34. Christopher Hill, *The English Revolution 1640*, 3rd edn, Lawrence & Wishart, 1955, p. 43.
35. E. P. Thompson, *The Making of the English Working Class*, Penguin, 1968, p. 9.
36. See Richard Johnson, 'Thompson, Genovese and socialist–humanist history', *History Workshop Journal*, VI, 1978, pp. 79–100, and Perry Anderson, *Arguments within English Marxism*, Verso, 1980.
37. E. P. Thompson, *The Poverty of Theory*, Merlin Press, 1978, especially pp. 110–19.
38. Ibid., p. 88.
39. Christopher Hill, *The World Turned Upside Down*, Penguin, 1975, p. 14.
40. Ibid., p. 386.
41. Thompson, *Making*, p. 13.
42. Marx, *Contribution*, p. 21.
43. Barry Hindess and Paul Q. Hirst, *Pre-Capitalist Modes of Production*, Routledge & Kegan Paul, 1975, pp. 308–13.
44. The classic refutation is Thompson, *Poverty of Theory*. For a more succinct statement, see Raphael Samuel, 'History and theory', in R. Samuel (ed.) *People's History and Socialist Theory*, Routledge & Kegan Paul, 1981, pp. xl–lii.
45. Compare Hill, *English Revolution*, with his *World Turned Upside Down*, separated by over thirty years.
46. H. R. Trevor-Roper, 'History: professional and lay', 1957, reprinted in H. L. Lloyd-Jones, V. Pearl and B. Worden (eds.) *History and Imagination*, Duckworth, 1981, p. 13.
47. Thompson, *Poverty of Theory*, p. 78.

Chapter 9

HISTORY BY NUMBERS

The revival of interest in theory which was discussed in the last chapter represents only one of the new trends in historical scholarship during the past twenty-five years – and one which, for all its brilliance, has engaged only a minority of historians. A far greater number has probably been actively involved in the other main development of the period – the attempt on several fronts to extend the technical resources of the discipline – to explore new types of source and to test new ways of exploiting familiar materials. One innovation, psycho-history, has already been briefly assessed (see above, pp. 73–4). In this chapter and the next I describe two approaches whose contribution is much more substantial and much less open to question. Both of them reflect the influence of the social sciences, but in each case historians have had to scrutinize very carefully the terms on which these innovative techniques should be practised.

I

The influence of quantitative history has been more pervasive than any other new approach. Almost no branch of historical research has been unaffected, and in the case of economic and social history something approaching a transformation has taken place. Two reasons account for this development. In the first place, the fundamental shift in emphasis from the individual to the mass which occurred earlier in this century (see Ch. 5) has major quantitative implications. For as long as historians concentrated on the doings of the great, they hardly needed to count. But once they became seriously interested in economic growth, social change and the history of entire communities, questions of number and proportion assumed a critical importance. Economic and social historians who turned for guidance to the social sciences had to face the fact that the quantitative element in both economics and sociology was pronounced. If historians proposed to deal with the same sort of questions as economists and sociologists, they could hardly avoid using – or at least testing – their methods. The second reason is technological. During the 1960s the computer came of age: it became cheaper and more accessible, while both the kind of data it could handle and the operations it could carry out were rapidly diversified, in ways which were well suited to the requirements of historical research. As a result a whole range of quantitative exercises which would have defied unaided human effort became practicable for the first time.

Quantitative history is founded on the conviction that in making quantitative statements historians should take the trouble to count rather than content themselves with impressionistic estimates. The Atlantic slave trade affords a good example of the difference which this can make. Until recently historians had assumed that the number of Africans shipped to the New World between the fifteenth and the nineteenth centuries totalled somewhere between fifteen and twenty million. This figure was based on little more than the guesswork of nineteenth-century writers, many of them prominent in the campaign to abolish the slave trade. In his quantitative study, *The Atlantic Slave Trade: A Census* (1969), Philip Curtin concluded that the number had been markedly exaggerated. By first critically evaluating and then adding together the figures available for particular periods and areas of the trade, he showed that the total was most unlikely to have been more than ten and a half million or less than eight million. This adjustment has no bearing on the moral outrage of posterity: whatever the total, it still represents an appalling blot on the record of Western civilization. But Curtin's figures provide for the first time a solid basis for considering the effects of the trade on the societies of tropical Africa and those of the Americas.[1]

In the course of their work historians make quantitative statements more frequently than might at first be supposed. Obviously a question such as 'what was Charles I's revenue in 1642?' or 'how large was the Liberal vote in the general election of 1906?' invites an answer as numerically precise as the sources will allow, and the reader of a reputable secondary work would expect nothing less. But many of the broader generalizations which historians habitually make are by implication quantitative also – for example, 'the British working class was literate by 1914' or 'women married late in early modern England'. A statement of this kind may echo the observation of a thoughtful contemporary, or it may arise from a comparison of a number of well authenticated examples. But how can we tell whether the contemporary was right, or that the examples cited are typical? Only a quantitative analysis can put these statements beyond reasonable doubt, by revealing the incidence of literacy and the range and frequency of the ages at which women actually married. Until quite recently most historians were reluctant to accept this argument. In the 1940s G. M. Trevelyan described the evidential base of his subject in these terms:

> The generalizations which are the stock-in-trade of the social historian must necessarily be based on a small number of particular instances, which are assumed to be typical, but which cannot be the whole of the complicated truth.[2]

The problem with this method is that the particular instances can all too easily be selected to confirm what the historian expected to find, and conviction may be lent to unwarrantable assumptions. Today the findings of the 'qualitative' historians such as Trevelyan are being increasingly modified or refined by the quantitative analysis of data systematically assembled to reflect an entire society. In this way not only the main trend is revealed but also the variations and exceptions which highlight the distinctive experience of a particular locality or group. Thus Curtin's work on the slave trade was important not only for establishing a total, but also for quantifying the concentration of the trade in the eighteenth century and the exceptional losses sustained by Angola and the Niger Delta region as compared with the other catchment areas. Finally, at its most ambitious, quantitative history seeks to elucidate an entire historical process by measuring and comparing all the relevant factors: why did the population of England increase so dramatically during the eighteenth century? What effects did the construction of railways in the mid-nineteenth century have on the development of the American economy? At this point, quantitative history stakes its claim to be not simply an ancillary technique, but to take over the centre ground of historical enquiry.

During the past twenty-five years an immense scholarly effort has been invested in quantitative research, and increasingly sophisticated statistical techniques have been applied. The findings are often presented in a highly technical and inaccessible manner, as will be clear from a glance at any recent volume of the *Economic History Review* or the *Journal of Economic History*. Undoubtedly this poses a problem for non-quantitative historians who are reluctant to take these findings on trust and yet are uncomfortably aware of the authority which is attached to quantitative statements of all kinds today. The call which is periodically made that all historians should have some instruction in statistics is scarcely realistic. But no specialized knowledge is required to understand where quantitative historians get their figures from, or in broad terms the uses to which they can be put. A non-technical discussion of these issues is sufficient to indicate both the strengths and the weaknesses of the quantitative approach – what it can achieve and what it cannot.

II

The field in which a quantitative approach is most essential and where arguably it has made its greatest contribution is *demographic history*. Demography without numbers is an absurdity, so in this area the quantitative historian can fairly claim to be indispensable. Demographic history involves a great deal more than merely working out the size of a given population in the past – difficult though even that can be in the absence of reliable census data. More significant than the total is the breakdown in terms of age, gender and household size. Calculations of this kind may reveal the ratio of producers to dependants, the proportion of households with living-in servants, and other indicators of importance to the economic and social historian. The most challenging task facing the demographic historian is to determine the causes of population change over time – or the lack of it. Here the first step is to reconstruct the birth-rate, the marriage-rate and the death-rate. Each of these 'vital' rates is in turn influenced by many different factors which lend themselves to quantification with greater or lesser ease – the incidence of contraception and abortion, the age of marriage, the illegitimacy rate, the impact of famines and epidemics, and so on. For many, the attraction of this kind of enquiry is that it uncovers patterns which relate to the whole of society, rather than just that segment of it illuminated by literary sources. In the case of pre-industrial societies which lived so much closer to the margin of subsistence than our own, it can be argued that demography was *the* determinant of social and economic life. On these grounds demographic history is central to the kind of 'total history' written by the *Annales* school with its primary interest in the early modern period.[3]

Demographic history mainly depends on two types of source. The first lists all the members of a country or community alive at any one time. This of course is the main function of the modern census, which was invented in the Scandinavian countries in the mid-eighteenth century. In Britain a census of the whole population has been taken at ten-yearly intervals since 1801, and it is generally conceded that after 1841 (when the name of each individual was noted for the first time) errors in the totals are statistically insignificant. Other listings survive from earlier periods – tax returns, returns of church communicants, declarations of political loyalty and the like. But, though comprehensive in intent, these were seldom so in practice, and the margin of error is very uncertain and inconsistent. One consequence of the relatively recent origin of census-taking is that it has proved extraordinarily difficult to establish the relationship between demographic change and the onset of industrialization in late eighteenth-century Britain. This is where the second type of source comes in – the recording in sequence of the 'vital' events in a given locality. For English history the most important source is the parish registers kept by Anglican incumbents who from 1538 were required by law to record all baptisms, marriages and burials in their parishes; the system persisted until the beginning of civil registration in 1837. From a sample of parish registers E. A. Wrigley and R. S. Schofield have calculated national rates of births, marriages and deaths, and have used these to project the total population of England back from 1801 as far as the mid-sixteenth century. As a result they are able to pinpoint small variations in the growth rate much more precisely than before, and to demonstrate the preponderant influence which changes in the marriage-rate had on the long-term rate of population growth.[4]

Wrigley and Schofield's work is an example of *aggregative* analysis, i.e. the interpretation of totals. But these same authors have applied a quite different approach to the parish registers which arises from the fact that every entry refers to named persons. The demographic history of a parish can therefore be reconstructed in terms of the growth and decline of its constituent families – or at any rate those that remained confined to a single parish. This technique, known as family reconstitution, is an example of *nominative* analysis, i.e. analysis through names rather than totals. It is immensely time-consuming: to reconstitute one parish of 1,000 persons over a period of three centuries requires about 1,500 hours, or a year's undistracted work.[5] But it has the advantage of showing patterns of fertility and mortality in much greater detail, and in a specific economic and social context. The knowledge that the birth-rate was rising or the death-rate declining in itself adds little to our understanding of the *causes* of population change; a good family reconstitution study may, however, show whether a rising birth-rate was due, for example, to a lowering of the age of first marriage among women, or to a decline in the incidence of lifelong spinsterhood. These findings can in turn be interpreted with reference to the conditions prevailing in the areas concerned.[6]

The second field in which quantitative methods have proved important is the history of *social structure*. There is in fact a close connection between this field and demographic history, because the same sources loom large in both. Any source which lists an entire population or records its 'vital' events offers, at least potentially, the possibility of classifying that population into social groups. This is most easily achieved in the case of groups defined by age or gender. But historians are becoming increasingly resourceful in abstracting other aspects of social structure from demographic data. The changing size and structure of the household is a case in point. The evidence of both pre-census listings and family reconstitution has effectively undermined the traditional notion that pre-industrial society in western Europe was characterized by large, complex households of the extended family type.[7] From the mid-nineteenth century the ever-increasing scope and precision of the questions asked in the census means that a whole range of social issues is opened up to quantitative analysis – occupation, status, religious affiliation, rural migration to the towns, and so on.[8] The 'new urban history' in the United States is largely based on the premise that the changing social structure of a city can be reconstructed by analysing the manuscript schedules of the US census in conjunction with other nominative data (notably tax records, city directories and registers of births, marriages and deaths).[9]

It may seem surprising that quantitative methods have much relevance to the third field to be considered here, namely *political history*. The traditional concern of the political historian is, after all, with 'unique' events and with the actions and motives of individual statesmen. But once the field of enquiry is broadened to include the political system as a whole, quantitative history comes into its own. This is most evident in the realm of electoral behaviour. Just as psephology – the study of present-day elections – is largely a matter of juggling with numbers, so too the study of elections in the past demands a quantitative approach. Admittedly, for any period up to the development of opinion polls in the 1950s the quantification of political attitudes presents major problems (and it can be argued that it still does). But the historian has other advantages which are denied to the modern psephologist. Prior to the Ballot Act of 1872 parliamentary elections in Britain were conducted in public and votes were individually recorded. Where registers of votes can be analysed in conjunction with other nominative data on income, status or religion, the way is open to firmer conclusions about the basis of party affiliation in nineteenth-century Britain.[10]

Quantitative techniques have also been usefully applied to one other concern of political historians – the study of political elites. It is too easy to allow our picture of an elite – as of any social group – to be determined by a handful of well-known case-histories. But in the case of a precisely defined elite such as the House of Commons, the salient biographical details of the entire membership can be assembled (see above, p. 75). This was Namier's most important contribution to historical method. Subsequent scholars have merely subjected collective biography to more rigorous quantitative analysis. Quantitative historians have been rather more original in their studies of the political behaviour – as opposed to the background – of legislative bodies. Most modern legislatures keep a record of votes taken: the division lists of the House of Commons extend back in an unbroken sequence to 1836. These can be tabulated according to the issues and then set against the findings of collective biography to clarify the basis of support for and opposition to particular policies. Studies of this kind have proliferated in America as part of the much-vaunted 'new political history'.[11]

Lastly, quantitative methods have had a decisive impact on *economic history*. The reasons are obvious enough. Economics – like demography – is a highly quantitative discipline. The principal elements in an economic system – prices, incomes, production, investment, trade and credit – all lend themselves to precise measurement; indeed, they demand it if the workings of the system are to be clearly understood. From the beginning of economic history as a distinct specialism in the late nineteenth century, economic historians collected quantitative economic data, usually as one aspect of whatever research they were engaged on. It is only in the last thirty years or so, however, that historians have tackled the problem of constructing extended statistical sequences, often from varied and imperfect sources, as a means of illuminating long-term economic trends. B. R. Mitchell and Phyllis Deane's *Abstract of British Historical Statistics* (1962) represents the most systematic attempt to do this for Britain so far. But it is some of the French quantitative historians who have pressed this approach furthest: the exponents of 'serial history' (*l'histoire serielle*) aim to build up extended sequences of prices, crop yields, rents and incomes which together will enable them to construct a model for France's development during the early modern period – and ultimately Europe's as well.[12] The claims of the 'new economic history' (or 'cliometrics') in the United States are, if anything, greater, and are critically evaluated in the fifth section of this chapter.

III

It is sometimes imagined that the application of quantitative methods on a large scale displaces the traditional skills of the historian and calls for an entirely new breed of scholar. Nothing could be further from the truth. Statistical know-how can only be effective if it is treated as an *addition* to the historian's tool-kit, and subject to the normal controls of historical method. Given the special authority which figures carry in our numerate society, the obligation to subject quantitative data to tests of reliability is at least as great as in the case of literary sources. And once the figures have been verified, their interpretation and their application to the solution of specific historical problems require the same qualities of judgement and flair as any other kind of evidence. Each of these two stages presents its own problems.

A historian is saved an immense amount of work if he or she is lucky enough to find a set of ready-made statistics – say a table of imports and exports or a sequence of census reports. Yet the reliability of such sources must never be taken for granted. We need to know exactly how the figures were put together. Were the returns made by the man-on-the-spot distorted by his own self-interest – like the tax-collector who under-stated his takings and pocketed the difference? Were the figures conjured out of thin air by a desk-bound official, or totted up by a subordinate who was not competent in arithmetic? Both these possibilities arise in the case of the impressive-looking statistics published by British colonial administrations in Africa which were often based on returns made by poorly educated and underpaid chiefs. How much scope was there for errors of copying as the figures were passed on from one level of the bureaucracy to the next? Could the same item have been counted twice by different officials? Where statistics were compiled from questionaires, as in social surveys or the census, we need to know the form in which the questions were put in order to determine the scope for confusion on the part of the respondents, and we have to consider whether the questions – on income or age, for example – were likely to elicit frank answers. Only an investigation of the circumstances of compilation, using the conventional skills of the historian, can provide the answer to these questions.

Often what interests historians is less a single set of figures than a sequence over time which enables them to plot a trend. The figures must accordingly be tested not only for their reliability but for their *comparability*. However accurate the individual totals in such a sequence may be, they can only be regarded as a statistical sequence if they are strictly comparable – if, that is, they are measuring the same variable. It needs only a slight discrepancy in the basis of assessment to render comparisons null and void. A classification which seems clear and consistent enough on paper may be applied differently over time, or between one place and another, which is one reason why comparative criminal statistics have to be treated so cautiously. In the case of the English census, the increasing refinement of the occupational schedule in every count since 1841 means that it is difficult to quantify the growth and decline of specific occupations. Even the most seemingly straightforward statistical sequences may conceal pitfalls of this kind. Comprehensive commercial statistics for England date back to 1696, when the post of Inspector-General of Imports and Exports was created. But because the official table of values drawn up by the first Inspector-General was applied almost without modification until the end of the eighteenth century, during which time some prices rose while others fell, the figures as they stand cannot be used to calculate the changing balance of trade.[13] Nor do modern statistical tables necessarily pass the test of comparability. Consider, for example, the official cost-of-living index which measures the cost of a typical 'shopping-bag' against the current wage-rate. In Britain the index, begun in 1914, ought to provide a reliable picture of the declining standard of living during the Depression of the 1930s. But during the inter-war period the price side of the index continued to be based on the same 'shopping-bag', even though changing patterns of consumption meant that the weighting given to the various items (fresh vegetables, meat, clothing, etc.) in 1914 no longer corresponded with the actual make-up of the average family budget.[14]

Most quantitative history, however, is not based on ready-made statistics. It was only in the late seventeenth century that the advantages of a statistical approach to public issues began to be canvassed, only during the nineteenth century that the state acquired the resources of manpower and money to undertake such work, and only in the present century that statistical information has been gathered in a really comprehensive way by both government and private bodies. For most of the questions that interest historians, the likelihood is that the figures will have to be laboriously constructed from the relevant surviving materials. To construct quantitative data in such a way that valid statistical inferences can be drawn from them is no easy matter. The issues of reliability and comparability will be posed, not once, but many times over as the historian seeks out data from varied and scattered source materials. The classification of the data in tabular form now becomes the task of the historian; and the criteria on which that classification is based raise questions of historical judgement rather than statistical method.

Above all, the construction of statistics raises acute problems of selection. There are, it is true, quantitative enquiries whose scope is so narrowly defined that all the relevant data can be assembled: W. O. Aydelotte's quantitative collective biography of all the members who sat in the Parliament of 1841–47 (the period of Sir Robert Peel's premiership leading to the split in the Tory Party over the Corn Laws) is a case in point.[15] But, as we have seen, one of the main attractions of the quantitative approach is the opportunity it offers for making statements not just about small elites, but about whole classes or societies over long periods of time. And whereas the vast bureaucracy employed by most modern states can gather comprehensive national statistics with relative ease, no historian, however well endowed with research assistants and computer time, can hope to survey *all* the primary sources needed for a quantitative study of, say, farm-size in Tudor England or personal incomes in early Victorian Britain. Modern statisticians have developed reliable techniques for taking a random sample, that is, one in which every element making up the whole has an equal chance of being included in the sample. In historical research it is often not practicable to apply these techniques to the letter, but the researcher must at least ensure that every variable is fairly represented in the sample. In a recently completed project the enumerators' returns for the 1851 Census were prepared for computer analysis in order to provide answers to a number of questions about social and economic structure which fell outside the scope of the report on the census published at the time; a 2 per cent sample was chosen which comprised the total population of one in every fifteen enumeration districts (945 in all). All the census information about these 415,000 individuals was fed into the computer, with the result that historians can now get a much clearer idea about variations in education, land tenure, household composition, the size of the labour force in different businesses, and many other issues.[16]

For the historian of periods earlier than the nineteenth century, the problem of selection is likely to have been partly or wholly solved by the ravages of time. But the residue that survives is still a sample of the original range of records, and it is important to recognize that it is often anything but a random sample. Some types of record are more likely to survive than others because their owners had a greater interest in their survival or better facilities for preserving them, for reasons which may introduce a manifest bias into the sample. Thus surviving business records are nearly always weighted in favour of the successful long-lasting firm, at the expense of smaller businesses which were unable to weather a crisis. Lawrence Stone was dogged by a problem of this kind in his study of the English aristocracy between 1558 and 1641. Although he had some information on all of the 382 individuals who held titles at that period, the proportion of noble families whose private papers survive in abundance never rose above one-third, and these families were mostly those of wealthy earls rather than minor barons whose estates were more subject to disintegration or dispersal. Stone was accordingly obliged to make allowances for the fact that many of his findings were drawn from an unrepresentative sample.[17]

IV

Having once established that the figures are reliable, comparable and representative, the historian can set about putting the data to work. Sometimes the figures amount to an unequivocal answer to the question in hand, and all that remains is to devise the best way of presenting them clearly on the printed page – whether by table, graph, histogram, 'cake' or pyramid. Some very elementary processing may be desirable, such as the calculation needed to work out percentages or averages. The findings of economic historians in matters such as exports or production often lend themselves to straightforward exposition, known in the trade as 'descriptive statistics'; an excellent example is the forty-odd pages of tables and charts which appear at the end of E. J. Hobsbawm's economic history of Britain since 1750, *Industry and Empire* (1968). But as historians have extended the application of quantitative methods they have increasingly found that what counts is not so much the explicit meaning of the figures as the inferences that can be drawn from them.

The drawing of such inferences may be essentially a statistical operation. In the case of an extended series of export statistics, for example, the researcher may wish to abstract the long-term trend of growth or decline, the regular fluctuations of slump and boom, and the irregular fluctuations caused by war, plague and the vagaries of government policy; only the sophisticated techniques of time series analysis will make this feasible.[18] Even more complex statistical techniques are employed by Wrigley and Schofield in their backward projection of the English population from the nineteenth to the sixteenth century: there must be few historians who can follow them through that labyrinth. From the historian's point of view, a particularly useful kind of statistical inference is the coefficient of correlation, i.e. the demonstration of a relationship between two variables. It is often important to know whether such a relationship exists and of what type – say between party affiliation and voting behaviour, or between the duration of marriage and the number of offspring. If reliable quantitative data are available for each variable, the relationship can be worked out by statistical means. The computer can be of great assistance in this kind of project. Suppose that, for every one of the five hundred members of a legislature, the researcher had assembled information under twelve headings (which might include age, education, party, constituency, income, occupation, and voting record on six different issues) and wishes to test each of these twelve variables against all the others. The working out by hand of each of these correlations would be an almost impossible task; a correctly programmed computer, on the other hand, would print out the required tables in minutes.[19] The result might be that a hitherto unsuspected correlation was revealed, suggesting a fruitful new line of research. It is important, nevertheless, not to exaggerate the significance of a statistically verified correlation: it does not take account of the possibility of coincidence, nor will it reveal which variable influenced the other; it may be, indeed, that the two variables are determined by a third, as yet unidentified variable. On all these points, historians must fall back on their common sense and their knowledge of the period and its problems.

But most historians who make inferences from quantitative data do not need to use statistics at all; instead they treat the figure as an indicator or 'index' of some other, usually much less tangible phenomenon for which direct quantitative evidence is not available. It is tempting to infer political attitudes from statistics of voting behaviour, or the influence of a book from its sales, or the intensity of religious belief from the returns of Easter communicants, but none of these inferences can be taken for granted, nor does their validity depend on statistical principles. In each case it depends on a historically informed awareness of other factors which may have affected the figures. Were voters open to corruption, or responsive to personalities rather than policies? Was the book bought as an item of conspicuous consumption and put away unread? Can we assume that taking Communion had the same significance for peasant congregations as it did for the clergy who compiled the returns?[20] The application of demographic data to family history has proved to be a minefield. To take just one example, it cannot be assumed without a great deal of supporting qualitative evidence that a narrow age-gap between husband and wife (as was already the case in early modern England) indicates a more affectionate and companionable marital relationship.[21] Thus, at the point where numerical data touch on a major historical question, quantitative methods in themselves often resolve nothing. As three leading proponents of quantitative history have conceded:

> Statistical manipulations merely rearrange the evidence; they do not, except on an elementary level, answer general questions, and the bearing of the findings upon the larger problems of interpretation in which historians are interested is a matter, not of arithmetic, but of logic and persuasion.[22]

Statistics may serve to reveal or clarify a particular tendency; but how we *interpret* that tendency – the significance we attach to it and the causes we adduce for it – is a matter for seasoned historical judgement, in which the historian trained exclusively in quantitative methods would be woefully deficient.

V

There is, however, one quantitative approach to history which claims to have transcended these limitations to some extent, and which has as a result generated heated controversy. Its first champions during the 1960s in the USA coined the word 'cliometrics' to distinguish their approach, and the term is now widely understood – although those who reserve judgement on its claims prefer to retain the inverted commas. 'Cliometrics' proceeds on the assumption that certain areas of human behaviour are best understood as a system in which both the variables and the relationship between them can be quantified; when the value of one variable changes, the effect which this has on the system as a whole can be calculated. The field of human behaviour which is most suited to this approach is economics. In fact 'cliometrics' is simply a fancy label for what is often called 'the new economic history'. It draws its inspiration from econometrics – that is, the techniques that statisticians have evolved to analyse economies of the present and to predict their future development. In proceeding from known to unknown variables the economist applies a theory of the relationship between the elements in an economic system (capital, wages, prices, etc.); when an economic theory is expressed in mathematical terms, it is known as a *model*. Econometrists are concerned to test and apply models by statistical means. For example, in input–output analysis a model is employed in order to calculate what inputs an economy (or one sector within it) requires to achieve a given production target.

For those historians with the necessary training in statistics, it is easy to see the appeal of econometric methods. They hold out the prospect of filling in some of the gaps in our existing historical knowledge which are due to the patchiness of firm quantitative data about the past. And, if carried to their logical limits, they allow historians to assess the economic effect of a given policy or innovation by measuring it against what *would* have happened if the policy had not been implemented or the innovation had proved stillborn: the system can be reconstructed to accommodate a different value for one or more variables. That at least is what the most advanced 'cliometricians' would claim. In *Railroads and Economic Growth* (1964), to take the most celebrated case, R. W. Fogel sought to measure the contribution which nineteenth-century railway construction made to the US economy by constructing a hypothetical (or 'counterfactual') model of what the American economy would have been like in 1890 if no railways had been built. He concluded that, even supposing no additional canals or roads were built, Gross National Product would only have been 3.1 per cent lower, and that 76 per cent of the land actually farmed in 1890 would still have been farmed. Previously most historians – including Fogel himself – had believed that the railways had had a much more dynamic effect on the American economy. Fogel maintained that counterfactual propositions are implicit in many historical judgements, and that what he had done was to expose this particular assumption as false by subjecting it to rigorous statistical testing.[23]

There are, however, several reasons why the work of the 'cliometricians' should be used with caution. To those historians who maintain that research questions should emerge from immersion in the widest possible range of primary sources, 'cliometric' history is inadmissible because its point of departure is always a clearly defined problem formulated in theoretical terms. But, as I argued in Chapter 8, there is no reason in principle why historians should not turn to theory in order to expose fresh problems or bring a new perspective to bear on familiar ones. The difficulty, of course, is that recourse to theory does not of itself confer authority on the findings; an inappropriate theory will naturally produce distorted results. This is plainly a relevant consideration in the case of the 'new economic history' because there are at least three well-established economic theories to choose from – the neo-classical, the Marxist and the Keynesian. But the objections to economic theory go farther than this. To the historian they are all suspect because they start from the premise that human beings in seeking to fulfil their material needs are governed by motives of a 'rational' profit-maximizing, cost-cutting kind. Yet often this is exactly what has to be demonstrated, not assumed: consumers may be deterred from buying in the cheapest market by calls to 'buy British' or to shun Jewish businesses; employers may pay wages over the odds or improve working conditions out of consideration for a paternalist self-image. An economc theory whch explains economic behaviour in 'ideal' conditions is unlikely to do so when confronted by the social and cultural factors which obtain in a historically specific situation, and historians who insist on using such a theory on the grounds that they are interested in purely economic problems are afflicted by a particularly disabling form of 'tunnel vision' (see p. 89).

The second objection applies to those econometric studies which, like Fogel's railway study, encompass an entire economy. It is humanly impossible to construct a model which takes account of every variable; indeed, models are useful precisely because they *simplify* reality. What can reasonably be demanded of a model is that it includes every *significant* variable. But in the case of a national economy even this requirement is in practice very difficult to fulfil, and just which variables are selected for inclusion becomes a crucial question. Fogel himself has been criticized for failing to include in his model the effects of railway construction on the mobility of the work-force and on technical advances in other sectors of the economy. Equally, once one factor (railway) is removed from the model for the purposes of counterfactual analysis it is virtually impossible to take account of all the consequent changes, direct and indirect, in the other variables; they cannot all be measured, and it remains an open question whether Fogel measured the most significant ones.[24]

Fogel's work also raises in an acute form the third objection to 'cliometrics' – that it leans too heavily on unverifiable inferences. Statistics itself is no more than a technique for making inferences from quantitative data, but most of them – like the coefficient of correlation and the time series analysis mentioned earlier – are mathematical inferences which can be demonstrated to follow from the data. The problem with 'cliometrics' is that too many of its inferences are not of this kind: they are valid only if the model on which they are founded is valid. And the danger is that the historian, instead of systematically testing the theory against the data to see if it works, takes the theory as given and uses it to construct new quantitative data. Each stage in the chain of reasoning whereby unknown quantities are constructed out of known quantities may be riddled with theoretical assumptions. This objection is clearest in the case of counterfactual models, such as Fogel's hypothetical American economy of 1890, which are by definition unverifiable; but it applies also to less virtuoso performances such as the calculation of overall levels of investment from miles of main railway-line constructed. It is easy for the unwary reader to forget that the calculations of the 'cliometricians' are no firmer than the theories which underpin them.[25]

The last point, which has been particularly emphasized by 'traditionalist' critics, is that 'cliometric' models tend to introduce serious, if unintended bias into the selection of sources. This is because, as mathematical models, they can take account only of numerical data. Non-quantifiable variables are automatically excluded, and the result may be a badly skewed interpretation. This point is not always squarely faced by advocates of 'cliometric' history. Thus Roderick Floud writes:

> The 'new' economic historian concentrates on measurable economic phenomena, and uses economic theory linking those phenomena, specifically because he wishes to cut through the complexity of history and to concentrate on those phenomena which best explain the events he is studying.[26]

It is precisely this equation of the measurable with the most significant phenomena which must be questioned. Some 'cliometricians' have preferred the problematical inferences which they make from quantitative data to the clear and emphatic evidence provided by nonquantitative sources. In their highly controversial book, *Time on the Cross* (1974), R. W. Fogel and S. L. Engerman abstracted statistical data from probate records, plantation records and census schedules which revealed the white planters of the American South in the midnineteenth century as a 'rational' and humane capitalist class, and their slaves as a prosperous and well-treated work-force. By ignoring the mass of 'qualitative' evidence in personal testimonies and correspondence, they exposed themselves to a devastating counter-attack from historians able to demonstrate the importance of aristocratic, 'precapitalist' values among the planters and the violence to which their slaves were subjected.[27] As this example shows, the non-quantifiable factors are often those same cultural and social factors which are excluded from the model as 'irrational'.

There are doubtless many historians who regard the public furore over *Time on the Cross* as a fitting nemesis for the 'cliometric' school as a whole. The book certainly illustrates the dangers of unwarranted inference and of bias in the choice of sources. But *Time on the Cross* is not typical. The 'cliometric' approach has made a real contribution to our understanding of a number of technical problems in economic history (which of course have not hit the headlines). What the record so far suggests is that the range of such problems is limited, and that in attempting to answer the really significant questions in economic history 'cliometrics' has highlighted particular factors of a formal kind rather than furnished comprehensive interpretations.

VI

During the 1960s quantitative history was a highly contentious issue. Some of the early proponents of the new approach got 'high' on figures, becoming 'statistical junkies' (to quote Lawrence Stone).[28] There was a certain presumption about their appropriation of labels such as 'the new political history', 'the new urban history' and 'the new economic history'. For a time history's scientific status was affirmed more unequivocally than at any time since the turn of the century; in 1966 a leading American quantitative historian was rash enough to predict that by 1984 the scientific study of the past would have reached the point when historians could set their sights on the discovery of general laws of human behaviour.[29] Comparable hostages to fortune were given by the 'cliometricians'. As a result, some of the traditionalists in the profession were provoked into making equally extreme rebuttals: in 1963 the President of the American Historical Association urged his colleagues not to 'worship at the shrine of that Bitch-goddess QUANTIFICATION' (sic).[30] Twenty years later the claims advanced for quantitative history are more modest, other historians feel less threatened, and a more dispassionate assessment is possible.

One undeniable achievement of the quantitative historians is to have increased the precision of many factual statements about the past, especially statements about people in the mass. In a great many fields impressionistic estimates have given place to rigorously controlled calculation which has revealed the overall trend, as well as the extent of variations and discrepancies within it. This represents clear gain. Beyond this, the gathering of large bodies of quantitative data on related issues has enabled historians to be much more confident about many of their descriptive generalizations. It is not true, as has sometimes been claimed,[31] that the result has simply been to re-state the obvious. A number of generalizations which were formerly taken for granted have been fatally undermined. Thus it seems to be established beyond reasonable doubt that the English household in the seventeenth and eighteenth centuries did not typically take the form of an extended family, and that slavery in the southern states of the USA had not ceased to be profitable to the owners on the eve of the Civil War (this much of Fogel and Engerman's thesis is sound). If these generalizations are cast in a negative rather than a positive form, this is because the effect of assembling comprehensive figures is often to highlight a diversity, or degree of variation from the norm, which confounds absolute pronouncements of any kind. Here too, the disposal of simplistic notions about the past represent a significant advance in knowledge.

It is sometimes argued that the preoccupation with aggregates and trends, by emphasizing the common factors in mass behaviour at the expense of the individual and the exceptional, has a 'dehumanizing' effect on history. Elton, for example, has detected in much of the 'new political history' an assumption that voting behaviour is a conditioned reflex, determined by economic and social conditions,[32] and it is certainly true that questions of motive may appear to be pre-judged by demonstrating a correlation between, say, the business interests of MPs and their record in the division lobbies. This argument needs to be considered in conjunction with another related objection – that quantitative history distorts our view of the past by directing attention to those sources which readily respond to statistical analysis at the expense of those which do not; as a result important historical questions may be posed in terms which exclude a total view. The debate which raged in the 1960s over the standard of living of the British working class during the Industrial Revolution brought out this difficulty well: critics of the quantitative approach pointed out that unquantifiable indicators of the quality of life were at least as significant as wage-rates and price-levels.[33]

But neither of these objections can stand unless it is proposed that legitimate historical enquiry be henceforth confined to those areas which can be illuminated by a quantitative approach. Although some zealots, with their talk of 'a revolution in historiographical consciousness', have come very close to adopting this position,[34] the majority of quantitative historians would not wish to claim exclusive rights. They would probably agree with Aydelotte, Bogue and Fogel when they write of quantitative history:

> What is attempted in this approach is to take more effective advantage of selected parts of the evidence: to seize on those parts of the data that can be handled more strictly, by mathematical means, and to subject them to a more refined analysis . . . Restriction of focus is the price that must be paid for being more sure of one's ground.[35]

The effect of any new and powerful technique is temporarily to put more familiar approaches at a discount. That phase probably already lies in the past. Political historians today are hardly less interested in the actions and motives of individual statesmen than they were before the advent of the 'new political history'. Social historians are supplementing broad quantitative surveys with 'in-depth' studies of particular communities or episodes for which rich documentation survives: the trend is exemplified by the shift in Emmanuel Le Roy Ladurie's work from the quantitative *Peasants of Languedoc* (1966) to his village study, *Montaillou* (1978), which depends for its effect on the evocative power of verbatim personal testimonies.

Underlying the more modest aspirations of quantitative history is a growing recognition that its contribution to historical explanation – as distinct from the verification of historical facts – is marginal. The generalizations yielded by analyses of numerical data tend to be descriptive rather than explanatory. To plot a trend, or to demonstrate a statistical correlation between this trend and another, does not *explain* it. Cause and significance remain matters for the interpretative skill of the historian in command of *all* the sources – not merely those which lend themselves to quantification. In the case of major historical problems, the effect of deploying quantitative techniques has been to clarify a number of relevant issues without 'closing' the question. Thus, after all the quantitative work which has been carried out on the economic position of the English aristocracy and the composition of the royal bureaucracy under Charles I, historians are no nearer a consensus on the origins of the English Revolution of the seventeenth century. The prospect that lies before historians, then, is not the solution of major questions by quantitative means, but new possibilities of synthesis, in which statistical inference is combined with the perceptions of traditional 'qualitative' history. On these more restricted terms the place of quantitative methods in historical enquiry seems assured.

NOTES

1. Curtin's figures are the subject of continuing debate among quantitative historians. See Paul E. Lovejoy, 'The volume of the Atlantic slave trade: a synthesis', *Journal of African History*, XXIII, 1982, pp. 473–501, and J. Inikori (ed.) *Forced Migration*, Hutchinson, 1982.
2. G. M. Trevelyan, *English Social History*, Longman, 1944, p. viii.
3. See, for example, Emmanuel Le Roy Ladurie, *The Peasants of Languedoc*, University of Illinois Press, 1974.
4. E. A. Wrigley and R. S. Schofield, *The Population History of England, 1541–1871*, Arnold, 1981.
5. E. A. Wrigley (ed.) *An Introduction to English Historical Demography*, Weidenfeld & Nicolson, 1966, p. 97.
6. See, for example, David Levine, *Family Formation in an Age of Nascent Capitalism*, Academic Press, 1977, which contains a detailed methodological discussion (pp. 153–74).
7. Peter Laslett (ed.) *Household and Family in Past Time*, Cambridge University Press, 1972.
8. The methodological issues are fully discussed in E. A. Wrigley (ed.) *Nineteenth Century Society*, Cambridge University Press, 1972.
9. See, for example, Leo F. Schnore (ed.) *The New Urban History*, Princeton University Press, 1975.
10. See J. R. Vincent, *Pollbooks: How Victorians Voted*, Cambridge University Press, 1967.
11. Allan G. Bogue, 'The new political history', in Michael Kammen (ed.) *The Past Before Us*, Cornell University Press, 1980. For the application of quantitative methods to British political history, see W. O. Aydelotte,

Quantification in History, Addison Wesley, 1971.

12. The clearest statement in English is Emmanuel Le Roy Ladurie, *The Territory of the Historian*, Harvester, 1979, Ch. 2.

13. G. N. Clark, *Guide to English Commercial Statistics, 1696–1782*, Royal Historical Society, 1938.

14. B. R. Mitchell and Phyllis Deane, *Abstract of British Historical Statistics*, Cambridge University Press, 1962, p. 466. For an account of the problems raised by cost-of-living indexes, see Roderick Floud, *An Introduction to Quantitative Methods for Historians*, 2nd edn, Methuen, 1979, pp. 125–9.

15. W. O. Aydelotte, 'On the business interests of the gentry in the Parliament of 1841–47', in G. Kitson-Clark, *The Making of Victorian England*, Methuen, 1962, and his *Quantification in History*, Ch. 5.

16. For a preliminary account, see Michael Anderson and others, 'The national sample from the 1851 Census of Great Britain', *Urban History Newsletter*, 1977, pp. 55–9.

17. Lawrence Stone, *The Crisis of the Aristocracy, 1558–1641*, Oxford University Press, 1965, p. 130.

18. Floud, *Introduction to Quantitative Methods*, pp. 88–122.

19. My example is adapted from one in Edwart Shorter, *The Historian and the Computer*, Prentice Hall, 1971, pp. 5–8.

20. Peter Burke, *Sociology and History*, Allen & Unwin, 1980, p. 40.

21. For a discussion on this and related issues, see Michael Anderson, *Approaches to the History of the Western Family, 1500–1914*, Macmillan, 1980, pp. 33–8.

22. W. O. Aydelotte, A. G. Bogue and R. W. Fogel (eds.) *The Dimensions of Quantitative Research in History*, Princeton University Press, 1972, pp. 10–11.

23. R. W. Fogel, 'The new economic history: its findings and methods', *Economic History Review*, 2nd series, XIX, 1966, pp. 642–56. For the application of this approach to British economic history, see G. R. Hawke, *Railways and Economic Growth in England and Wales, 1840–1870*, Oxford University Press, 1970.

24. Peter Mathias, 'Economic history: direct and oblique', in Martin Ballard (ed.) *New Movements in the Study and Teaching of History*, Temple Smith, 1970, pp. 83–4, and E. H. Hunt, 'The new economic history', *History*, LIII, 1968, pp. 15–16.

25. John Habakkuk, 'Economic history and economic theory', *Daedalus*, C, 1971, pp. 305–22.

26. Roderick Floud (ed.) *Essays in Quantitative Economic History*, Oxford University Press, 1974, p. 2.

27. See Herbert G. Gutman, *Slavery and the Numbers Game*, University of Illinois Press, 1975, and Paul David and others, *Reckoning with Slavery*, Oxford University Press, 1976.

28. Lawrence Stone, *The Past and the Present*, Routledge & Kegan Paul, 1981, p. 94.

29. Lee Benson, *Toward the Scientific Study of History*, Lippincott, 1972, pp. 98–104.

30. Carl Bridenbaugh, 'The great mutation', *American Historical Review*, LXVIII, 1963, p. 326. For a more extended attack, see Jacques Barzun,

Clio and the Doctors, Chicago University Press, 1974.
31. G. R. Elton, *The Practice of History*, Fontana, 1969, pp. 49–51.
32. G. R. Elton, *Political History*, Allen Lane, 1970, pp. 48–9.
33. For a review of the controversy, see Arthur J. Taylor, (ed.) *The Standard of Living in Britain in the Industrial Revolution*, Methuen, 1975.
34. François Furet, 'Quantitative history', *Daedalus*, C, 1971, p. 160.
35. Aydelotte, Bogue and Fogel, *Dimensions of Quantitative Research*, p. 9.

Chapter 10

HISTORY BY WORD OF MOUTH

The last of the new directions in historical enquiry to be explored in this book is the growing recourse to oral evidence. The previous two chapters reflected the concern of historians to strengthen the explanatory side of their work, whether by the application of theory or by the quantitative analysis of their evidence. Here we return to the location and evaluation of sources – but sources of a kind more familiar to social scientists which require a further broadening of the historian's skills. However, oral sources do not all present the same kind of challenge to the conventionally trained historian. They fall into two distinct categories, with differing implications for their status as historical evidence. The first and more familiar category is oral reminiscence – the first-hand recollections of people interviewed by a historian, usually referred to as *oral history*. Since the late 1960s oral history has been increasingly exploited in Britain and other Western countries, particularly for the light it can shed on recent social history. Then secondly there is *oral tradition*, that is, the narratives and descriptions of people and events in the past which have been handed down by word of mouth over several generations. Although practically extinct in highly industrialized countries, oral tradition is still a living force in those countries where literacy has not yet displaced a predominantly oral culture; since the 1950s it has been studied with growing assurance by historians of Africa.

I

It is only very recently, then, that professional historians have acquired any experience of collecting oral sources. Even today the mainstream of the historical profession remains sceptical and is often not prepared to enter into discussion about the actual merits and drawbacks of oral

research. As recently as 1970, Arthur Marwick's otherwise comprehensive list of primary sources in his *The Nature of History* made no
mention of oral sources.[1] Yet oral sources of both kinds provided the
bulk of the evidence used by those who are now looked back to as the
first historians – Herodotus and Thucydides. The chroniclers and
historians of the Middle Ages were hardly less dependent on oral
testimony; and although written sources grew rapidly in importance
from the Renaissance onwards, the older techniques still survived as a
valued adjunct to documentary research. It was only with the emergence of modern academic history in the nineteenth century that the
use of oral sources was entirely abandoned. The energies of the new
professionals cast in the Rankean mould were taken up by the study of
written documents, on which their claim to technical expertise was
based, and their working lives were largely confined to the library and
the archive.

Ironically, many of the written sources cited by today's historians
were themselves oral in origin. Medieval chroniclers like William of
Malmesbury in the twelfth century incorporated oral traditions as well
as first hand testimonies into their writings. Social surveys and official
commissions of enquiry, which loom so large in the primary sources for
nineteenth-century social history, are full of summarized testimonies
which historians draw on, often with little regard for the selection of
witnesses or the circumstances in which they were interviewed. Yet the
idea that historians might add to the volume of available oral evidence
by conducting interviews themselves continues to arouse misgivings.
The reason is partly that historians are reluctant to see any com-
promise with the principle that contemporaneity is the prime requirement of historical sources (see above pp. 29–30) – and oral sources
have an inescapable element of hindsight about them. But perhaps
there is a more deep-seated aversion to any radical change in the habits
of work required for historical research, and a reluctance to grapple
with the implications of scholars sharing in the creation (and not just
the interpretation) of new evidence.

In the meantime the interview method has become an important
research tool in the social sciences. In social anthropology, which came
to maturity during the 1920s and 1930s, researchers typically adopt the
role of participant-observer. They aim as far as possible to lead the life
of a member of the community under study, and in order to make sense
of their experience engage in constant dialogue with their hosts, including the collection of life-histories. In studying contemporary
Western society, sociologists have tended to become less personally
involved with their subject-matter, but the in-depth interviewing of
respondents has nevertheless been an important source of data alongside the more commonly practised social survey by questionnaire. The
interview techniques of social anthropology and sociology have proved
helpful to historians, though – as we shall see – they have needed to

develop their own distinctive approach to the material recorded.

The fact that oral techniques have made any headway at all among professional historians is due almost entirely to the reticence of conventional written sources on a number of areas which are now engaging scholarly attention. Recent political history is one such topic. Whereas in the Victorian and Edwardian periods public figures commonly conducted a voluminous official and private correspondence, their modern counterparts rely much more on the telephone, and when they do write letters they seldom have the leisure to write at length. There have been major public figures in recent times who have left no private papers to speak of – Herbert Morrison, a leading member of the Labour Party in the 1930s and 1940s, being a notable example.[2] In order to fill out the evidence to the proportions appropriate to a biography, historians have had to collect the impressions and recollections of such figures from their surviving colleagues and associates. The same applies to many lesser figures in political and other walks of life. The British Oral Archive of Political and Administrative History was set up at the London School of Economics in 1980 to collect this kind of material in a systematic way.[3] The second area concerns what might be termed the recent social history of everyday life, and particularly those aspects of working-class life in the family and the work-place which were seldom the subject of contemporary observation or enquiry. In Britain the oral history movement is dominated by social historians whose interest in these topics is in many cases sustained by an active socialist commitment, evident in their house journal, *Oral History*. The third area which cries out for an enlargement of the conventional historian's technical skills is the history of pre-literate societies which have generated little or no written evidence of their own and are known in the documents only through the statements of literate – and usually prejudiced – outsiders. In the African case, not only is the everyday experience of Africans themselves recoverable by no other means; much of the more formal content of history, such as the rise of entrepreneurial trade or the evolution of political institutions, requires substantial oral work too. Of these three broad areas, it is in the last two that the most substantial contribution has been made and the most significant implications for historical method have arisen.

II

When I came to this village with my father, I was in lodgings as well, so there were no real home comforts to come back to after the pit. I remember being in one set of lodgings: there were six or seven other miners lodging there. It was only a house with three bedrooms, so you can imagine that we were sleeping on a rota basis.

If five or six of us were on the same shift, as soon as I got out of the pit I'd gallop home to be the first to have a bath. There were no bathrooms: all you had was an old zinc tub, and the landlady would have a couple of buckets of water on the fire. If there were five or six of you together, first of all five of you would bath the top half of the body. Everybody bathed the top half of the body in a rota, and then you stepped back into the bath and washed the bottom part of your body. What used to amuse me in those days – well, not amuse – what used to embarrass me was that you'd get the women from next door or from each side of the terraced house. They'd come in there, and they'd sit down in the kitchen, and they wouldn't bloody move – when even you were washing the bottom part of your body. As a youngster and not being used to that, I was not only shy but embarrassed, because you learnt the differences even in those days between the sexes.[4]

This narrative, collected from a retired collier in South Wales as part of a research project on the history of mining communities, conveys something of the qualities which recommend 'oral history' to historians. It is a fragment of autobiography by someone who would never otherwise have dreamed of dignifying his reminiscences in that way. As an individual experience which is commonplace and yet at the same time particular, it offers a vivid insight into a way of life which now survives in Britain only in the memories of the very old. Contemporary written sources for the Edwardian period – the reports of social investigators and charitable bodies, for example – provide copious information about the homes of the poor, but it is information derived at second hand and glossed by 'expert' opinion, a description from outside rather than a product of experience. Oral history allows the voice of ordinary people to be heard alongside the careful marshalling of social facts in the written record.

Domestic routine is only one of the many aspects of the past for which oral history can provide a corrective to the bias of the written sources. Social history aspires to treat the history of society as a whole, not just the rich and the articulate. But, as we saw in Chapter 5 (pp. 84–5), the records to which the social historian instinctively turns carry the stamp of the organizational preoccupations which brought them into being. As a result, labour history features the full-time union official rather than the rank and file; the history of housing emphasizes speculative building and sanitary reform rather than the tenants' quality of life; and agricultural history is taken up with estate management and the rural economy, not the working conditions of the farm labourers. Written documents are also primarily the work of adult men: women who did not belong to the leisured letter-writing class wrote little that has survived, and the experience of childhood finds almost no overt expression in the documentary record. And some social groups which were prominent only sixty or seventy years ago are almost entirely absent from the conventional sources – itinerant traders, unorganized wage-earners of all kinds, and poor immigrant communities.

The testimony which can be gleaned from surviving members of these groups, like the memories of most old people about their youth, is often confused as regards specific events and the sequence in which they occurred. Where it is most reliable is in characterizing recurrent experience, like the practice of a working skill or a child's involvement in a network of neighbours and kin. The routines of daily life and the fabric of ordinary social relationships were commonplace and therefore taken for granted at the time, but now they seem of compelling human interest, and oral enquiry offers the readiest means of access. What it also uniquely conveys is the essential *connectedness* of aspects of daily life which the historian otherwise tends to know of as discrete social facts. Through the life histories of the very poor, for instance, the way in which casual labour, periodic destitution, undernourishment, drunkenness, truancy and familial violence formed a total social environment for thousands of people before the First World War (and later) can be vividly portrayed. Oral history, in short, tries to give social history a human face.

How do oral historians come by their informants? The sampling techniques of sociology have had some influence here. In the most ambitious attempt yet made to incorporate the findings of oral history into a general social history, Paul Thompson took a carefully constructed sample of 500 surviving Edwardians from all classes and regions of Britain, and some of the resulting material is presented in his book, *The Edwardians* (1975).[5] But few historians have followed his example. Most recent oral history has been emphatically local in focus, and for this there are sound practical reasons. In a strictly local study all the elderly who are willing and able can be canvassed; less trust has to be placed in the reliability of the individual informant since the testimonies can be tested against each other; and the purely local references which always feature prominently in life-histories can be elucidated with the help of other source materials. But it is also significant that oral history has from the outset been practised by amateur local historians. The English tradition of amateur local history (which extends back to the sixteenth century) has stressed topography and the world of the squire, parson and – more rarely – businessman. Oral history promises a sense of place and community accessible to ordinary people, while at the same time illuminating broader features of social history. Very fine work of this kind has been done under the auspices of the History Workshop movement (see above, (pp. 6–7). Raphael Samuel has reconstructed the economic and social milieu of Headington Quarry near Oxford before it was enveloped by the expansion of the motor industry in the 1920s; without the rich oral testimony he collected, Samuel would have found it difficult to penetrate far beyond the stereotype of 'Quarry roughs' in newspapers of the time to understand the range of trades and social networks which sustained the independent spirit of the villagers.[6] In the field of urban local history, perhaps the best oral work has been the two London studies by Jerry White, an accomplished amateur: one on a notorious Holloway street between the Wars, the other about a single tenement block in the East End around the turn of the century.[7]

Underlying the current practice of oral history are two powerfully attractive assumptions. First – and most obviously – personal reminiscence is viewed as an effective instrument for *re-creating* the past – the authentic testimony of human life as it was actually experienced. Paul Thompson revealingly entitles his book on the methods and achievements of oral history *The Voice of the Past* (1978), and – notwithstanding all the reservations made in the text – the notion of a direct encounter between historians and their subject-matter is central to Thompson's outlook and is even more explicit in his principal foray into oral history, *The Edwardians*. At one level, therefore, oral history simply represents a novel means of fulfilling the programme laid down by professional historians since the early nineteenth century – 'to show how things actually were' and to enter into the experience of people in the past as fully as possible (see above, pp. 10–12).

But many oral historians are not content with being grist to the mills of professional history. They see oral history rather as a democratic alternative, challenging the monopoly of an academic elite. Ordinary people are offered not only a place in history, but a role in the *production* of historical knowledge with important political implications. In east London the People's Autobiography of Hackney is an open group of local residents who record each other's life histories and publish the transcriptions in pamphlets marketed through a local bookshop. Although educated people participate, no academic historians are involved; if they were, the confidence of people in their own perceptions of the past might be undermined. The idea is that through oral work the community should discover its own history and develop its social identity, free from the patronizing assumptions of conventional historical wisdom. Ken Worpole, co-ordinator of the group, recalls the circumstances in which it began in the early 1970s: 'producing shareable and common history from the spoken reminiscences of working-class people seemed a positive and important activity to integrate with various other new forms of "community" politics'; he sees this and other similar projects as essential to the task of 'reviving the historical component of an affirmative class consciousness'.[8] The same might be said of ethnic consciousness, and it is quite likely that black history in Britain will develop along these lines, as blacks draw on their recent experience of migration, settlement and discrimination.[9]

III

However, both these formulations – oral history as 're-creation' and as 'democratic' knowledge – present major difficulties. The problems which arise from the oral method are perhaps most evident in the research project conducted by a professional historian. It is naive to suppose that the testimony represents a pure distillation of past experience, for in an interview each party is affected by the other. It is the historian who selects the informant and indicates the area of interest; and even if he or she asks no questions and merely listens, the presence of an outsider affects the atmosphere in which the informant recalls the past and talks about it. The end-product is conditioned both by the historian's social position *vis-à-vis* the informant, and by the terms in which he or she has learnt to analyse the past and which may well be communicated to the informant. In other words, historians must accept responsibility for their share in creating new evidence.

But the difficulties are far from over when the historian is removed from the scene. For not even the informant is in direct touch with the past. His or her memories, however precise and vivid, are filtered through subsequent experience. They may be contaminated by what has been absorbed from other sources (especially the media); they may be overlaid by nostalgia ('times were good then'), or distorted by a sense of grievance about deprivation in childhood which only took root in later life. To anyone listening the feelings and attitudes – say of affection towards a parent or distrust of union officials – are often what lends conviction to the testimony, yet they may be the emotional residue of later experience rather than the period in question. As one critic of Paul Thompson's work put it:

> His 'Edwardians' after all, have lived on to become 'Georgians' and, now, 'Elizabethans'. Over the years, certain memories have faded, or, at very least, may have been influenced by subsequent experience. How many of their childhood recollections were, in fact, recalled to them by their own elders? What autobiographies or novels might they have since read that would reinforce certain impressions at the expense of others? What films or television programmes have had an impact on their consciousness? . . . to what extent might the rise of the Labour Party in the post-war decade have inspired retrospective perception of class status and conflict?[10]

Whatever the evidence it rests on, the notion of a direct encounter with the past is an illusion, but perhaps nowhere more than in the case of testimony from hindsight. The 'voice of the past' is inescapably the voice of the present too.

Yet even supposing that oral evidence were somehow authentic and unalloyed, it would still be inadequate as a representation of the past. For historical reality comprises more than the sum of individual experiences. It is no disparagement of the individual to say that our lives are largely spent in situations which, from our subjective perspective, we cannot fully understand. How we perceive the world around us may or may not amount to a viable basis for living, but it never corresponds to reality in its entirety. One of the historian's functions is to advance towards a fuller understanding of the reality of the past; access to a much wider range of evidence than was available to anyone at the time, together with the discipline of historical thinking, enables the historian to grasp the deeper structures and processes which were at work in the lives of individuals. The vividness of personal recall which is the strength of oral evidence also therefore points to its principal limitation, and historians need to be wary about becoming trapped within the mental categories of their informants. It is not that those categories are necessarily wrong, merely that they are more confined than they need be. In the words of Philip Abrams:

> The close encounter may make the voices louder; it does not . . . make their meanings clearer. To that end we must turn back from 'their' meanings to our own and to the things we know about them which they did not know, or say, about themselves.[11]

This limitation applies with particular force to the democratic or populist tendency in oral history. The idea behind projects of the 'people's autobiography' type is that an articulate and authentic historical consciousness will enable ordinary working people to take more control over their lives. But to do so they need an understanding of the forces which have actually moulded their world – most of them not of their making or directly manifest in their experience. The problem with collective oral history is that it is likely to reinforce the superficial way in which most people think of the changes they have lived through, instead of equipping them with deeper insights as a basis for more effective political action. Jerry White makes this point cogently:

> Because it [the group project] is locked in an autobiographical mode – with absolute and inviolable primacy given to what people say about themselves – it does little, if anything, to capture those levels and layers of reality outside individual experience.[12]

Or, as a Marxist might put it, contemporary Western society is permeated by capitalist values which distort people's perception of themselves and each other: oral history, far from undermining these values, may subtly reinforce 'false consciousness' and thus further lower the revolutionary potential of the working class.

What place, then, does oral history have in the practice of historians? The problems raised here are not grounds for having nothing to do with oral history. What they suggest is rather that oral evidence, like all verbal materials, requires critical evaluation, and that it must be deployed in conjunction with all the other available sources; in other words, the canons of historical method described in Chapter 3 apply here too. Transcriptions of testimonies, like Thea Thompson's

Edwardian Childhoods (1981) or the *Working Lives* published by the People's Autobiography of Hackney (1972, 1976), are not 'history', but raw material for the writing of history. Like some other primary sources, they often display evocative and expressive qualities which make them well worth reading for themselves, but they are no substitute for the work of historical interpretation.

Oral sources are in fact extremely demanding of the historian's skills. In his book *The Edwardians* Paul Thompson, by introducing the oral evidence alongside his findings from more conventional sources, may appear to have done all that is required; but for the most part quotations from interviews are presented in an impressionistic manner as illustrative support for the various themes discussed in the book.[13] If the full significance of an oral testimony is to come across, it must be evaluated in conjunction with all the sources pertaining to the locality and people spoken of, or else much of the detail will count for nothing. Sometimes oral research itself unearths new documentary material in private hands – family accounts or old photographs – which add to the amount of supporting evidence. It is mastery of the local context which makes the oral work of Raphael Samuel and Jerry White so striking. White describes his book on tenement life in London's East End, *Rothschild Buildings* (1980), in these terms:

> This may be primarily a work of oral history but documents have played a large part in its conception. Written sources and oral sources interact throughout: finding a new document has led me to ask different questions of the people I interviewed, and the oral testimony has thrown fresh light on the documents. The rules printed on the first tenants' rentbooks led me to ask if they were obeyed and how; finding the original plans of the Buildings made me wonder what was kept in the fitted cupboard behind the living-room door; people's memories of shopping led me to take street directories with a large pinch of salt; autobiographical details cast doubts on census classifications, sociologists' assumptions and standard historical reference works, and so on.[14]

Command of the full range of relevant sources is no less important for 'democratic' oral history. The more traditional inventory of local historians' sources – business archives, newspapers, census returns, the reports of charitable bodies, etc. – provides an entry into the economic and social context of the informants' lives and may reveal something of the historical processes which have shaped the observable changes in the locality. The limitations inherent in the amateur group project mean that, to be politically effective, it requires the participation, if not of professional historians, at least of people familiar with the methods and findings of mainstream social history.[15]

What recent work suggests, however, is that oral research may be less important as *histoire vérité* or as an expression of community politics than as precious evidence of how popular historical consciousness is constructed. Of course most oral testimony worth recording has factual content, but the departures from verifiable fact and the manner in which experience is re-interpreted to conform with a familiar world-view are significant in themselves. The very subjectivity of the speaker may be the most important thing about his or her testimony. As we saw in Chapter 1, popular historical consciousness is a battleground in which the legitimacy of competing ideologies and authorities may be at stake (see above, pp. 6 – 8). The sense of the past which individuals carry around with them comprises a selection of their immediate experience, together with some conception of the nature of the social order in which they live. Historical biographies sometimes show how these two elements bear on each other in the thinking of leaders and intellectuals, but we know very little about their place in the historical awareness of ordinary people. Yet the way in which social groups assimilate and interpret their own experience is a historical factor in its own right, at the heart of political culture. From this perspective, the mental transition from 'Edwardians' to 'Georgians' and on to 'Elizabethans' is an object of study for its own sake, instead of being merely an obstruction in the way of a direct encounter with the past. An oral history which is informed by psychological insight and supported with the full resources of historical scholarship has a major contribution to make here – and one that takes it far beyond the life-histories of the social sciences from which the oral history method is derived. But as yet that contribution has hardly begun.[16]

IV

While oral history has been enlarging the scope of recent social history in industrialized societies (and not only in Britain), a comparable exercise in recovery has been going on in sub-Saharan Africa (and other regions of the Third World). Yet although the oral nature of the material means that the two share several common problems of technique and interpretation, there has been little scholarly contact across the North–South divide, mainly because the circumstances in which the two enterprises began and their characteristic subject-matter are quite different.[17] In fact Africa is as good a territory as any other for the practice of 'oral history' in the sense understood in the West. The memories of the colonized are an essential corrective to the written sources which so often reflect the view from the district commissioner's verandah or the mission compound. In many parts of Africa the colonial period was so brief that until a few years ago firsthand testimony about the imposition of white rule was still widely available. Several studies of colonialism in Africa have deployed oral material to very good effect.[18] But the greatest challenge to historians has been to

181

equip Africa with a more extended past – to demonstrate that modern Africa, like all other societies, is the outcome of historical processes whose roots lie deep in the past. Given the almost complete ignorance which prevailed only thirty years ago, this has been a formidable undertaking, in which the development of a scholarly approach to oral tradition has featured prominently.

The first manifestoes for African history during the 1960s called for an ambitious multi-disciplinary approach to pre-colonial history: linguistics, ethno-botany, palaeo-climatology and epidemiology were all invoked, as well as the more familiar archaeology, so that African history looked set to become 'the decathlon of social science'.[19] But the more esoteric disciplines have on the whole remained the province of their respective specialists, and most of them relate to environmental changes measured in millenia rather than centuries or generations – the relevant timespan for most historians. In Africa as elsewhere, verbal materials have retained their central position in historical research. This is partly because the documentary base proved much broader than had at first been supposed. The European trading companies and missionary societies, which had been in contact with Africa since the fifteenth century and by the nineteenth century had penetrated deep into the interior, were found to have extensive records. In the Islamic regions of the Sahel, the western Sudan and the East African coast, where the frontiers of literacy extended far into black Africa, there are local chronicles dating back in some cases to the sixteenth century, and even – in a few states like the Sokoto caliphate of northern Nigeria – a nucleus of administrative records. But the veneer of literacy was very thin in Islamic Africa, and interest in conservation – in an environment where documents do not easily survive – was slight. At the same time, the European sources, although much more plentiful, present essentially an outsider's view of African culture: they may document the external relations of a kingdom and major milestones like a rebellion or the death of a ruler, but by themselves they are quite inadequate for understanding the structure and evolution of African societies. And many parts of Africa had no contact with literate outsiders at all until the arrival of the first colonial administrators at the very end of the nineteenth century. Inevitably, therefore, historians found themselves drawn to the other main type of verbal source – oral tradition.

Oral tradition may be defined as a body of knowledge which has been transmitted orally over several generations and is the collective property of the members of a given society. In those parts of the world which have known near-universal literacy for two or three generations, oral tradition has practically died out. One of the few forms in which it survives in Britain is the rhymes and riddles of schoolchildren – precisely because they are too young to be fully assimilated into the prevailing literate culture.[20] But in many African societies ethnic identity, social status, claims to political office and rights in land are still validated by appeals to oral tradition; what in Western society would be formalized by written documents in oral societies derives its authority from the memories of the living. Historians are by no means the first observers to record oral tradition in Africa. Since the beginning of the colonial period it has attracted the interest of ethnographers – and indeed of literate Africans too. More recently social anthropologists have studied oral tradition for the light it sheds on the social values of African societies today. But only in the 1950s did historians begin to evaluate oral tradition carefully for its historical content and to lay down procedures for its collection and interpretation. From the start their work carried a note of urgency: as literacy spread and young men increasingly left the countryside for the town or the labour compound, the chain of oral transmission was evidently nearing its end, and the traditions would die with the elders unless recorded in the field. (Literacy and labour migration made less impact on women, but the transmission of traditions in African society is nearly always a male preserve.)

This was an immensely exciting enterprise. Historians collected detailed bodies of tradition which by genealogical reckoning extended back four or five centuries, complete with named individuals and their exploits – the very stuff of conventional historiography. Their faith in the reliability of the traditions was greatly strengthened by the discovery that in the more centralized and elaborate chiefdoms the recital of traditions was the business of trained specialists; fixed texts with vivid poetic imagery helped to imprint tradition in the memory, while in some instances material relics like royal tombs or regalia were used as mnemonic devices to ensure that the reigns of earlier rulers were recalled in correct sequence. The high-point of this new-found confidence was the publication in 1961 of Jan Vansina's methodological treatise, *Oral Tradition*.[21] On the strength of his fieldwork in Rwanda and among the Kuba people of Zaire, Vansina maintained that the methods required to evaluate a formal oral tradition were in principle no different from those required by written documents. He likened the African historian's position to that of the Medievalist confronted by several corrupt variants of an original text (see above, p. 53): through close analysis of the form of the document, the variant texts and the chain of transmission, the historian could in each case arrive at the original 'primary' version. At the same time, comparison of the traditions of neighbouring chiefdoms sometimes revealed a striking degree of agreement, and the independent evidence of archaeology provided further confirmation of the truth of tradition. In the case of the Bantu-speaking kingdoms of pre-colonial Uganda (Buganda and her neighbours) the outcome was a continuous political history of some four centuries' depth.[22] Although oral tradition could hardly be viewed as a *direct* encounter with the past in the manner of 'oral history', it was hailed as a truly indigenous source – the voice of the African past uncontaminated by colonialism.

V

Unfortunately longer experience of oral tradition and reflection on the nature of oral society have shown that the position is not nearly so straightforward as this. Some of the reservations expressed earlier about the re-creative claims of oral history apply here too – notably the new and potentially distorting presence of the professional historian as the recorder of the testimony. But there are more serious problems peculiar to tradition. These arise from the repeated tellings through which any tradition has been transmitted to the present, and from its social function which is a much more central issue here than in the case of personal reminiscence.

However much the recital of a tradition may be governed by a wish to repeat accurately what has been handed down, it always entails an element of *performance*. Like story-tellers everywhere, the performer is alert to the atmosphere among his audience and his sense of what is acceptable to them. Each retelling of the story is likely to be textually distinct from the one before, as the content becomes subtly adjusted to social expectations. Traditions are not kept alive by story-tellers who, by some mysterious faculty beyond the grasp of literate people, are able to remember great epics and lists without effort; they are handed down because they hold meaning for the culture concerned. In the last resort, the traditions are valued not for themselves, but because other more important things depend on them.

Broadly speaking oral traditions fulfil two social functions. They may be a means of teaching the values and beliefs which are integral to the culture – the proper relationship between humans and animals, for example, or the obligations of kinship and affinity. Secondly, they may serve to validate the particular social and political arrangements which currently prevail – the distribution of land, the claims of one powerful lineage to the chiefship, or the pattern of relations with a neighbouring people. Traditions about origins and great migrations usually fall into the first category, while those which recount the doings of particular groups and individuals belong to the second, but there is no hard-and-fast division: many traditions are both cosmological statements and political charters. By the time a tradition has been handed down over four or five generations, its social function is likely to have modified the content considerably, by suppressing detail which no longer seems relevant and by elaborating the rhetorical or symbolic elements in the story. And this process can continue indefinitely, as changes in social or political circumstances leave their imprint on the corpus of oral tradition. It may be politic to excise certain rulers from the record, or to alter the genealogies which 'explain' the present relations between lineages.[23] Sometimes these adjustments are made quite deliberately. Among the Kuba a dynastic tradition could only be recounted after its content had been carefully vetted in private by a council of notables; as one of them put it, 'After a while, the truth of the old tales changed. What was true before, became false afterwards.'[24] More commonly, the process of assimilating tradition to current realities is more gradual and less calculated. David Henige sums up the position like this:

> In societies that depend on flexibility and ambiguity in their social and political activities (and this really means all societies, of course) orality can free the present from imprisonment by the past because it permits the remembrance of aspects of that past – like the sequence and activities of former rulers – to accord with ever-changing self-images.[25]

The experience of colonialism introduced further distortion. European over-rule in many instances changed the balance of power between neighbouring societies and led to a remodelling of their political structures to fit administrative needs – with predictable consequences for oral tradition. In British territories astute African rulers soon realized how respectful of 'tradition' their new masters were, and they manufactured king-lists and supporting traditions to demonstrate the antiquity of their authority and so advance their claims for special treatment. Furthermore the new schools run by Christian missionaries introduced a novel element into the conditions of oral transmission. In societies where literacy is a recent accomplishment and is associated with the ruling group, the written word carries immense and indiscriminate prestige. In Africa the earliest published versions of oral tradition, regardless of quality, acquired authority at the expense of other versions, and they often became the standard form in which the tradition was repeated orally. The outcome was a permanent distortion – particularly serious if, as in Buganda, the African chiefly elite propagated an 'official' version designed to buttress its own political position.[26] Far from being a pristine 'authentic' source, oral tradition – like most features of African culture – has been deeply affected by the experience of colonialism and the social changes that came with it.

The sensitivity of oral tradition to the demands of its audience and the prestige of the written word was strikingly borne out when the black American writer Alex Haley went to the Gambia in 1966 in search of his slave-boy ancestor, Kunta Kinte. Although the oral traditions current in the region do not contain information about real people before the nineteenth century, Haley duly found an elder who recited a tradition about the boy's capture into slavery by 'the king's soldiers' in the mid-eighteenth century. Haley had made no secret of his story and what he was looking for, and there seems little doubt that the 'tradition' was concocted for him. Several years later, as a result of the publicity surrounding Haley's best-seller *Roots* (1976), many more specialists in tradition were able to recite the story of Kunta Kinte with further lively embellishments.[27]

Using oral traditions for historical reconstruction therefore raises major problems. Not only are they mostly narratives intended for the edification of posterity – and thus rather low down in the historian's hierarchy of sources (see Ch. 3); they have also been constantly reworked to articulate their meaning more clearly, and sometimes to change it. Unlike primary documentary sources, oral tradition does not convey the original words and images from which the historian may be able to re-create the mental world of the past. In fact it makes more sense to regard oral tradition as a *secondary* source, but with the added twist that it has erased all the earlier versions. It is as if the publication of the latest historical monograph was marked by the destruction of all copies of the previous work on the subject.

The remodelling over time which all oral traditions undergo is such that the basic facts are in doubt. Among the Lango people of northern Uganda, most recitations of tradition begin with the statement 'We Langi came from Otuke' – the impressive hill in the extreme north-east of their country. This may mean that 500,000 people are descended from migrants who came from Otuke *en masse*; it may be a compressed statement referring to a gradual movement of people from a general north-easterly direction; or – as was probably the case – it could mean that the dominant groups within Lango society came from the north-east and later were able to impose the Otuke tradition as a badge of Lango identity on everyone else; it could conceivably have no historical content at all and reflect a world-view in which, say, the north-east represented cattle-keeping – the most prestigious form of subsistence in Lango – as against the south (= fishing) and the west (= crop husbandry).[28] To interpret the significance of such a tradition requires considerable immersion in the culture of the people concerned. Placing it in time may be even more difficult, in view of the arbitrary lengthening and telescoping of genealogies and lists which is so characteristic of oral tradition.[29] Perhaps most frustrating of all is the tendency for oral tradition to validate the social institutions of the day and only rarely to admit that these institutions have ever been different, for it is in just this area that other types of evidence like archaeology and external documentary sources have least to offer.

The result is that historians are now very cautious indeed about advancing interpretations of oral traditions which purport to refer to events several centuries ago. They know the danger of accepting at face value what may be no more than the community's present-day self-image put into time perspective. Indeed there are signs of convergence here with the preoccupations of some of the more advanced exponents of oral history. For if the subtle modifications by which ordinary people re-interpret their indivudual life experience provide insight into the formation of historical consciousness, how much richer must the evolving oral tradition of an entire community be as evidence of how the past can be manipulated for social ends. Some recent work is concerned less with using oral tradition as historical evidence than with seeking to understand the cultural and political context in which images of the past are constructed.[30] This has very promising implications for the study of collective mentality in Africa.

Valuable though this perspective on historical consciousness is, it does not, however, exhaust the scholarly uses of oral tradition. As a historical source in the conventional sense, oral tradition will continue to be exploited for at least three reasons. In the first place, it is wrong to assume that there is necessarily a complete 'fit' between present and past. In fact the representation of society in tradition is more likely to lag behind the reality, particularly in times of rapid social change such as Africa has lived through in the past hundred years. We all interpret the present in the light of models derived from past experience, and oral societies are no exception. Thomas Spear points out that the values and assumptions which are manifest in the traditions of the Mijikenda peoples of Kenya relate to circumstances around 1850, before their social system had been disturbed by the new wealth earned by young men from the caravan trade with the coast; the time-lag offers valuable insight into their earlier political culture.[31]

Secondly, traditions which have been glossed time and time again are unlikely to have been changed in every particular. Stories about the distant past may have been moulded to conform to changing social perceptions, but they also carry information which is incidental to the meaning of the text and affords a glimpse of conditions in the past, such as archaic styles of dress and weaponry, or the arrival of the first exotic goods by long-distance trade from the coast. Even stories whose significance seems to be primarily as mythical symbols may yield valid historical inferences. A case in point is the tradition told by the Shambaa of north-east Tanzania about the foundation of their mountain state. This is attributed to a heroic leader called Mbegha who killed wild pigs, distributed free meat, and settled major disputes. Steven Feierman concedes that at one level this story is a myth rich in symbolic statements about Shambaa culture (expressing, for example, the opposition of wilderness to homestead, and of meat to starch); but reference to the traditions of neighbouring peoples confirms that the tale of Mbegha also deals with the resolution of a crisis in Shambaa society in the eighteenth century, caused by the arrival of large groups of immigrants from the plains.[32] Oral traditions, like written documents, can be 'witnesses in spite of themselves' (see above, p. 31).

Thirdly, and perhaps most important of all, many of the features which make the interpretation of oral tradition so problematic are much less evident the nearer they approach the present. Myths of origins have a fascination all of their own for both fieldworkers and armchair scholars, but the area in which oral tradition has made the greatest impact on historical knowledge is nineteenth-century African history. All oral tradition, however stylized and abstract it eventually becomes, begins as description of actions and events as they were experienced in life. From the historian's point of view, the great merit of traditions pertaining, say, to the lifetime of the grandparents of today's elders is that the process of abstraction has not yet gone very far: details which meant a great deal to the original participants may have been dropped, and the stories may have been affected by the perspective of hindsight, but the exploits of named individuals and their social world remain clearly visible. In a valuable discussion of how oral tradition evolves, Joseph Miller refers to this material as 'extended personal recollections', implying an intermediate category between firsthand testimony and oral tradition proper.[33] The experience of many historians shows that shallow traditions about the nineteenth century respond well to the critical skills in which the profession is trained.

The historian of the nineteenth century holds another advantage, namely the *plurality* of traditions surviving from that period. For more remote epochs the only traditions likely to survive are those associated with the ruling lineage or – in the case of chiefless societies – tribal epics of migration and warfare. But the period immediately preceding the Scramble for Africa lies within the remembered past of smaller social groups – the clan, lineage or petty chiefdom. This material not only allows the historian to apply the principles of comparative source criticism by setting one tradition against the others; it also does much to offset the otherwise pronounced tendency for oral tradition to portray African society from the top as seen through the eyes of the ruling elite. Something of the tension which divided opposing interests and rival centres of authority can be reconstructed from the varied oral materials surviving from the nineteenth century, as David Cohen has demonstrated so well in his micro-study of Bunafu.[34] In short, historians can now attempt a broader social analysis than the mainstream court traditions permit by themselves.

In Africa the nineteenth century was a period of major social change, due to the spread of long-distance trade, the renewed expansion of Islam, and – in the south and east – the convulsions set in train by the meteoric rise of the Zulu kingdom. As the work of recovering the oral traditions for this period proceeds, historians are greatly enlarging their understanding of these themes and of the circumstances in which Africans confronted the colonial intrusion at the close of the century.[35]

VI

As a new trend in historical enquiry, the use of oral evidence stands in sharp contrast to the developments discussed in Chapters 8 and 9. Whether specializing in oral tradition or oral reminiscence, oral historians are drawn by their sources to an interest in the particular and an inclination to the narrative mode. Oral history in the West is particularly opposed to the tendency of quantitative history to deal in broad categories and general explanations in a 'dehumanizing' way. Oral historians of both kinds tend to follow where their data lead and to keep theories and models at arm's length. It is as though their purpose was to restore the particularities of human experience to their central place in historical discourse and to sharpen our perception of individuals and their predicaments. A technique which owes its modern development to sociology and anthropology has been enlisted in support of an enterprise foreign to the generalizing, theory-oriented nature of social science.

The practice of both oral history and oral tradition, then, has had more to do with the re-creational than the explanatory side of historical enquiry. Like other academic innovators oral historians have tended in the past to advance exaggerated claims for their expertise, maintaining that they are uniquely – perhaps exclusively – qualified to recover 'lost' areas of human experience. Both oral history and oral tradition have been presented as the voice of those who have been denied a proper hearing by the conventional materials of historical research – in one case the bottom tier of industrialized society, in the other the non-European peoples who were at the receiving end of colonialism. In both these areas the vital contribution of oral sources can hardly be denied. What cannot be sustained, however, is the notion that the historian, by listening to 'the voice of the past', can re-create these neglected territories of history with an authentic immediacy. The term 'oral history' – sometimes used to cover work on oral tradition as well as personal reminiscence – is particularly unfortunate, suggesting as it does a new specialism analogous to diplomatic or economic history. Oral history is not a new branch of history but a new *technique* – a means of bringing into play new sources to be evaluated alongside written sources and material remains.

But at the same time oral sources merit more attention than they currently receive from the profession at large, or the wider public. They are, after all, *verbal* materials, and they share many of the strengths and weaknesses of written sources – the wealth of detail and nuance of meaning, as well as the distortions of cultural bias and political calculation. Oral sources are therefore particularly appropriate materials for the exercise of the historian's traditional critical skills. And they have the further attraction of affording a unique

189

insight into the formation of popular historical consciousness – something which should be of abiding interest to all historians.

NOTES

1. This omission is partly rectified in two sentences on oral history in the second edition of *The Nature of History*, Macmillan, 1981, p. 141, but oral tradition is still ignored.
2. Bernard Donoughue and G. W. Jones, *Herbert Morrison*, Weidenfeld & Nicolson, 1973.
3. Anthony Seldon and Joanna Pappworth, *By Word of Mouth*, Methuen, 1983.
4. Christopher Storm-Clark, 'The miners, 1870–1970: a test-case for oral history', *Victorian Studies*, XV, 1971, pp. 65–6.
5. Thompson describes his sampling procedure more fully in his methodological work, *The Voice of the Past: Oral History*, Oxford University Press, 1978, pp. 122–9.
6. Raphael Samuel (ed.) *Village Life and Labour*, Routledge & Kegan Paul, 1975.
7. Jerry White, 'Campbell Bunk: a lumpen community in London between the Wars', *History Workshop Journal*, VIII, 1979, and *Rothschild Buildings: Life in an East End Tenement Block, 1887–1920*, Routledge & Kegan Paul, 1980.
8. Ken Worpole, 'A ghostly pavement: the political implications of local working-class history', in Raphael Samuel (ed.) *People's History and Socialist Theory*, Routledge & Kegan Paul, 1981, p. 28.
9. *Oral History*, VIII, 1980, no. 1, reports the proceedings of a conference on black history and oral history in 1979 which was attended by both professional historians and black activists.
10. Stephen Koss, review of Paul Thompson's *The Edwardians* in *Times Literary Supplement*, 5 December 1975, p. 1436.
11. Philip Abrams, *Historical Sociology*, Open Books, 1982, p. 331.
12. Jerry White, 'Beyond autobiography', in Samuel, *People's History*, p. 35.
13. See the review of Thompson's book by Robert Gray in *Social History*, V, 1977, pp. 695–7.
14. White, *Rothschild Buildings*, p. xiii.
15. For a small-scale but promising example of this approach, see Tottenham History Workshop, *How Things Were: Growing Up in Tottenham 1890–1920*, 1982.
16. For an exploration of what might be involved here, see Luisa Passerini, 'Work ideology and consensus under Italian Fascism', *History Workshop Journal*, VIII, 1979.
17. Oral history and oral tradition are considered together in a fruitful way, however, in B. Bernardi, C. Poni and A. Triulzi (eds.) *Fonti Orali: Antropologia e Storia*, Franco Angeli, 1978: some of the major contributions are in English.

18. John Iliffe (ed.) *Modern Tanzanians*, East African Publishing House, 1973, includes a number of recorded life-histories. Oral evidence is skilfully woven into Charles Perrings, *Black Mineworkers in Central Africa*, Heinemann, 1979.

19. Wyatt MacGaffey, 'African history, anthropology, and the rationality of natives', *History in Africa*, V, 1978, p. 103.

20. See Iona and Peter Opie, *The Lore and Language of Schoolchildren*, Oxford University Press, 1959.

21. Published in French in 1961, the English version appeared as *Oral Tradition*, Routledge & Kegan Paul, 1965.

22. M. S. M. Kiwanuka, *A History of Buganda*, Longman, 1971, and S. Karugire, *A History of the Kingdom of Nkore in Western Uganda to 1896*, Oxford University Press, 1971.

23. In this and the previous paragraph, I have drawn heavily on Joseph Miller, 'Listening for the African past', which forms the introduction to J. C. Miller (ed.) *The African Past Speaks*, Dawson, 1980.

24. Jan Vansina, *The Children of Woot*, Wisconsin University Press, 1978, p. 19.

25. David Henige, ' "The disease of writing": Ganda and Nyoro kinglists in a newly literate world', in Miller, *African Past Speaks*, pp. 255–6.

26. Michael Twaddle, 'On Ganda historiography', *History in Africa*, I, 1974.

27. Donald R. Wright, 'Uprooting Kunta Kinte: on the perils of relying on encyclopaedic informants', *History in Africa*, VIII, 1981.

28. John Tosh, *Clan Leaders and Colonial Chiefs in Lango*, Oxford University Press, 1978, pp. 13, 24–34.

29. David Henige, *The Chronology of Oral Tradition*, Oxford University Press, 1974. See also his *Oral Historiography*, Longman, 1982, pp. 97–102.

30. See, for example, Paul Irwin, *Liptako Speaks*, Princeton University Press, 1981.

31. Thomas Spear, 'Oral traditions: whose history?', *History in Africa*, VIII, 1981. See also his *Kenya's Past: an Introduction to Historical Methodology in Africa*, Longman, 1981.

32. Steven Feierman, *The Shambaa Kingdom: A History*, Wisconsin University Press, 1974, Chs. 2–3.

33. Miller, 'Listening for the African past', p. 10.

34. David W. Cohen, *Womunafu's Bunafu: A Study of Authority in a Nineteenth-Century African Community*, Princeton University Press, 1977.

35. Notable examples are Andrew Roberts, *A History of the Bemba*, Longman, 1973, and Jan Vansina, *The Tio Kingdom*, Oxford University Press, 1973.

191

CONCLUSION

During the 1960s the outlook for historical studies looked bleak and uncertain. Historians were preoccupied by the prospect of a declining interest in their work, among both students and the wider public. It seemed as though sociology was on the way to displacing history as the core discipline for non-scientists. There was talk of a 'crisis in the humanities'.[1] But the American historian who in 1964 looked forward to an imminent period of rapid advance and exciting achievement was nearer the truth.[2] The self-doubts which afflicted the profession at that time were resolved by a surge of innovations which greatly increased the scope of historical enquiry; twenty years later the invigorating effects are still with us.

The last three chapters have assessed the contribution of sociological and economic theory, the quantitative analysis of historical data, and the use of oral evidence. But this list is very far from being exhaustive. Other new departures like the use of landscape and film as historical sources, and the adoption of interpretative frameworks from cultural anthropology and human geography, have been only lightly touched on in this book, because in my judgement their impact has not been so pronounced, nor do they hold such interesting implications for the nature of historical enquiry; but in a comprehensive survey they would certainly merit extended discussion. And this is not to mention experiments like psycho-history whose value is more dubious (see above, pp. 73 – 74). Together all these innovations amount to the most significant methodological advance since Ranke laid the foundations of modern historical scholarship a century-and-a-half ago. As a result the content of historical study has been vastly extended too. It now embraces social structures in their entirety, the history of collective mentalities, and the evolving relationship between society and the natural environment. And for the first time historical research now extends to every corner of the globe; no culture is deemed too remote or too 'primitive' for the attention of historians.

This record of innovation over the past twenty years evokes varied

192

responses within the profession. Some like Lawrence Stone, who has been in the vanguard for much of the period, argue that a 'heroic age' of historiography has come to an end, and that we are now entering a period of quiet consolidation of received wisdom.[3] By contrast, a few brave spirits like Geoffrey Barraclough claim that we are about to witness a breakthrough to 'scientific history'.[4] I do not find either of these assessments very convincing. Quantitative history has probably now reached the stage of quiet consolidation, but that is hardly true of historical research in general. There are no signs of the interest in theory being confined to a few tried and trusted models. Oral historians have only just begun to register the full implications of the status of their evidence. One of the reasons why nothing has been said in this book about the history of diet and disease is that the agenda for these areas has scarcely been drawn up. And the call for 'total history' remains as challenging as before. Could it be that talk of a golden age in the past reflects an assumption by senior scholars approaching retirement that nothing their juniors may do can equal the excitement of the years spanned by their own careers? Whatever the explanation, this appraisal seems unduly pessimistic. But that is no reason to embrace Barraclough's vision of a brave new world. Talk of 'scientific history' seems to rest on a confusion between technique and explanation. The effect of adopting some of the procedures of the social sciences has not been to place major issues of historical interpretation beyond dispute in our own time; what it has done is to alert historians to new factors in history, and to make some of their descriptive statements about the past more precise and more comprehensive. Historians are as far as ever from the kind of consensus implied by 'scientific history', and – for reasons which were explained in Chapter 7 – it is in the nature of their discipline that they will remain so.

Other historians have objected strongly to the new-fangled inter-disciplinary approaches on the grounds that they undermine the integrity of history as a discipline and the cultivation of a truly historical awareness.[5] But the traditional approach has been supplemented, not displaced. Despite the exaggerated claims made for some of the new techniques in their early days, they have not wiped the slate clean. Older approaches tend to persist long after their novelty has worn off, and the traditional canons of historical method retain their central position in scholarly practice. As a result, the range of orientation among today's historians is quite unprecedented. A glance at any of the recent stock-taking symposia will show how richly varied is the present-day output of historians.[6]

But the enlargement in the scope of historical enquiry has one undeniable implication: history has become a discipline with very little apparent coherence. During the nineteenth century it was possible in practice to fence off history from other disciplines and to confine its brief to the narrative presentation of political events. The rise of economic history in the early twentieth century would have imposed greater strain on this convention, had it not been for the fact that political and economic history tended to remain in separate compartments. But today the situation is very different. Not only has the range of approaches to the past expanded, with the maturing of social history and the coming of environmental history and the history of collective mentalities. More and more research is conducted on the frontiers between thematic specialisms, and the traditional claim of political history to be the core of the subject is almost impossible to sustain any longer; history has become a house of many mansions, with numerous doors and passageways inside.[7]

History has always been inimical to the definitions of the logician. But now more than ever it can only be adequately characterized in terms of paired opposites. It concerns both events and structures, both the individual and the mass, both mentalities and material forces. Historians themselves need to combine narrative with analytical skills, and to display both empathy and detachment. Their discipline is both re-creation and explanation, both art and science; in short – to return to one of the starting-points of this book – history is a hybrid which defies classification. These distinctions should be seen not as warring opposites but as complementary emphases, which together hold out the possibility of grasping the past in something like its real complexity. Nothing is to be gained from defining history in terms of lucid absolutes – except perhaps rhetorical support for some new approach whose credentials have yet to be established. A great deal will be lost if, in the interests of a spurious coherence, historians close their eyes to a whole dimension of their subject.

Last but not least, the diversity of current practice reflects a central ambivalence in the function of history. For as long as men and women retain any interest in human nature and human creativity, they will recognize that every manifestation of the human spirit in the past has some claim on their attention, and that history is worth studying as an end in itself. Some of the new approaches during the past twenty years are recognizably part of this humanistic tradition. The study of collective mentalities is concerned in the first instance to re-create the emotions and intellect of people living in conditions very different from our own, so that their humanity can be more fully realized. Oral historians in Britain and other industrialized societies are committed to the recovery of everyday experience in the recent past as something of value in itself.

But the innovative strain in recent historiography has been much more strongly influenced by the conviction that the record of the past holds lessons for contemporary society. The signs are that the retreat from topical concerns which characterized the historical profession in the first half of the twentieth century has ended. Quietly but persistently, historians are now reasserting their subject's claim to offer guidance and perspective. The conviction is there, and it influences research priorities, even if the results are seldom communicated to a lay readership as forcefully as they should be. Macro-economic history, and the quantitative methods which it has brought to greater sophistication than any other branch of history, is principally concerned to explore the dynamics of growth and stagnation in national economies. The sense of crisis about the management of the world's natural resources has prompted the growth of environmental history, just as the entry of black Africa into the international arena has directed attention to African history. The theories of social structure and social change which historians have drawn from the social sciences were originally propounded by thinkers like Marx and Weber as a contribution to contemporary problems; it is no accident that they have been applied with such interesting results to areas like urban history and the history of the family which directly address contemporary problems today.

What gives most cause for optimism about the future of historical studies is that more and more historians are now investigating themes of topical relevance. They do so not as a propaganda exercise, but in the conviction that there are valuable insights to be learnt from the findings of historical scholarship. No doubt those insights are less clear-cut than the champions of 'scientific history' would care to admit. If society looks to historians for 'answers' in the sense of firm predictions and unequivocal generalizations, it will be disappointed. What will emerge from the pursuit of 'relevance' is something less tangible but in the long run more valuable – a surer sense of the possibilities latent in our present condition. For as long as historians hold that end in view, their subject will retain its vitality and its claim on the support of the society in which they work.

NOTES

1. J. H. Plumb (ed.) *Crisis in the Humanities*, Penguin, 1964.
2. H. Stuart Hughes, *History as Art and as Science*, Chicago University Press, 1964, pp. 20–21.
3. Lawrence Stone, *The Past and the Present*, Routledge & Kegan Paul, 1980, p. xi.
4. Geoffrey Barraclough, *Main Trends in History*, Holmes & Meier, 1979, p. 207. See also Lee Benson, *Toward the Scientific Study of History*, Lippincott, 1972, pp. 98–104.
5. This is especially true of Jaques Barzun, *Clio and the Doctors*, Chicago University Press, 1974. But see also G. R. Elton, *The Practice of History*, Fontana, 1969.
6. See Michael Kammen (ed.) *The Past Before Us*, Princeton University

Press, 1980, and George C. Iggers and Harold T. Parker (eds.) *International Handbook of Historical Studies*, Methuen, 1980. These works present a revealing contrast to H. P. R. Finberg (ed.) *Approaches to History*, Routledge & Kegan Paul, 1962.

7. For some stimulating reflections on this theme, see Theodore K. Rabb, 'Coherence, synthesis and quality in history', in T. K. Rabb and Robert I. Rotberg (eds.) *The New History: the 1980s and Beyond*, Princeton University Press, 1982.

FURTHER READING

The notes at the end of each chapter indicate where supplementary information on particular points may be found. This section is intended to indicate where the reader can turn for further discussion of the main themes raised in the book. Only works in English are included. Where a book has appeared in more than one edition, I cite the most accessible one (usually a paperback); in the main text of the book, dates of publication refer to the first edition in any language.

Historians are not much given to reflecting at length on the nature of their discipline, though they are certainly more self-conscious than they used to be. Expounding the principles of historical enquiry can be left to the philosophers, and W. H. Walsh, *An Introduction to Philosophy of History* (3rd edn, Hutchinson, 1967) is much the best work of this kind. Works by historians themselves tend to fall into two categories. Firstly, there are the personal statements by distinguished historians which are often very illuminating but make no claim to be comprehensive. Much the most impressive of these is E. H. Carr, *What is History?* (Penguin, 1964), still unsurpassed as a stimulating and provocative statement by a radically-inclined scholar. Marc Bloch, *The Historian's Craft* (Manchester University Press, 1954) has deservedly attained the status of a classic, but is rather less accessible to English-speaking readers. G. R. Elton, *The Practice of History* (Fontana, 1969) is a vigorous manifesto by a leading conservative. David Thomson, *The Aims of History* (Thames & Hudson, 1969), is briefer and less combative.

The second approach is to raise questions to do with the nature and scope of history through the history of historical writing, or assessments of individual historians. John Cannon (ed.) *The Historian at Work* (Allen & Unwin, 1980) is a good introductory work of this kind. Fritz Stern (ed.) *The Varieties of History* (2nd edn, Macmillan, 1970) traces the development of historical consciousness through the statements of leading historians from the eighteenth century to the present.

The Pursuit of History

J. R. Hale (ed.) *The Evolution of British Historiography* (Macmillan, 1967) is also useful. Pre-modern historiography is lucidly presented in Denys Hay, *Annalists and Historians* (Methuen, 1977). Herbert Butterfield, *Man On His Past* (Cambridge University Press, 1955) is the nearest we have to a good treatment in English of the Rankean revolution in historical studies. John Kenyon, *The History Men* (Weidenfeld & Nicolson, 1983) is a very readable account of the growth of professional history in England since the Renaissance, but its coverage of twentieth-century scholarship is perversely selective. The historical approach is fascinating, but it is beyond the brief of any of these authors to present a critical discussion of the methods and scope of history.

Apart from these two categories, there are very few satisfactory introductory works. The best brief account is the Open University's course booklet, *Introduction to History* (1977), prepared by Arthur Marwick. Marwick's *The Nature of History* (Macmillan, 1970) is much more comprehensive, but despite a second edition in 1981, it now has a rather dated air.

The use of history is one topic which does lend itself rather well to a historical approach, as is demonstrated by Pieter Geyl, *Use and Abuse of History* (Yale University Prss, 1955) and J. H. Plumb, *The Death of the Past* (Macmillan, 1969). Michael Howard's recent inaugural lecture, *The Lessons of History* (Oxford University Press, 1981), offers a measured defence of the relevance of history. Gordon Connell-Smith and Howell A. Lloyd, *The Relevance of History* (Heinemann, 1972) is a more polemical work, argued from a position similar to my own. *Making Histories* (Hutchinson, 1982), edited for the Centre for Contemporary Cultural Studies by Richard Johnson and others, develops the argument that popular historical consciousness is a central battleground between competing ideologies.

For a British readership the best introduction to the principal categories of documentary source is J. J. Bagley, *Historical Interpretation*, in two volumes: vol. I, *Sources of English Medieval History, 1066–1540* (Penguin, 1965), and vol. II, *Sources of English History, 1540 to the Present Day* (Penguin, 1971). The critical evaluation of primary sources is well described in a number of works, notably G. Kitson Clark, *The Critical Historian* (Heinemann, 1967). V. H. Galbraith, *An Introduction to the Study of History* (C. A. Watts, 1964) considers the topic from the point of view of a Medievalist. Also recommended are Jacques Barzun and Henry F. Graff, *The Modern Researcher* (3rd edn, Harcourt, Brace Jovanovich, 1977), Louis Gottschalk, *Understanding History: A Primer of Historical Method* (Knopf, 1950), and the previously cited works of Bloch and Elton. L. P. Curtis (ed.) *The Historian's Workshop* (Knopf, 1970) gathers together firsthand accounts by a number of historians of how they set about their research.

The range of historical studies is best conveyed by a number of symposia in which different specialists advertise their wares. Among the best are Felix Gilbert and S. Graubard (eds.) *Historical Studies Today* (Norton, 1972) and Michael Kammen (ed.) *The Past Before Us* (Cornell University Press, 1980). H. P. R. Finberg (ed.) *Approaches to History* (Routledge & Kegan Paul, 1962) and Martin Ballard (ed.) *New Movements in the Study and Teaching of History* (Temple Smith, 1970) are also worth consulting. G. R. Elton, *Political History* (Allen Lane, 1970) is an uncompromising defence of the traditional core of the discipline. W. G. Hoskins, *Local History in England* (2nd edn, Longman, 1972) is the best introduction to its subject. The aspirations of the influential *Annales* school are presented in Emmanuel Le Roy Ladurie, *The Territory of the Historian* (Harvester, 1979) and Fernand Braudel, *On History* (Weidenfeld & Nicolson, 1980). Lawrence Stone, *The Past and the Present* (Routledge & Kegan Paul, 1981) provides a sympathetic review of recent trends in historical scholarship, as does George C. Iggers, *New Directions in European Historiography* (Wesleyan University Press, 1975). Jacques Barzun, *Clio and the Doctors* (Chicago University Press, 1974) is the most forceful statement of the conservatives' hostility to inter-disciplinary history.

The controversy between Carr *(What is History?)* and Elton (*The Practice of History*) is the best starting-point for the debate about the standing of historical knowledge. Walsh is also particularly acute here. B. A. Haddock, *An Introduction to Historical Thought* (Arnold, 1980) surveys the ebb and flow of philosophical debate on this issue since the Renaissance, but ignores the interventions of historians themselves. R. G. Collingwood, *The Idea of History* (Oxford University Press, 1946) is the classic statement in English of the Idealist position, though it is far from easy reading. Herbert Butterfield, *The Whig Interpretation of History* (Penguin, 1973) is still well worth reading, although it was first published in 1931.

Much the most stimulating discussion of the place of theory in historical interpretation is Philip Abrams, *Historical Sociology* (Open Books, 1982). Peter Burke, *Sociology and History* (Allen & Unwin, 1980) is a much briefer and less searching account. David Bebbington, *Patterns in History* (Inter-Varsity Press, 1979) is a particularly clear review of the main theories of history from ancient times to the present. Most of the standard introductions to Marx's thought glance fairly lightly over his theory of history. G. A. Cohen, *Karl Marx's Theory of History: A Defence* (Oxford University Press, 1978) and Melvin Rader, *Marx's Interpretation of History* (Oxford University Press, 1979) are two more specialized works by philosophers which put forward contrasting interpretations. E. P. Thompson, *The Poverty of Theory* (Merlin Press, 1978) is a blistering attack on rigidity in historical theory by a master of polemic.

The best introduction to quantitative history is the Open University's course booklet, *The Quantitative Analysis of Historical Data* (1974), prepared by Michal Drake. Roderick Floud, *An Introduction to Quantitative Methods for Historians* (2nd edn, Methuen, 1979) takes the reader further into the complexities of statistical method. William O. Aydelotte, *Quantification in History* (Addison Wesley, 1971) is a discriminating defence of quantitative history.

Paul Thompson, *The Voice of the Past: Oral History* (Oxford University Press, 1978) is a very readable introduction to oral history from a social historian's perspective. Anthony Seldon and Joanna Pappworth, *By Word of Mouth* (Methuen, 1983) considers the uses of oral history for recent political history. The best introduction to oral tradition is David Henige, *Oral Historiography* (Longman, 1982), which can be supplemented by the classic account, Jan Vansina, *Oral Tradition* (Penguin, 1973).

Finally, two works which introduce topics not discussed in this book: Paul Smith (ed.) *The Historian and Film* (Cambridge University Press, 1976), and W. G. Hoskins, *Fieldwork in Local History* (Faber & Faber, 2nd edn, 1982) which shows how the landscape can be used as a historical source.

INDEX

Abrams, Philip, 199
  quoted, 134, 179
Acton, Lord, 51, 112, 119
  quoted, 101, 112
administrative history, 69
Africa, history of, 4, 13, 14, 16, 20, 21,
    27–8, 55, 61, 99–100, 101, 118, 153,
    174, 181–8, 195
agrarian history, 61, 175
Althusser, Louis, 147
America, history of, 4, 70, 102, 153
analysis, 95, 98–9, 106, 113
Anderson, Perry, 146
Annales school of historians, 79, 82, 86,
    89–90, 98, 103, 143, 155, 199
anthropology, 86–8, 132, 135, 173–4, 183,
    189, 192
archaeology, 28, 41, 182, 186
archives, 34–5, 42–5, 67
  see Public Record Office
art history, 28, 70–1
art, history as an, 95, 105–6, 110
Asquith, H. H., 56
  quoted, 39
autobiography, 32, 54–5
  see also oral sources
Aydelotte, William O., 160, 200
  quoted, 163, 168

Bagley, J. J., 198
Bailyn, Bernard, 70
Ballard, Martin, 199
Bancroft, George, 4
Barraclough, Geoffrey, 22, 98, 193
  quoted, 22
Barzun, Jacques, 198, 199
Bebbington, David, 199
Becker, Carl M.,
  quoted, 120

bias
  in historians, 21, 114, 117–22, 123–5,
    128, 131, 166
  in primary sources, 54–6, 111, 121
biography, 38, 58, 71–4, 79, 174, 181
  collective, 75, 157, 160, 177, 179, 180
black history, 2, 123, 177
Blake, Robert, 74
Bloch, Marc, 15, 61, 79, 197, 198
  quoted, 31, 51, 61, 100, 115
Blue Books, 40, 58
British Library, 42
British Museum, 42, 44
Bogue, Allan G.,
  quoted, 163, 168
Braudel, Fernand, 90, 95, 103, 138, 199
  quoted, 103
Bridenbaugh, Carl, quoted, 167
Brogan, D.W., quoted, 32
Burckhardt, Jacob, 71
  quoted, 117
Burke, Peter, 88, 199
  quoted, 17
Bury, J.B., 119
  quoted, 119, 127
business history, 81
Butterfield, Herbert, 120, 122, 124, 198,
  199
  quoted, 95, 120

calendars, 42
Cambridge Modern History, 100–1
Camden, William, 50
  quoted, 50
Cannon, John, 197
Carlyle, Thomas, 95
Carr, E.H., 23, 113, 122, 197, 199
  quoted, 23, 122, 124
causation, 97–9, 116–17, 130, 169